CRIME WITHOUT PUN

In this compelling book, the author looks at a cluster of situations where, in the past, the official law condemned the taking of life; but the killing was rarely or never punished. The examples include the actions of vigilante and lynch mobs, along with crimes of passion justified by the so-called "unwritten law." The book covers the killing of the newborn at the very beginning of life, and "mercy killing" at the very end. The book asks why, in each case, the legal system in action allowed what the legal system in theory condemned, and how and why crimes without punishment changed in form and content over the course of time.

Lawrence M. Friedman is the Marion Rice Kirkwood Professor at Stanford Law School, Stanford University. He has written or edited over 30 books on legal history and the relationship between law and society.

Crime Without Punishment

ASPECTS OF THE HISTORY OF HOMICIDE

LAWRENCE M. FRIEDMAN

Stanford University

CAMBRIDGE
UNIVERSITY PRESS

CAMBRIDGE
UNIVERSITY PRESS

University Printing House, Cambridge CB2 8BS, United Kingdom

One Liberty Plaza, 20th Floor, New York, NY 10006, USA

477 Williamstown Road, Port Melbourne, VIC 3207, Australia

314-321, 3rd Floor, Plot 3, Splendor Forum, Jasola District Centre, New Delhi - 110025, India

79 Anson Road, #06-04/06, Singapore 079906

Cambridge University Press is part of the University of Cambridge.

It furthers the University's mission by disseminating knowledge in the pursuit of education, learning and research at the highest international levels of excellence.

www.cambridge.org
Information on this title: www.cambridge.org/9781108446280
DOI: 10.1017/9781108686679

© Lawrence M. Friedman 2018

First published 2018
First paperback edition 2019

A catalogue record for this publication is available from the British Library

ISBN 978-1-108-42753-1 Hardback
ISBN 978-1-108-44628-0 Paperback

For Leah, Jane, Amy, Sarah, David, Lucy, and Irene

Contents

Acknowledgments   *page* viii

Introduction   1

1   **Popular Justice and Injustice**   4

2   **The Unwritten Law**   20

3   **Dead on Arrival**   60

4   **The Quality of Mercy**   88

5   **Black Swans**   125

6   **The Meaning of Unwritten Law**   129

Index   141

Acknowledgments

I would like to thank a number of research assistants, including Julio Pereyra, Vivek Tata, Lauren Gorodetsky, and Shih-Chun Chien, who helped me very much in the work on this book; also the staff of the Stanford Law Library, for their invaluable service in dredging up books and sources. I am grateful to Stewart Macaulay for his extremely useful comments and to two anonymous reviewers for *their* useful comments. Special thanks, first, to my wife, Leah Friedman, who read the entire manuscript and helped me immensely; and second, to William Havemann, who coauthored and made essential contributions to an article that formed an earlier version of Chapter 2 on the unwritten law.

Introduction

Murder is the king of crimes. No crime is worse, except (perhaps) treason. Murder is defined, basically, as the unlawful killing of another human being, but every society has its own understanding of which killings are lawful and which are not. Only law and custom can tell us exactly what "murder" means in a given legal order. A justified or excusable killing is not murder. For example, in California, a killing is "excusable" if it was "committed by accident or misfortune" and is "justifiable" when done in self-defense (or in the "lawful defense" of a member of the family).[1] You can kill someone who, for no good reason, is about to plunge a dagger into your heart. In wartime, during battle, soldiers have a positive duty to kill the enemy. But soldiers are not supposed to kill prisoners of war or enemy soldiers who surrender.

These excuses and exceptions are well known. American law also classifies types of unlawful killing into grades and classes. Murder comes in "degrees." "First-degree" murder is the worst, the most serious. A planned, deliberate murder is first-degree murder. Other homicides are classified as second-degree murder or manslaughter. These are one or two steps down from first-degree murder. Killing that results from reckless behavior – by a drunk driver, say – is seriously criminal, but is not first-degree murder. Homicide law, in the American states (and elsewhere), is full of subtle distinctions. Nonetheless, it is generally the case that the most serious punishments are reserved for killing that meets the legal definition of murder, especially first-degree murder.

Penal codes do not come from outer space. They are catalogs of behaviors that society condemns, and catalogs of the prices that violators should or must pay. The codes, on the whole, reflect the moral sense of their communities. A person who kills an innocent stranger in cold blood, or who robs a convenience store (for example) and shoots to death a trembling store clerk – that person, most of us feel, deserves the full fury of the law. A man who breaks into a house to rob it and vandalize it, and who kills the owner without a qualm when the owner comes

---

[1] Cal. Penal Code, §§195, 197.

suddenly home – this man has committed an appalling crime and deserves strong punishment.

Penal codes are long and complex, because societies are complex. Legal norms can be confused, ambiguous, contested. The same is true of social norms, probably even more so. Moreover, a country or state usually has a single penal code, which (in theory at least) applies to everybody and covers all situations. But there is no single "code" of social norms. Norms can vary from group to group. They might be in flux. Citizens might disagree about what the norms mean and when they apply. Many devoutly religious people strongly believe that it is murder plain and simple to kill an unborn child in its mother's womb. But abortion, in the United States and in most countries at this point in time, is perfectly legal under many circumstances. Indeed, according to the Supreme Court of the United States, in the famous case of *Roe v. Wade*,[2] a woman has a constitutional right to an abortion, at least in the early stages of pregnancy. The decision was and is extremely controversial. Many people long for the time when the Court might overrule this decision and wipe it from the books.

This book is about a different situation. It is about killings that, historically, the formal law plainly condemned, but social norms (apparently) did not. To put it another way: if we simply read the language of the penal codes, these killings seemed to be murder; they did not fall into any known and recognized exceptions. But the behavior of the system was quite different. These killings were rarely or never punished. They were in this sense crimes without punishment. The law *assigned* them a punishment, but the punishment was never or only rarely imposed. Obviously, the law is not a machine that runs automatically; it is a system, and actual people run it. A clause in the penal code is mere words if police, or prosecutors, or judges and juries, or some combination of these, simply ignore it.

This book deals with forms of homicides that fit this pattern: murder in theory, but something else in practice. It is largely, but not exclusively, historical, largely, but not exclusively, about American law in the nineteenth century, and the first half or so of the twentieth. As we see in what follows, the situation has changed a great deal between then and now.

This book asks: What situations fall or have fallen into this category? How did the legal system, in practice, respond to these situations and how have actions and reactions changed over time? Why did these crimes escape punishment in the first place, and why have these changes taken place?

The situations seem, on the surface, quite different, and to have very little in common. We begin with a brief look at the vigilante tradition, particularly in the Old West, and lynch law, particularly in the Old South. We move on to cases of the so-called unwritten law: a man kills his wife's lover, or a woman kills her abusive spouse. Then we examine cases of unmarried women accused of killing their newborn children, and, finally, so-called mercy killings – cases, where, for example, a family member

[2] *Roe v. Wade*, 410 U.S. 113 (1973).

(or doctor) eases a dying, pain-wracked person into the other world. A short chapter also considers what I call "black swan" cases, unusual situations that do not fit into a common pattern. Two well-known cases arose out of trouble on the high seas – in one, men, adrift in the Atlantic and starving, killed a teenager and ate his flesh to stay alive; in another, crew members in an overloaded boat simply tossed people into the sea.

At the other end of the scale, people who kill police officers can expect particularly harsh punishment. Blacks who kill whites are more likely to get a death sentence than whites who kill blacks. In the Old South, an African-American accused of injuring or killing a white person was liable to be lynched; if tried in court, he was almost certain to be condemned to death. A second book could be written, which you could call *Crimes with Huge Punishment*, or *Overpunished Crimes*, or some such title.

But our topic here is homicide that results in no punishment at all, or, at best, light punishment. The instances I mentioned seem to have nothing much in common, except for the punishment or lack of it. And, to be sure, they are very different. In the final chapter, I try to answer a few basic questions. First and foremost is the question: what explains the gaps between the formal law and the behavior of the system? I argue that most of these gaps represent a particular type of clash, between norms and cultures. And I try to show how the structure of the legal system – the jury system, very notably – acts as an enabler and permits, in short, this kind of split between law and practice.

Most of my examples, as I said, are historical, and also, for the most part, no longer part of the living law. This, then, is also a study of social change: What led to the rise and fall of these unwritten laws? What do they tell us about the evolution of American society? This too is a theme of the final chapter.

1

Popular Justice and Injustice

On display in the Carbon County Museum in Rawlins, Wyoming, is a pair of shoes made of human skin. The skin belonged to an outlaw, Big Nose George Parrott, who was lynched in March 1881. Big Nose George was a bandit, part of a gang of desperados. He was complicit in the murder of a deputy sheriff; he was also involved in the murder of a detective who had chased Big Nose and his gang. Big Nose was arraigned in Rawlins, tried, found guilty, and sentenced to hang. Ten days before the date of his appointment with the gallows, he managed to escape. Big Nose did not get very far. A group of men caught him, tied his hands behind his back, put a noose around his neck, and forced him to climb a ladder: he died on this makeshift gallows; a crowd of some 200 people watched him choke to death. Dr. John Osborne, who was there, skinned the corpse and made shoes from the skin. Dr. Osborne became governor of Wyoming in 1893; supposedly he wore the shoes on inauguration day.[1]

This morbid tale combines elements of two types of action: the vigilante movement in the American West and lynching in the American South. Big Nose was the victim of a lynch mob; the mob killed him, even though ordinary legal process would have produced, and was about to produce, the same result (perhaps less flamboyantly). In many ways, his fate was similar to the fate of many African-Americans, lynched by angry white mobs, at roughly the same period of time. The mob that lynched Big Nose was ad hoc, hastily put together. Otherwise, his fate was like the fate of many outlaws, or presumed outlaws, who were put to death by groups of men who called themselves vigilantes.

BELOVED ROUGHNECKS

Most people, I imagine, have heard of the vigilantes and the vigilante movement; it is part of the mystique of the Old West. One of the highlights of the year in Helena,

---

[1] Lori van Pelt, "Big Nose George: A Grisly Frontier Tale," www.wyohistory.org/encyclopedia/big-nose-george-grisly-frontier-tale, visited Sept. 2, 2016.

Montana, is the Vigilante Parade, which has been held for many years. Vigilantes figure in a number of movie "Westerns." Vigilante movements, in Richard Maxwell Brown's definition, are "organized, extralegal movements, the members of which take the law into their own hands."[2] This definition can be stretched to cover all sorts of actions and activities, including some in the present day. It can cover outbursts of group action that go far back in American history: for example, the South Carolina Regulators of the late 1760s, an organized group who took "relentless and harsh" action against those that the group considered outlaws.[3]

But what we might think of as the golden age of vigilantes came almost a century later, in the period from the 1850s on, and mostly (though not entirely) in the American West. The most famous instances of all were the two San Francisco "vigilance committees" of the 1850s. The term "vigilante," which is of course a Spanish word, seems to date from this period; the first usage of the word is indeed recorded in San Francisco, in 1856.

In the wake of the Gold Rush, thousands of people poured into San Francisco. The city exploded in a kind of demographic stampede. It was a rough, raw, turbulent place, bursting at the seams. Crime was, or seemed to be, rampant. Law and order had broken down. At least this is what many people thought. Hubert Bancroft, writing about San Francisco as it was in December 1850, described a city in chaos: "Crime stalked boldly in the public thoroughfares"; frequent fires caused "confusion" and "plunder." The police force was "small and inefficient. In case of an arrest the law was powerless; false witnesses were suborned ... not more than one in ten was ever convicted."[4]

In February 1851, a store was robbed; the owner, C. J. Jansen, was beaten and knocked unconscious; $2,000 was stolen. Two Australians were arrested. A mob gathered in Portsmouth Square; they held a "popular court," and a trial of sorts; the leader of the mob, a merchant named William T. Coleman, acted as prosecutor. But the evidence was flimsy, and the "jury" deadlocked; the two Australians escaped with their necks. In June, however, a "Committee of Vigilance" was formed. It put a certain John Jenkins on trial; he was hanged after this "trial" and twenty-eight other bad characters were simply chased out of town.[5]

The second "vigilance committee" came into existence in 1856; this one had more than 6,000 members; it hanged two men, and banished about thirty others. Bancroft reprints a document (which he insists is "genuine") which the committee gave to a man named James Cusick, telling him to get out of town: "The Committee of

[2] Richard Maxwell Brown, *Strain of Violence: Historical Studies of American Violence and Vigilantism* (Oxford, New York: Oxford University Press, 1975), pp. 95–96.
[3] Manfred Berg, *Popular Justice: A History of Lynching in America* (Chicago: Ivan R. Dee, 2011), p. 15.
[4] Hubert Bancroft, *Popular Tribunals*, Vol. 1 (San Francisco, CA: The History Company, 1887), p. 137.
[5] There is a sizeable literature on the subject of the San Francisco vigilance committees; see Kevin J. Mullen, *Let Justice Be Done: Crime and Politics in Early San Francisco* (Reno: University of Nevada Press, 1989); Robert M. Senkewicz, *Vigilantes in Gold Rush San Francisco* (Stanford, CA: Stanford University Press, 1985).

Vigilance, after full investigation and deliberation, have declared you guilty of being a notoriously bad character and dangerous person." Cusick was warned to "leave the state of California ... never to return, under the severest penalties."[6] To save their necks, people like Cusick accepted their sentence of banishment.

The 1856 Committee of Vigilance, and other vigilante movements, had a good press in their day. Men sang their praises and insisted that the vigilantes had done a good job, had restored law and order, had tamed the wild spirit of criminality and corruption. Hubert Bancroft, their most noted chronicler, was particularly lavish in his praise of the "beloved rough-necks," who brought about a "speedy and almost bloodless cure" for the epidemic of crime and lawlessness.[7] Another contemporary, Nathaniel Langford, writing in 1890, chiefly about Montana, thought communities owed their "peace and security" to "the prompt and decisive measures adopted by the Vigilantes." People, he wrote, "had perfect confidence in the code of the Vigilantes."[8]

In the years after the formation of the San Francisco vigilance committees, vigilante action spread through the West like wildfire. Vigilance committees were formed in Montana and in other states and territories; more of these vigilante episodes took place in Texas than anywhere else. Mostly, they shared a common goal: quick, merciless justice for thieves, murderers, and all manner of desperados. Sometimes there was no trial at all – nothing but a quick trip to the gallows. At other times, the vigilantes did conduct something more or less resembling a trial, though hardly one that a common law lawyer would recognize, and hardly one that met normal legal standards. In Nevada City, Montana, James Brady was accused of shooting a saloonkeeper, Thomas Murphy. Brady admitted it; said he was drunk at the time. The vigilantes conducted a quick and dirty "trial," convicted him, and sentenced him to death. They gave him time to write a letter to his daughter, but that was all. There was no appeal from the judgments of vigilance committees. Brady was doomed. "A butcher's hoist was used for Brady's hanging with a box and a plank rigged for his drop"; he was executed in front of a crowd of people on June 15, 1864.[9] In Montana, two men arrested for horse-stealing actually got a two-day trial in 1868.[10]

Richard Maxwell Brown counted more than 300 instances of vigilante action.[11] Of these, something in excess of 200 took place in the western United States, in the period between 1850 and the beginning of the twentieth century. Not all of them made heavy use of the hangman's rope; an 1884 movement in Montana, however, directed against horse and cattle thieves, claimed thirty-five victims.[12] Warnings to get out of town were another common tactic of the vigilantes. Most of the men

---

[6] Bancroft, *Popular Tribunals* 2 (1887), p. 276.

[7] Hubert Bancroft, *Popular Tribunals* 1 (1887), pp. 11, 16.

[8] Nathaniel Pitt Langford, *Vigilante Days and Ways: The Pioneers of the Rockies* (New York: Merrill, 1890), p. 537.

[9] Mark C. Dillon, *The Montana Vigilantes, 1863–1870: Gold, Guns, and Gallows* (Logan: Utah State University Press, 2013), pp. 301–302.

[10] Ibid., p. 304. [11] Brown, *Strain of Violence*, p. 96. [12] Ibid., p. 101.

fingered by vigilance committees were guilty of some crime, often murder. But this was not always the case. One striking incident concerned Captain J. A. Slade, at least as Thomas Dimsdale recounted it.[13] Slade also figures, in a very colorful way, in Mark Twain's book *Roughing It*, his history of his "variegated vagabondizing," which he published in 1871. Slade, according to Dimsdale, came to Virginia City in 1863. He could be a "kind-hearted and intelligent gentleman," but when he drank, he turned into a "reckless demon." He would gallop through the streets, shouting and yelling, firing his revolvers, breaking into taverns and shooting at the lamps, and in general vandalizing and terrorizing the town. One morning, the sheriff tried to arrest him and began to read a warrant: Slade tore it up and, with his buddies, ended any talk of arrest. This defiant behavior amounted to a kind of "declaration of war," and the vigilance committee, after Slade continued to commit various outrages, decided to get rid of him once and for all. Slade, seized by the committee, begged for his life; he pleaded for a chance to see his wife, who was living at their ranch. A messenger rode off to tell her what had happened; when she heard, she drove on a "fleet charger," as fast as she could, over "twelve miles of rough and rocky ground," in a desperate attempt to save her husband's life. Too late. Slade was hanged. The body was cut down and carried to a hotel, at which point his wife arrived to discover that "she was a widow. Her grief and heart-piercing cries were terrible evidences of the depth of her attachment." But Slade's execution "had a most wonderful effect upon society," at least in Dimsdale's view.

In Mark Twain's account, Slade had been a serial killer before his Virginia City days. Twain recounts the story of his hanging, quoting directly from the "bloodthirsty interesting little Montana book" of Thomas Dimsdale. But all Slade's murders were in the past (if they existed at all). Slade died for other sins. The men who strung up Captain Slade, and the men who led, or who took part in, vigilante actions, acted as judge, jury, and executioner. Slade might have been a murderer, he might have deserved to die on the gallows. But there was no trial, no proceedings before the courts, no juries, no judges, no due process.

Vigilantes had nothing but contempt for the formal system of justice. Dimsdale's account makes this clear; he sneers at the ordinary brand of justice, with its long delays, its "wearisome proceedings." He accuses local juries of being lawless themselves: paying no attention, for example, to the judge's instructions. If what the defendant did was "a crime against the Mountain Code," it would be punished; if not, the jury would not convict. Judges and juries would punish thieves, but "in affairs of single combats, assaults, shootings, stabbings, and highway robberies," the law was "worse than useless."[14] This low opinion of ordinary legal process was widely shared – widely shared, that is, among the vigilantes and their backers. Bancroft, for example, claimed that (in San Francisco at least) crime wove around itself "the

---

[13] Thomas J. Dimsdale, *The Vigilantes of Montana* (reprint edition, Montana: Two-Dot, 2003), pp. 170–180; see also Dillon, *Montana Vigilantes*, pp. 321–327.

[14] Dimsdale, *Vigilantes of Montana*, pp. 8–9.

threads of law, as the larva spins the protecting cocoon ... [U]nprincipled demago-
gues were placed around the bench, and ruffians made court officers ... Police
officers connived with professional house-breakers and shared the spoil." In the
"interior" it was hard to convict anybody of murder. Juries came from "the hangers-
on about court-rooms, men fit for nothing else ... too lazy to work."[15]

Nathaniel Pitt Langford, who had himself been one of the vigilantes – indeed,
a member of the executive committee of the Virginia City vigilance committee –
gives us an enlightening story about one James Daniels. Daniels, living in
Helena, Montana, got into a quarrel during a card game; the upshot was, he
stabbed and killed a man named Gartley. The vigilantes arrested him and turned
him over to the "civil authorities." He was tried for murder; the jury found him
guilty only of manslaughter. The judge sentenced him to three years in prison.
A "petition for his pardon, signed by thirty-two respectable citizens of Helena,"
was given to the acting governor, who "under mistaken sense of his own powers,
issued an order for his release." Daniels left the prison and went back to Helena.
At this point, the vigilantes arrested Daniels and hanged him.[16] The ordinary
processes of justice had been at work – but the results were not what the vigilantes
wanted.

None of these actions by the vigilantes was authorized, yet no one was ever
charged with murdering Captain Slade, or for stringing up James Daniels, or for
what was done to the other victims of vigilante actions. In fact, many vigilantes were
town elites, respectable men in the community. Leading citizens, in instance after
instance, stood at the head of vigilante movements. Richard Maxwell Brown quotes
from a message sent by a man in Denver, Colorado, in 1859: "There is to be
a Vigilance Committee organized in the town this evening. All of the leading men
of the town has [sic] signed the Constitution." All of the "first men of the town are
determined to punish crime."[17] "Leading men" were also at the head of the San
Francisco vigilance committees. The members, the rank and file, might be drawn
from the (male) population as a whole; but the leadership was not. Vigilante
membership was also no bar to later success in life. Brown lists a number of men
who went on to have distinguished careers. Fennimore Chatterton, like John
Osborne, became governor of Wyoming. Two former vigilantes served as governors
of New Mexico.[18] Granville Stuart, a Montana vigilante leader, became (among
other things) American minister to Uruguay and Paraguay, and president of the
Montana Historical Society. Stuart, by the way, organized a group of vigilantes
called the "Stranglers"; he also put together a fourteen-man group, in the
Musselshell Valley region in Montana, to do something about horse and cattle

---

[15] Bancroft, *Popular Tribunals* 1, pp. 129–130.
[16] Langford, *Vigilante Days and Ways*, pp. 473–475. Interestingly, Langford, otherwise an apologist for
the vigilantes, disapproved of what the vigilantes had done in this case; here they "had exceeded the
boundaries of right and justice and became themselves the violators of law and propriety."
[17] Quoted in Brown, *Strain of Violence*, p. 107.   [18] Ibid., pp. 164–166.

rustling. They shot and hanged rustlers because the law "was powerless to deal with" such thieves.[19]

What lay behind the vigilante movement? The obvious answer, and the one repeated over and over again during vigilantes' prime time, was the assertion that law and order had fatally broken down in Western communities. The towns and mining camps were raw, rowdy, and lawless sites of bloody anarchy. Those who were supposed to uphold the law – sheriffs, for example – could not always be trusted; they were either ineffectual or, what was worse, criminals and highwaymen themselves. Henry Plummer, at one time a county sheriff, was (according to Dimsdale) "chief of the road agent gang." He ended up on the gallows. The vigilance committee condemned him to death. He was seized at his house, and marched off to execution. He begged for his life, and "seemed almost frantic at the prospect of death." Standing on the gallows, he "slipped off his necktie and threw it over his shoulder to a young friend who had boarded at his house," who "threw himself weeping and wailing upon the ground." Plummer asked for "a good drop," and he got it; he "died quickly and without much struggle." His death brought positive results: men "breathed freely" because people like Plummer were "dreaded by almost everyone."[20]

Today, in the cool light of history, there is reason to be skeptical about some of these claims. Was Plummer really the criminal Dimsdale described?[21] Plummer was at one time an elected sheriff; the Democratic Party had nominated him for the territorial assembly.[22] The evidence against Plummer, in the view of one modern authority, was "shockingly weak."[23] And, while no doubt there were law-and-order problems in the West, men like Bancroft and Dimsdale probably exaggerated these problems. The vigilante movements were often *political* movements; some were culture clashes between elites and non-elites, and some were colored by ethnic or religious conflict. This was certainly true in San Francisco. Merchants and leading citizens were at the forefront of the San Francisco vigilance committees: "the most eminent local community leaders," the "leading businessmen of the city."[24] The executive committee of the 1856 vigilantes had thirty-seven members. Most of them can be identified, and they were primarily importers and merchants; four of the members were bankers.[25] The San Francisco vigilance committee of 1856 was in a battle against the Irish and Catholic elements in the city; the goal was to smash the

---

[19] Dillon, *Montana Vigilantes*, pp. 341–342.
[20] Dimsdale, *Vigilantes of Montana*, pp. 129, 130–131, 133. For another account along the same lines, see Langford, *Vigilante Days and Ways*, chapter 10, p. 162ff, and Dillon, *Montana Vigilantes*, pp. 141–146.
[21] On the doubts about Plummer's criminality, see the discussion in the foreword to the 2003 edition of *Vigilantes of Montana*, by R. E. Mather.
[22] Dimsdale, *Vigilantes of Montana*, p. 224.
[23] Christopher Waldrep, *The Many Faces of Judge Lynch: Extralegal Violence and Punishment in America* (New York: Palgrave Macmillan, 2002), p. 95.
[24] Brown, *Strain of Violence*, p. 97.
[25] Robert M. Senkewicz, *Vigilantes in Gold Rush San Francisco* (Stanford, CA: Stanford University Press, 1985), p. 170.

political machine run by Irish-Catholic Democrats.[26] In this, the committee of 1856 was quite successful.

In short, these were not simply "popular tribunals," spontaneous eruptions from ordinary citizens. In Dimsdale's famous account of the vigilantes of Montana, the element of a culture war is obvious to the careful reader. The book is astonishingly prudish. You have to wonder: is this the Wild West? Dimsdale seems shocked by society in the raw. He talks about saloons, where "poisonous liquors," with names like "Tangle-leg" and "Tarantula-juice," are "vended to all comers"; he talks about the "absence of good female society . . . an evil of great magnitude," the tawdry dance halls, the presence of women of "easy virtue . . . promenading through the camp," the "all-pervading custom of using strong language," and that very general sin, "habitual Sabbath breaking."[27] Dimsdale and the vigilantes represented (in a way) polite society; Dimsdale lived in a rough and tough environment, but he seemed curiously unreconciled to it. Yet this man, who wags his finger in disapproval of "Sabbath breaking" and "strong language," was comfortable with the fact that his group killed people whom it branded enemies of the people, and all without trial or process.

Whatever the underlying motives, what is important to note is the fact that hardly anybody was ever punished for taking part in a vigilante movement. There were criticisms, to be sure, but no one was ever put on trial. And the critics, such as they were, were swimming against the tide. The men who hanged Captain Slade, the men who hanged Henry Plummer, and the men who supported the men who hanged them, hardly stopped to consider that they were committing a crime. These were in fact crimes, but crimes without punishment.

The Western movements are the most famous; they are the ones that gave their name to the vigilantes. But, as we pointed out, the vigilante idea (and practice) goes back as far as the eighteenth century. And movements have cropped up here and there, in every part of the country, that were more or less like the Western vigilantes. The Ku Klux Klan was, in a sense, a vigilante group. Lynch mobs (which we turn to next) were a kind of vigilante group.

The underlying idea still appears to have a certain appeal: citizens, fed up with crime and disorder, take the law into their own hands. At the end of 1920, jewelers in New York formed a "vigilance committee"; they stationed armed guards at jewelry stores, and offered a reward for information that might lead to the arrest and conviction of whoever had killed a fellow jeweler Edwin Andrews.[28] Brown gives examples from the 1960s – groups like the North Ward Citizens' Committee, in Newark, New Jersey, made up mostly of Italian-Americans. These groups patrolled city streets and kept watch in their areas. In 1990, Robert Neely, the chief justice of West Virginia, published a book entitled *Take Back Your Neighborhood*. Neely

---

[26]   Brown, *Strain of Violence*, p. 141.   [27]   Dimsdale, *Vigilantes of Montana*, pp. 3, 4, 9.
[28]   "Jewelers Form Vigilantes," *New York Times*, Dec. 18, 1920.

advocated a modern type of vigilantism, "not old-fashioned hang-'em-high justice," and not the justice of the Ku Klux Klan, but the justice of ordinary people at work, unarmed foot soldiers pounding a beat in their own neighborhoods, keeping the peace and fighting crime in an efficient and professional way.[29] Neely's "neovigilantes" would be useful – and, in the opinion of many people, benign; essentially, they would be doing what the police are supposed to do, but apparently do not do, or do adequately, by Neely's standards.

Some neovigilante groups have a more sinister cast. The "Minute Men," formed originally in 2005 in Tombstone, Arizona, were meant to help seal the porous Mexican border, fighting smugglers and illegal migrants, but the tactics and techniques of the Minute Men often seemed to cross over to the dark side. In this case – as in Neely's idea of "modern" vigilantes, the point is the failure of the formal, the official, the "legal." The role of the vigilante is to plug holes in the dyke of justice. But often, both past and present, this would be too simple an explanation for the movement. The vigilantes thrive in a domain of clashing norms and cultures. We return to this theme.

LYNCHING

The vigilantes had their champions; their champions in fact dominated the older literature. In their day, there was certainly opposition to the vigilantes, but as time went on, the vigilantes, as one author put it, retreated into history, and "constructed a picture of themselves that was overdrawn and legendary."[30] Only in the last half of the twentieth century did a certain amount of revisionism set in. Historians today look at the vigilantes with a somewhat jaundiced eye. The literature is mixed at best.

On the other hand, nobody today will say a kind word – nor should they – for a related phenomenon, lynching and the lynch mob, and their actions, mostly in the American South.[31] This too was a disease of the late nineteenth century and the first part of the twentieth. The lynch mobs were roughly contemporaneous with the vigilantes, and the two movements had more in common than one might want to admit.

Judge Lynch did his dirty work in every part of the country; there were brutal and savage examples in such unlikely places as Michigan;[32] nonetheless, in most regions

---

[29] Dana Parsons, "Modern-Day Vigilantes Take Back the Neighborhoods," *Los Angeles Times*, Feb. 7, 1992.

[30] Senkewicz, *Vigilantes in Gold Rush San Francisco*, p. 193.

[31] There is a large literature on lynching; see, for example, Berg, *Popular Justice*; Leon Litwak, *Trouble in Mind: Black Southerners in the Age of Jim Crow* (New York: Alfred A. Knopf, 1998), pp. 280–312; Philip Dray, *At the Hands of Persons Unknown: The Lynching of Black America* (New York: Random House, 2002).

[32] Michael J. Pfeifer, "Lynching in Late-Nineteenth-Century Michigan," in Michael J. Pfeifer, ed., *Lynching beyond Dixie: American Mob Violence outside the South* (Champaign: University of Illinois Press, 2013), p. 211. The book, as the name suggests, contains other essays on the subject, dealing with Kansas, Arizona, Illinois, Ohio, and Maine, among other places.

of the United States, lynching was sporadic and occasional. It was in the states of the Old South, and the border states, and mostly in small, rural towns, that a virtual orgy of lynching took place. Most of the victims were black men. Some of them were accused of raping or assaulting white women – this almost guaranteed a lynch mob. Others were accused of injuring or killing white men, or of other kinds of behavior that, for whatever reason, offended white opinion in their town. Rape and assault dominated discussions of lynching; the South seemed almost obsessed by lurid (and purely imaginary) images of African-American savages with an insatiable desire to rape white women. Men did the actual lynching, but women watched the mob at work, and (usually) did not disapprove. Rebecca Latimer Fenton, a prominent suffragette (she later served as a U.S. senator from Georgia, though only for a day), was also a rabid racist, and a devoted fan of lynching. She described the black victims as "ravenous beasts" whose death was richly merited. She wrote to an Atlanta newspaper in 1905 that if a "black rapist . . . was torn to pieces limb by limb and burnt with slow fire," this would be simple justice; it would be, after all, less than the "revolting torture" he had "inflicted upon a harmless victim."[33] In point of fact, most lynchings had nothing to do with sexual assault, but sexual assaults, or at least claims about sexual assaults, were used to justify the horrors of lynching.

The line between lynching and vigilante action was not always clear; lynching, after all, is a form of vigilante action. It would not violate the English language to say that Captain Slade was lynched. In Leadville, in 1881, one Charles Morman, with two "companions," entered a "theatre and gambling-house," and fired off his revolver, killing "Polk Prindle, a peaceful citizen." Morman ran away, but he was caught and put in jail. "Late at night some unmasked vigilants took the prisoner from the jail and hanged him to a tree, in the presence of several hundred citizens." The story (in the *New York Times*) was headlined "Lynched for Wanton Murder."[34] In the Southwest, in Texas and New Mexico, the line between the two almost disappears. This is particularly true because of the darkly racial aspects of both lynching and vigilante action in that region. Mexicans were notoriously the victims. In 1877, two men, Andres Martinez and Jose Maria Cordena, were arrested for horse theft in Collin County, Texas. They were in the hands of the authorities when ten masked men grabbed them and shot them dead. The "authorities" were fully complicit in many of these incidents. In 1881, the Texas Rangers crossed the border into Mexico and seized Onofrio Baca, who was accused of murder. He was handed over to a mob and "strung up to the cross beams of the gate in the court house yard."[35]

[33]　Quoted in Charles Crowe, "Racial Violence and Social Reform – Airings of the Atlanta Riot of 1906," *Journal of Negro History* 53 (1968), p. 234, reprinted in Paul Finkelman, ed., *Lynching, Racial Violence and Law* (New York: Garland, 1992), p. 252.

[34]　"Lynched for Wanton Murder," *New York Times*, Apr. 14, 1881. In the same month, the *Times* reported that a "Nebraska Ruffian" had been "lynched" by "vigilants." *New York Times*, Apr. 4, 1881.

[35]　William D. Carrigan and Clive Webb, "The Lynching of Persons of Mexican Origin or Descent in the United States, 1848 to 1928," *Journal of Social History* 411 (2003).

In Georgia, we are told, "night riders" – fifty masked horsemen – rode into the town of Dalton in 1884 and attacked five houses thought to be brothels, destroying the furnishings; they beat up the men and women in these houses; they also shot and killed a black man, Tom Tarver, who lived with a white woman. In this area, there were at least sixty-six raids by vigilantes between 1889 and 1894. They horsewhipped prostitutes and shot "three blacks in Dalton who were organizers for the Populist Party."[36] The mayor of Dalton never condemned the raids and the county grand jury never bothered to indict anybody who took part in these incidents. The night riders gave "notice" to the citizens of Dalton, telling them that their aim was to get rid of "thieves, prostitutes, and miscegenationists."[37] This "notice" neatly encapsulated three aspects of the work of this type of vigilante. They stood for law and order (the war on thieves), for the moral order (the war on prostitutes and brothels), and for white supremacy (the war on "miscegenation"). The first two of these were close to the work of the Western vigilantes; the third comes close to lynch law.

Nobody prosecuted the "night riders." Moreover, there is a shameful history of race riots in the United States, and, in almost every case, it was the whites who touched off the riots and the blacks who were overwhelmingly the victims. This was true, for example, of the infamous Colfax massacre in Louisiana (1873). About 150 blacks died in this riot (and three whites); this was perhaps the worst race riot during the period of Reconstruction. The federal government indicted ninety-seven men, who were charged with murder and conspiracy. Only nine actually went on trial. The white community raised money for the defense; one local man raffled off a fancy watch, proceeds to be used for the defendants; there was even a gala benefit in New Orleans. The jury acquitted all of the defendants of murder; three were convicted of conspiracy, but even that was reversed on appeal.[38] Race riots were crimes without punishment.

Lynching lacked the chaos and raucousness of a race riot, but it was, if anything, more barbaric. It sometimes involved torture and brutality to an incredible degree; simply seizing a man, dragging him out of jail, and hanging him was bad enough, but often the mob was guilty of more sadistic behavior. The victims sometimes got the treatment Rebecca Felton advocated: they were burned alive. This was the fate of Charlie Wright, an African-American in Perry, Florida, in 1922; he was burned at the stake in front of a large mob. A white schoolteacher had been found dead, with her throat cut, alongside a railroad track. Wright was accused of the crime. He was arrested, and after he was "taunted and tortured" by a crowd, he confessed. At that point, he was "strapped to a stake. Pine wood and grass were placed at his feet" and set afire. "All classes of citizens" in the town "were present at the burning. Pictures of

---

[36] William F. Holmes, "Moonshining and Collective Violence: Georgia, 1889–1895," *Journal of American History* 67 (1980), pp. 589, 593; Randolph Roth, *American Homicide* (Cambridge, MA: Belknap Press of Harvard University Press, 2009), p. 422.
[37] Holmes, "Moonshining and Collective Violence," p. 593.
[38] LeeAnn Keith, *The Colfax Massacre* (New York: Oxford University Press, 2008), pp. 136, 142–143.

Wright's charred body were taken."[39] In Paris, Texas, in 1893, a young black man, Henry Smith, accused of killing a little girl named Myrtle Vance, was lynched before an enormous crowd; he was first tortured with hot irons, then set on fire. Afterward, people searched for buttons, teeth, and other mementos.[40] Jesse Washington was lynched in Waco, Texas, in 1916; he too was burned to death, in front of a crowd of some 10,000 or so. Before he died, his fingers, toes, and genitals were cut off. A man on horseback "dragged the corpse through the streets of Waco, followed by a throng of young boys. Some of the body parts were sold to onlookers."[41]

Lynching was, of course, always against the law; nothing in the codes of Georgia or Texas or Mississippi gave men the right to kill a prisoner. Many state statutes made this point crystal clear. One of the clearest was the law in Kentucky. In Kentucky, any group of more than three people "assembled for the purpose of doing violence, injury to or lynching any person in custody" was to be "regarded as a mob," and if the person in custody "meets death at the hands of any such mob," the people who took part in the mob were guilty of lynching. The "penalty for lynching shall be death or life imprisonment."[42] In Virginia too, lynching was defined as a form of murder.[43] In other states, the matter was left to implication. Special statutes in these states were aimed at the prevention of lynching, in one way or another. In Georgia, if a judge sniffed the danger of a lynch mob, he could change the prisoner's venue. Also under Georgia law, officers of the law could "summon" citizens to prevent "mob violence," and were told to "use every means in their power to prevent" this sort of violence; failure to follow the dictates of the statute was labeled a misdemeanor.[44]

These statutes were nothing more than words on paper. Despite the Kentucky statute, more than 300 people, mostly black (73 percent), were lynched in Kentucky;[45] lynching, like vigilante action, was almost never punished, in Kentucky and elsewhere. As an Ohio paper put it in 1935, "Officials ... offer little resistance to a lynching mob." The "ringleaders" are fairly obvious, but there is "seldom" any kind of effort to identify who was in the mob and who led it. The leaders (and everybody else who might be involved) were rarely brought to

[39] "Lynched: Knew White Family's Hidden Secrets," *Chicago Defender*, Dec. 16, 1922. The headline refers to a statement by a friend of Wright, claiming Wright was not guilty, but "possessed some valuable information concerning one of the influential white families of the district." He was killed to "get him out of the way."

[40] Dray, *At the Hands of Persons Unknown*, p. 78.   [41] Berg, *Popular Justice*, p. 103.

[42] The statutes as of the 1930s are set out in James Harmon Chadbourn, *Lynching and the Law* (Chapel Hill: University of North Carolina Press, 1933), pp. 149–214. The Kentucky statute, Ky. Stats Ann. (1930), section 1151a-1, is discussed at pp. 166–167. The statute also includes elaborate provisions for the protection of prisoners from lynching.

[43] Ibid., p. 209. Similarly, in West Virginia, ibid., p. 210. In Alabama, the punishment for the "crime of lynching" carried a potential death sentence (ibid., p. 149).

[44] Ibid., pp. 154–155.

[45] George C. Wright, *Racial Violence in Kentucky, 1865–1940: Lynchings, Mob Rule, and "Legal Lynchings"* (Baton Rouge: Louisiana State University Press, 1990), pp. 70–71.

trial, and a "conviction is almost unknown."[46] In Modoc County, California, five people ("three of them half-Indians") were lynched for petty theft in 1901. This was one of the rare cases in which the authorities actually tried to do something. But when a first trial ended in acquittal, the authorities simply gave up.[47]

Indeed, if lynchers were, by some chance, indicted, they were rarely convicted. Records of the Tuskegee Institute for the years between 1900 and 1930 found only twelve cases where anybody at all was convicted – sixty-seven individuals in total. This meant that conviction of a lyncher – any conviction, of any lyncher – occurred in less than 1 percent of the lynchings in the United States after 1900.[48] As late as 1946, four African-Americans were lynched near Monroe, Georgia – Roger Malcolm, his wife, his wife's sister, and his sister-in-law's husband, George Dorsey. Malcolm had gotten into a fight with a white man, had injured him, and was arrested. The four were delivered to an armed mob, which riddled all of them with bullets. There was an outcry and an investigation, and some suspects were identified, but nobody was arrested; a culture of silence and actual fear prevented anybody from being brought to justice.[49] In the same year, a lynch mob in Minden, Louisiana, tortured and killed an African-American veteran, John C. Jones. A federal grand jury handed down indictments, but a jury of twelve white men acquitted the defendants.[50] Lynch mobs were not even deterred by the U.S. Supreme Court: in 1906, Eddie Johnson, a twenty-three-year-old black man, was lynched by a mob in Tennessee, even though Justice Harlan of the Supreme Court had agreed to hear his appeal and announced he was under federal protection.[51]

Local authorities did not, very often, even try to avoid lynching and protect their prisoners. Indeed, it was dangerous, even for whites, to resist a lynch mob. Few ever made the effort. There were occasional exceptions. In a town in Georgia in 1937, two "level-headed white farmers" thwarted a mob of about 100 men who were intent on lynching Willie Hopkins, "21 years old and reputedly feeble-minded, who was charged with attacking a white farm woman." The two farmers "kidnaped the

[46] "A Tennessee Lynching," from the Dayton, Ohio *News* of Nov. 7, 1935, quoted in *Chicago Defender*, Nov. 23, 1935, p. 16.

[47] Michael J. Nolan, "Defendant, Lynch Thyself: A California Appellate Court Goes from the Sublime to the Ridiculous in People v. Anthony J.," 4 *Howard Scroll: The Social Justice Law Review* 53 (2001), p. 73.

[48] Barbara Holden-Smith, "Lynching, Federalism, and the Intersection of Race and Gender in the Progressive Era," *Yale Journal of Law & Feminism* 31 (1996), p. 40.

[49] Doyle Murphy, "FBI Questions Elderly Georgia Man in Connection with Unsolved 1946 Lynching at Moore's Ford Bridge," *New York Daily News*, Feb. 17, 2015.

[50] Lynda G. Dodd, "Presidential Leadership and Civil Rights Lawyering in the Era before Brown," *Indiana Law Journal* 85 (2010), pp. 1599, 1617.

[51] Dray, *At the Hands of Persons Unknown*, pp. 150–159. The Supreme Court did not take this defiance lying down. In *United States v. Shipp*, 203 U.S. 563 (1906), the court upheld a judgment of contempt of court against the sheriff, who (it was claimed) had connived at and permitted the lynching, along with the jailer and a group of citizens. The sheriff and the others in fact went to jail. See "Sheriff Shipp Now in Washington Jail," *New York Times*, Nov. 14, 2006.

intended victim, gave him to a sheriff, and helped rush him to Savannah for safe keeping."[52]

Of course, throughout the period, there were people, in the South as well as in the North, who found lynching barbaric and disgusting. Anti-lynching bills of one kind or another were introduced over and over again into Congress, but they never became law. Powerful Southern senators and congressmen were able to block these bills. States' rights was the usual excuse for opposing anti-lynching laws. The real reason, aside from plain bigotry, was the fear that a federal law, unlike state laws, might possibly be enforced. And on the whole, as far as we can tell, white Southerners were in favor of lynching, or, at the least, thought it was often justified. In 1942, a black congregation in Chicago protested when Willie Vinson, accused of an "attempt" to assault a white woman, was lynched in Texarkana. The mayor of Texarkana, William Brown, reacted with anger. A "criminal of your race," the mayor said, "committed a vile crime ... When rapes stop, then lynching will stop. If you don't play with fire you will not be burned." "I hate lynchings," he said, "but it is like removing a cancer; it is painful to have the cancer (rape) and it is painful to cut it out (lynching)."[53]

What explains Southern lynch law? Not weakness of law and order – law and order were in fact not weak. To be sure, some lynchings did occur in reaction to what the mob considered leniency; this was true in the notorious case of Leo Frank (who was white and Jewish), and was lynched in Georgia in 1915. Frank was accused of murdering Mary Phagan, a thirteen-year-old girl who worked in a pencil factory owned by Frank's uncle. Frank was almost certainly innocent. He was tried and convicted on the flimsiest of evidence in an atmosphere of rabid anti-Semitism. His appeals failed in the courts, but the governor, John Slaton, commuted his sentence to life imprisonment. An angry and hysterical mob seized Frank and lynched him in Marietta, Georgia.[54]

This incident was exceptional in a number of ways. First of all, Leo Frank was white; that made him a minority among lynching victims. Apparently, more than 4,700 lynchings took place between the 1880s and the Second World War. Blacks made up 73 percent of the victims, more than four out of five lynchings took place in the South, and, in the South, black deaths "were a staggering 83% of the total."[55] And leniency was almost never an issue. After all, a black man accused of killing a white man or raping a white woman stood no chance at all in court in the Jim Crow South. No blacks served on juries; all-white juries were absolutely certain to return verdicts of guilty against black defendants, and certain too, in appropriate cases, to impose

[52] "Dixie Reporters Relate Eye Witness Story of Lynching That Was Halted," *Kansas City Plaindealer*, May 14, 1937, p. 1.
[53] "Texarkana Mayor Writes in Defense of Lynching," *Chicago Defender*, Aug. 29, 1942, p. 1.
[54] There is a sizeable literature on this case; see, for example, Leonard Dinnerstein, *The Leo Frank Case* (New York: Columbia University Press, 1987); Steve Oney, *And the Dead Shall Rise: The Murder of Mary Phagan and the Lynching of Leo Frank* (New York: Pantheon Books, 2003).
[55] Berg, *Popular Justice*, p. 92.

a death sentence. In one case, indeed, in 1916, in Waco, Texas, Jesse Washington, a black teenager, whom we mentioned earlier, accused of killing a white woman, agreed to waive his right to ask for a change of venue or to appeal. He was told he would be "protected from lynch law ... As the jurors were called, members of the crowd yelled, 'We don't need any jury!'" The trial was short; the jury took three minutes to find him guilty. He was sentenced to hang "in a few hours." The sheriff disappeared and the mob had its way: he was burned at the stake, in a particularly gruesome way, as we noted.[56]

This trial was a mockery of justice – but it reveals a fundamental fact about white opinion in the South. Regular legal process was biased and exceedingly harsh, but this did not satisfy white mobs. Formal law was too fastidious and its message (apparently) too wishy-washy. It did not strike enough terror and teach a strong enough lesson to the black community. The message and the lesson were about white supremacy.

In one notable lynching in 1918, the victim was a twenty-nine-year-old German immigrant, Robert Prager. The site was Collinsville, Illinois – not the deep South. This was during the First World War and Prager had aroused suspicion of disloyalty in a period of intense anti-German feeling. A mob grabbed Prager, but the police rescued him and took him into custody. Still, that night, a mob of hundreds seized Prager and hanged him on the outskirts of town. According to one account, his "dying request" was to "be permitted to kiss the American flag."[57]

Lawrence Yates Sherman, a Republican senator from Illinois, denounced this lynching as the work of a "drunken mob masquerading in the garb of patriots," as a "deliberate willful act of murder, and the men who participated in it ought to be hung."[58] No such thing happened. The grand jury of Madison County, Illinois, indicted sixteen people for their role in the lynching, including Joseph Riegel, a former soldier, "now a cobbler," who "confessed at the coroner's inquest." At the trial, the judge, in his instructions, told the jury not to consider the war as a factor; this was a case "in which a helpless prisoner was taken from a jail and murdered." The court recessed; a band from the Great Lakes Naval Training Station, present by coincidence, played the Star-Spangled Banner. The jury deliberated all of forty-five minutes and declared all of the defendants not guilty.[59]

The only thing unusual about this case was that there was any sort of legal proceeding at all. Normally, leaders and followers were immune from punishment. This was clear in the Leo Frank case, the Robert Prager case, and countless other

---

[56] Chadbourn, *Lynching and the Law*, p. 8. Chadbourn does not identify the victim of this lynching, but the reference makes clear it was Jesse Washington.

[57] "Says Prager's Dying Wish Was to Kiss Flag," *Chicago Daily Tribune*, May 30, 1918, p. 14; on the Prager case, see Berg, *Popular Justice*, pp. 136–137.

[58] "Sherman Calls Prager Slayers a 'Drunken Mob,'" *Chicago Daily Tribune*, Apr. 9, 1918, p. 6.

[59] "16 Indicted for Participation in Prager Killing," *Chicago Daily Tribune*, Apr. 26, 1918, p. 7; "'Not Guilty' is Jury's Verdict in Prager Case," *Chicago Daily Tribune*, June 2, 1918, p. 10.

cases where white mobs lynched black victims. In most cases, everybody knew who
was involved. In most cases, photographic evidence of the lynching was widely
circulated.[60] Often you can see the faces of the lynch mob clearly. But nothing
was ever done to bring them to justice. In a few cases, there were half-hearted
attempts at some kind of reckoning; these usually dribbled out into nothingness.
In the Leo Frank case, there was a grand jury hearing after the lynching. Testimony
was given. The result was a foregone conclusion. The grand jury of Cobb County,
Georgia, was "unable to connect anybody with the perpetration of this offense," and,
as a consequence, "we find it impossible to indict anyone." Seven members of the
lynch mob, apparently, were serving on this grand jury.[61]

There was also immunity for men who, for whatever reason, were accused of
committing *any* sort of crime against an African-American. White juries simply
acquitted these men. This happened again and again. Alexander Salley,
a "conscientious white sheriff," deplored this state of affairs in his state, South
Carolina (1889); he felt he was powerless to do anything about it: "it is the height
of folly to try to convict a white man for killing a poor negro. A certain class think it is
something to be proud of."[62]

This attitude lasted deep into the twentieth century. The murder of Emmett Till
is a case in point. Till was a fourteen-year-old boy, raised in Chicago, who was
visiting relatives in Mississippi. Apparently, Till was naïve or foolish enough to flirt
with a white woman – probably on a dare or as a joke. This was not a wise move for an
African-American boy in Mississippi in 1955. The woman's husband, along with his
half-brother, snatched Till, and a few days later, his mauled and mutilated body was
found in the river. His mother in Chicago brought the body back and showed it to
the world; a storm of protest arose. The two men were put on trial. The all-white jury
acquitted them.

Emmitt Till's death was murder, not lynching; it was done quietly and
privately at night and no mob was involved. This is hardly progress, but it
does suggest that, by this time, lynching had become something of an anachron-
ism. Murder of blacks would still go unpunished, but mob action would be less
and less common. As a social phenomenon, lynching could not survive in the
age of the civil rights movement, and, perhaps, in an age in which the federal
government had gotten serious about black rights in general. Hate crimes did
not disappear, but they went underground. Race killing was, in some ways, still
a crime without punishment, but it lacked the overt, mass, community aspects of
lynch law.

The vigilante movement also disappeared – at least the Western form.
It survived, to be sure, elsewhere. Both lynching and the vigilante movement
were never exclusively American. Lynching has appeared, for example, in Latin

---

[60]   For any number of horrifying examples, see Amy Louise Wood, *Lynching and Spectacle: Witnessing
       Racial Violence in America, 1890–1940* (Chapel Hill: University of North Carolina Press, 2009).
[61]   Oney, *And the Dead Shall Rise*, p. 589.   [62]   Quoted in Litwak, *Trouble in Mind*, p. 254.

America.[63] And notorious "death squads" have flourished in Central and South America and elsewhere as well – in the Philippines under President Duterte, for example, where thousands of (alleged) drug dealers and users have been dispatched through extremely dubious means. Death squads are, in a way, a form of vigilantism. They are "groups composed of police or other agents of the state who are assigned, with varying degrees of secrecy, to carry out the extra-judicial extermination of … 'public enemies' and 'undesirables.'"[64] They flourish mainly in right-wing autocracies. The crimes they commit are, of course, crimes without punishment.

We still hear, in the United States, about "vigilantes" from time to time. The term still refers to groups whose goal is to enforce norms and laws that the state, for whatever reason, has not handled or has not handled well, or where law and order have broken down (at least in the eyes of the "vigilantes"). In Port Chester, New York, in 1964, twenty-four residents formed a "vigilante group" to deal with "teen-age drinkers from Connecticut," who swarmed into a neighborhood of "small and dingy barrooms," where underage boys and girls could buy drinks. These vigilantes accused the police of "ineptness."[65] In New Orleans, in 2010, after Hurricane Katrina devastated parts of the city, some white, upper-income people banded together to form "vigilante" groups; in one white "enclave" in a mostly black neighborhood, "armed white militias" cordoned off many of the streets, and there was police violence too against African-American residents of the city. The "suffering population" of poor African-Americans was "far more brutalized than many were willing to believe."[66] And, recently, as we noted, informal militias and patrols have formed at the country's southern border, ostensibly to protect the border from invading hordes.[67] The constant theme is ineffective law enforcement. Most modern "vigilantes," however, would never dream of hanging anybody. Their work is preventive, not reactive. But violence, or the threat of violence, is always a possibility.

---

[63] See, for example, the essays (mostly about Guatemala) collected in Carlos Mendoza and Edelberto Torres-Riva, *Linchamientos: Barbarie o "Justicia Popular"?* (Guatemala: FLACSO: Proyecto Cultura de Paz de UNESCO, 2003).

[64] Ray Abrahams, *Vigilant Citizens: Vigilantism and the State* (Cambridge: Polity Press, 1998), p. 123.

[65] Merrill Folsom, "Vigilantes Form in Port Chester," *New York Times*, Dec. 10, 1964, p. 1.

[66] Trymaine Lee, "Rumor to Fact in Tales of Post-Katrina Violence," *New York Times*, Aug. 26, 2010.

[67] See Austin Bunn, "Homegrown Homeland Defense," *New York Times*, June 1, 2003.

2

The Unwritten Law

In the late 1850s, Daniel Edgar Sickles, a congressman from New York, received an anonymous letter.[1] The contents of the letter shocked him deeply.[2] Sickles was thirty-seven years old; his young and attractive wife, Teresa, was about half his age. The letter (nobody knows who sent it) claimed that Teresa was committing adultery; she was involved in a torrid affair with a man named Philip Barton Key.[3] Sickles confronted his wife; could this be true? In tears, she confessed: yes, this was true. She used to meet Key, she said, in a house on Fifteenth Street, where, on a bed in the second floor, she "did what is usual for a wicked woman to do." Sickles was nothing if not a man of action. He took a weapon and looked for Key on the streets of the capital. When Sickles found Key, he shouted, "Key, you scoundrel . . . you have dishonored my bed – you must die!" And Key did die; one bullet pierced his thigh, another his liver.[4] Sickles was arrested and charged with first-degree murder.[5] At the end of the trial, the jury, in almost indecent haste, brought in its verdict: not guilty.[6]

Fifty years later, on a crowded street in Los Angeles, a woman named Margaret Finn shot and killed J. E. Mahaffey.[7] Finn and Mahaffey were engaged to be married. Moreover, Finn was pregnant with Mahaffey's child. The problem was, Mahaffey was getting cold feet. He had money problems, he told her, and he wanted

---

[1] An earlier version of this chapter was Lawrence M. Friedman and William E. Havemann, "The Rise and Fall of the Unwritten Law: Sex, Patriarchy, and Vigilante Justice in the American Courts," *Buffalo Law Review* 61 (2013), p. 997.

[2] See William Andrew Swanberg, *Sickles the Incredible: A Biography of Daniel Edgar Sickles* (New York: Scribner's, 1956), pp. 46–54.

[3] Ibid., p. 46. Key was the son of Francis Scott Key, who wrote the Star-Spangled Banner. Philip Barton Key was young, good looking, and a widower.

[4] Ibid., p. 55. Of course, as is well known, the double standard was in full flower in this period. Daniel Sickles was hardly the model of a faithful husband. He spent a number of evenings at a Baltimore hotel with a woman who registered as Mrs. Sickles, but was not Teresa; he was plainly guilty of "adulterous intercourse." See Nat Brandt, *The Congressman Who Got Away with Murder* (Syracuse: Syracuse University Press, 1991), pp. 90–91.

[5] Swanberg, *Sickles the Incredible*, pp. 55–58.   [6] Ibid., p. 66.

[7] See "Woman Murders Man on Crowded Street," *Los Angeles Times*, July 6, 1908, p. 14.

to postpone the wedding indefinitely. Finn, apparently anguished by what she felt was a betrayal, tracked down Mahaffey and shot him dead. Her mind, she claimed, had gone blank at the time; what happened was "a mystery" to her, and she had no memory of pulling the trigger. She also said that Mahaffey deserved to die because of the way he had treated her: "I had placed my honor and my life in his trust and he betrayed that trust."[8] The judge seemed to agree and dismissed the case. Finn never went to trial.[9]

On January 13, 1912, John Beal Sneed shot and killed Captain Al Boyce Sr., a millionaire banker, in the lobby of the Fort Worth Hotel.[10] Sneed, from a prominent Texas family, had a young wife, Lena. Lena fell in love with Boyce's son, Al Jr.; they met as university students.[11] Lena confessed this fact; she told her husband she loved Boyce and wanted to elope with him to South America.[12] But Sneed had her committed to a sanitarium. Al Jr. managed to arrange for her to escape and the couple ran off to Canada, hoping to start a new life together. Sneed, however, found out, retrieved Lena, and came back to Texas – jealous, ashamed, and eager for revenge. He was convinced that young Boyce's father had played a part in this sordid drama; for this reason, he shot and killed the senior Boyce, saying later that "it had to be done."[13] Sneed's trial for murder ended up with a hung jury; the judge declared a mistrial.[14] Before Sneed could be retried, Sneed, disguised as a tramp "with a heavy growth of beard and wearing overalls," tracked down young Boyce in front of a Methodist church in Amarillo, Texas, and shot him. Boyce, wounded and bleeding, pleaded for his life, but Sneed shot him dead.[15] A jury acquitted him of both killings.[16]

These three cases illustrate aspects of what has been called the "unwritten law." The Sickles trial is perhaps the classic example; it is also one of the earliest on record. In these cases, typically, the defendant is on trial for murder. The crime: a man kills another man who had sexual relations with the first man's wife or who had dishonored the defendant's mother or sister. Formally and technically, this is murder. If the case goes to a jury, the defendant's lawyers will advance this or that legal argument. Often, they will plead "temporary insanity" (of which more later). But the real defense, and a powerful one, is the "unwritten law." A man is entitled to protect the sanctity of marriage and home; honor and manhood require firm action. And the dead man, moreover, was a scoundrel, a seducer, who deserved to die. In the cases that went to trial, the jury acquitted, sometimes with amazing speed.

[8] "Tells Why She Killed Lover," *Los Angeles Times*, July 7, 1908, p. l13.
[9] "Margaret Finn Is Acquitted," *Los Angeles Times*, Oct. 17, 1908, p. II2.
[10] "Unwritten Law Issue in Trial," *Atlanta Constitution*, Feb. 6, 1912, p. 8.
[11] Thomas H. Thompson, *Boyce–Sneed Feud*, Texas State Historical Association, www.tshaonline.org /handbook/online/articles/jcbo2, visited Sept. 23, 2013.
[12] "He Slew Wife's Lover; Sneed Is Acquitted," *Atlanta Constitution*, Feb. 26, 1913, p. 9.
[13] "Unwritten Law Issue in Trial."
[14] "Sneed Kills Young Boyce," *Boston Globe*, Sept. 15, 1912, p. 2.
[15] "Wounded Boyce Begged for Life," *Atlanta Constitution*, Sept. 24, 1912, p. 1.
[16] See "He Slew Wife's Lover: Sneed Is Acquitted."

State penal codes, of course, never recognized any defense to these honor kill-ings – at least not officially. Texas law in the nineteenth century came about as close as any. First of all, under the Penal Code of 1857, a killing, if committed "under the immediate influence of sudden passion arising from an adequate cause," was defined as manslaughter, not murder.[17] And what qualified as a sudden passion? "Adultery of the person killed, with the wife of the person guilty of the homicide, provided the killing occur as soon as the fact of an illicit connection is discovered."[18] And if a husband killed a man who was "taken in the act of adultery" with his wife, this was neither murder nor manslaughter, but "justifiable," and not a crime at all, provided the killing took place "before the parties to the act of adultery have separated."[19] As one author put it, sarcastically, to kill a deer, or a duck, quail, or turkey, you needed a hunting license, but to "kill some lesser species," including "common varmints such as possums, coons, rabbits and the like," no permit was needed, and the "season is always open"; this was also true of a male human varmint, if you "could catch one between the sheets with your wife."[20]

Taken literally, this last defense was a very narrow one. The husband had to make his move before the guilty couple had "separated." In short, the scoundrel had to be very unlucky in his love-making, very careless, or totally carried away. He would, in other words, have to be caught in the act. This had to be a rare defense. Texas courts in some cases did stretch the statute – but only a bit: the statute was, after all, quite explicit. And in one rather bizarre 1922 case, the court refused to go beyond a literal reading of the statute. The defendant, Sensobaugh, entered his house and found the victim "under circumstances justifying the conclusion that he was about to have criminal relations" with Sensobaugh's wife. But Sensobaugh decided not to kill the man; instead he tied him up and "cut off his penis with a razor." Arrested, fined, and ordered to jail, Sensobaugh argued that, since he could have killed his rival, doing something less than that was entitled to the same immunity. The court, however, refused to buy this argument. The statute specifically talked about killing a rival, and nothing else. Sensobaugh had maimed, but not killed. The conviction was affirmed.[21]

A few states had statutes similar to the Texas law. Under the New Mexico Code of 1915, for example, a man was justified in killing someone "who is in the act of having carnal knowledge of such person's legal wife" (sec. 1458). And the Utah statutes of 1898 made homicide justified, "when committed in a sudden heat of passion,"

[17] Penal Code of the State of Texas, 1857, Article 594, pp. 116–117.
[18] Ibid., Article 599 (3), pp. 117–118. Also "insulting words or conduct of the person killed, towards a female relation of the party guilty of the homicide," qualified for manslaughter, not murder, Art. 599 (4).
[19] Ibid., Article 562, p. 110. See also Hendrick Hartog, "Lawyering, Husbands' Rights, and 'the Unwritten Law' in Nineteenth-Century America," *Journal of American History* 84 (1997), pp. 67, 68.
[20] Bill Neal, *Sex, Murder and the Unwritten Law: Courting Judicial Mayhem, Texas Style* (Lubbock: Texas Tech University Press, 2009), p. 3.
[21] *Sensobaugh v. State*, 244 S. W. 379 (Ct. of Crim. Appeals of Texas, 1922).

caused by an attempt "to commit a rape upon or to defile the wife, daughter, sister, mother, or other female relative . . . of the accused" (sec. 4168).[22] In any event, no such law was in effect in the District of Columbia; there was no *legal* way for Congressman Sickles to claim "justifiable" homicide. Key was fully dressed and going about his business; Sickles shot him on the streets of Washington. The formal law was no use to Sickles. Killing a rival was murder, plain and simple.

There was, of course, the concept of sudden passion, which might have dropped the crime from murder to manslaughter. But manslaughter, even though it did not carry the death sentence or life imprisonment, was still a serious crime with serious consequences. The living law, in Texas and elsewhere, did not bother making distinctions between degrees of homicide. It simply let defendants go. That was the "unwritten law." Killing a rival who had sex with a wife or who dishonored a mother or sister was basically a crime without punishment.

The "unwritten law" came in a number of versions. The Sickles version was the most common: killing your wife's lover. But a kind of unwritten law also applied to women who killed brutal husbands or lovers, or to men who "ruined" a woman and refused to marry her. American juries from New York to Georgia to California, in the nineteenth century and in the early twentieth, faced with these situations, would not and did not convict. And many judges apparently approved of this position.

In a jury trial, lawyers for defense and prosecution will each try to convince the jury of their case. They make arguments that judge and jury (they hope) will find sympathetic and persuasive. At the end of the trial, the jury goes behind closed doors to talk the case over. When the jurors come out, they announce a brief, laconic verdict. They never give reasons. They almost never tell us why they decided as they did. The jury room is the blackest of black boxes. Still, we can make educated guesses about the minds of the jurors – about which arguments persuaded them. Context, culture, prejudices, and stereotypes of the day: these were probably decisive.

Of course, the arguments of the lawyers and the patterns of jury verdicts are hardly rigorous evidence of norms, culture, and social attitudes. But often this is the best we can do. This is especially true for the dark ages before opinion polls. Any single trial, any particular verdict, might be idiosyncratic. But *patterns* of verdicts and decisions are different; they tell a tale.

In cases that invoked the "unwritten law" between 1850 and 1950, the patterns are quite obvious. For nearly a century, jury behavior announced, in no uncertain terms, that a man had a right to kill his wife's lover or seducer. A man like Congressman Sickles was not to be punished at all, and never mind what the penal code said. This "unwritten law" was in fact unwritten, but in one key sense

---

[22] The section adds "or when the defilement has actually been committed," but this does not really codify the unwritten law because the statute still requires a "sudden heat of passion," and this implies that the "defilement" and the killing had to be very close in time. *State* v. *Botha*, 27 Utah 289, 75 P. 731 (1904).

it was certainly not law. Yet the evidence suggests it was a "law" in another sense: it was well understood, even routine; it was invoked whenever the facts fit a certain pattern, and it led to predictable results.

The unwritten law is, nonetheless, a rather shadowy subject. If a case went to trial, juries almost always acquitted. In our system, the state cannot appeal from an acquittal. As soon as the jury says, "not guilty," the case is over, and the defendant walks out of the courtroom. Since only appeal cases are reported, the unwritten law was not openly discussed in standard legal texts. The evidence, then, lies buried deep in the files of county courts all over the country. Scholarship on the unwritten law, although it is fairly substantial,[23] has to rely, in large part, on other sources – very notably, newspaper accounts of incidents and trials. This is where we learn about the rise and fall of the unwritten law.

We begin to hear about the "unwritten law" roughly around the middle of the nineteenth century. A few sensational cases, at the very beginning of the twentieth century, amounted to a kind of climax. By about 1950, the "unwritten law" was in decline, and it is now, at least in its classic form, quite extinct. The unwritten law assumed a specific cluster of social and cultural norms, and when these decayed, the unwritten law as such fell into terminal disuse.

The unwritten law was in effect in every part of the country, though perhaps more common in the South, with its stronger sense of masculine honor.[24] A search of three major newspapers, the *Atlanta Constitution*, the *Los Angeles Times*, and the *New York Times*, for the period focused on, yielded a total of 201 reported instances where the defendant invoked the unwritten law as part of his case.[25] These 201 instances have to be taken as a sample, nothing more. Many more instances must have occurred – unreported except in the back pages of newspapers in other parts of the country, or not important or interesting enough to get the attention of the press in these three cities. Still, the 201 cases are a big enough sample to yield insights into the nature of the beast.

Men were the defendants in the overwhelming majority of the cases. In 163 cases (81.1 percent), men were on trial for killing or trying to kill a man who had wronged his wife or female relative; in thirty-eight cases (18.9 percent), the defendant was a woman on trial for killing or trying to kill a man who "betrayed" her, or a woman

[23] See generally Carol Haber, *The Trials of Laura Fair* (Chapel Hill: University of North Carolina Press, 2013); Neal, *Sex, Murder, and the Unwritten Law*; Hartog, "Lawyering, Husbands' Rights, and 'the Unwritten Law' in Nineteenth-Century America"; Robert M. Ireland, "Insanity and the Unwritten Law," *American Journal of Legal History* 32 (1988), p. 157; Robert M. Ireland, "'The Libertine Must Die': Sexual Dishonor and the Unwritten Law in the Nineteenth-Century United States," *Journal of Social History* 23 (1989), p. 27; Martha Merrill Umphrey, "The Dialogics of Legal Meaning: Spectacular Trials, the Unwritten Law, and Narratives of Criminal Responsibility," *Law & Society Review* 33 (1999), p. 393.

[24] See Edward L. Ayers, *Vengeance and Justice: Crime and Punishment in the Nineteenth-Century American South* (New York: Oxford University Press, 1984).

[25] The method used was to search the databases for every instance in which the terms "unwritten law" and "trial" appeared in a newspaper article.

who stole away her husband. A majority of the cases came from the South (51.7 per-cent); most of the rest came from the West or the Northeast. It seems likely that the South did produce more than its fair share, but the choice of newspapers naturally skews the results. There was also a noticeable spike in numbers in the first two decades of the twentieth century, especially in the years right after 1906.

Each case, of course, is unique. Nor did they all come out in quite the same way. The cases can be divided into three categories. The *first* consists of all the cases where the defendant escaped scot-free. These were cases where the jury acquitted, or where a grand jury declined to indict the defendant, or where a coroner's jury found that no crime had been committed, or a prosecutor simply did not bring charges. In the *second* group, the defendant was found guilty, but the punishment was so mild that the unwritten law might well have been a factor. In these cases the defendant paid a fine, or was released on probation, or was sentenced to eight years or less. Since the charge was usually first-degree murder, a short sentence has to be con-sidered unusually lenient. This category also includes cases where the defendant was convicted, but the governor granted clemency. The *third* category consisted of cases in which the unwritten law did not seem to help the defendant; the defendant was convicted and sentenced to death or to a long term in prison – to terms longer than eight years, the (somewhat arbitrary) cutoff point.[26]

On the whole, the unwritten law was hugely successful – or so it seemed. Of course, there might be selection bias: newspaper editors might find cases of acquittal more newsworthy than cases where the defense failed. This is possible. If I had to guess, I would guess that the sample undercounts the success of the unwritten law. Newspapers did not always follow through on coverage. A defendant might be convicted and sentenced later to a trivial sentence, or granted a pardon and this might go unreported. In three cases, the *Atlanta Constitution* reported that the jury convicted, but recommended "mercy" in sentencing.[27] There was no follow-up story on the actual sentence. These cases have to be put down as cases where the unwritten law failed to help the defendant; this might be somewhat misleading, but it is hard to be sure of the actual outcome.

In general, the evidence suggests that the unwritten law was a national phenom-enon. The tilt toward the South and the West also seems fairly clear. Contemporaries seem to have thought so too. Mary Ertell ran away with a man who "fascinated" her.[28] When he abandoned her, she shot him down, admitted the crime, and expressed no remorse. A New York jury acquitted her. Newspapers

[26] In one case, a defendant received an eight-year sentence and thanked the judge for the judge's "leniency." See "J. H. Hartley Gets 8-Year Sentence," *Atlanta Constitution*, Dec. 8, 1911, p. 3. This seemed as good a reason as any to choose eight years as a dividing line between lenient and severe sentences.

[27] See "Manslaughter Was the Verdict," *Atlanta Constitution*, Oct. 3, 1908, p. 11; "Pleaded the Unwritten Law," *Atlanta Constitution*, June 30, 1907, p. C5; "Unwritten Law Plea Fails to Save Short," *Atlanta Constitution*, May 11, 1913, p. 1.

[28] "The Unwritten Law," *Atlanta Constitution*, Apr. 1, 1901, p. 4.

commenting on the case called it "an importation of Kentucky law."[29] A reporter for the *Atlanta Constitution* wrote that human nature was "very much the same everywhere."[30] "There is unwritten law in New York as well as in the south and west." This was in 1901. Later, in 1909, an editorial in the same newspaper bemoaned the "increase in the number of acquittals of men charged with murder in this state." Georgia, it was feared, could develop "as great a disregard for human life . . . as ever existed in the lawless days of the west."[31]

To some people, the unwritten law was if anything a source of pride. The reference to "Kentucky law" is not wholly fanciful. Governor Brown of Kentucky endorsed the unwritten law even after his own son became a victim. And, after pardoning Nancy May for killing Alice Smith, another Kentucky governor remarked that the unwritten law had "prevailed in many cases" and that it conformed to a "certain sentiment in Kentucky."[32] After acquitting John Sneed in the murder of Al Boyce Jr., the foreman of the Texas jury was asked why the jury handed down this verdict. He said it was because "this is Texas. We believe in Texas a man has the right and the obligation to safeguard the honor of his home, even if he must kill the person responsible."[33]

The South was, it seems, quite hospitable to the unwritten law, but there were plenty of examples from other parts of the country. Two of the most notable defendants, George Cole and Harry Thaw (more on these two later), were tried in New York. And while Congressman Sickles faced a court in the District of Columbia, he was himself a New Yorker. In 1913, a jury in St. Paul, Minnesota, acquitted Professor Oscar Olson in the murder of Clyde N. Darling, "alleged wrecker of the Olson home," on the basis of the unwritten law.[34] In 1938, Rudolph Sikora, a dispatcher's clerk in Chicago, killed Edward Solomon, described as the "rival for his wife's love."[35] A jury of "eleven husbands and one bachelor" heard the case. The prosecutor asked for the death penalty. The jury was out for two hours and then announced a verdict of not guilty. A crowd of some 200 in the courtroom, "most of them women," screamed and cried in delight; many "burst into wild tears."[36] "Above the noise came the piercing hallelujah of a tall woman in black, who cried 'Bless his sweet heart . . . !'" Sikora himself shouted, "It's swell," before he was rushed from the courtroom.[37]

[29]   Ibid.   [30]   Ibid.

[31]   "The Elasticity of the 'Unwritten Law,'" *Atlanta Constitution*, Jan. 22, 1909, p. 6.

[32]   "Pardon for Murderess," *New York Times*, July 8, 1904, p. 1.

[33]   Thompson, *Boyce–Sneed Feud* (internal quotation marks omitted).

[34]   "Prof Olson Freed by Jury: 'Unwritten Law' Plea Wins," *Chicago Daily Tribune*, Apr. 9, 1913, p. 2.

[35]   Marcia Winn, "Sikora Free in Love Murder," *Chicago Daily Tribune*, Oct. 22, 1938, p. 1.   [36]   Ibid.

[37]   Ibid. But in 1901, Thomas G. Barker was convicted of attempted murder, after trying to kill his wife's lover in New Jersey. "Barker Convicted of Shooting Mr. Keller," *New York Times*, June 22, 1901, p. 1. A reporter for the *New York Times* thought that this meant that there was no unwritten law in New Jersey (ibid.). The reporter spoke too soon. In four later cases in New Jersey, the unwritten law succeeded. For example, in 1937, Margaret Drennan, a woman from New Jersey, killed Paul Reeves. "Margaret Drennan Acquitted in Slaying of Married Man," *Atlanta Constitution*, Oct. 23, 1937, at 1. She claimed he was the father of her unborn child – even though he was married to another woman

In short, results in the Northeast, in those cases that went to trial, do not seem different from the cases in the South. What we do not know – and cannot know – is whether there was simply more of this sort of honor killing in the South, compared to the Northeast. In some cases in the Northeast, defendants came from the upper classes; they were men who could afford a stellar legal team, a team that could mount and pull off a defense based on the unwritten law.[38] In the South and West, the unwritten law may have been more routine. Defendants were a cross-section of society – farmers,[39] airport workers,[40] miners,[41] immigrants.[42] In the South and West, there were also occasional nonwhite defendants. In 1911, James J. Manuel, an African-American in Denver, was acquitted after killing the Rev. Alexander Edwards, his pastor, who had confessed to "improper relations" with Manuel's wife.[43] In 1915, a black man from Georgia, Will Maxon, killed Dud McGregor, who had accused Maxon's wife of stealing McGregor's chickens, apparently a grave affront to a woman, at least in Georgia. Maxon was acquitted.[44] And surprisingly, two decades earlier, the governor of South Carolina had pardoned Robert Stenhouse, a black man who killed a white man, after finding him *in flagrante delicto* with Stenhouse's wife.[45] Stenhouse had been sentenced to two years' imprisonment – not much for a homicide case. The governor pardoned him on the grounds that "the unwritten law on this subject was as good for the negro as the white man." This clemency was extraordinary; this was the Jim Crow South in the age of lynching, after all.

But it might be hasty to claim that the unwritten law was an equal-opportunity doctrine. In 1925, a young Filipino waiter, Yatko, shot and killed Harry L. Kidder, a white man; Kidder, according to Yatko, was having an affair with Yatko's (white) wife.[46] The wife wanted to testify against her husband; in California, under the doctrine of marital privilege, the defendant could invoke the privilege and block his wife from giving testimony. The judge, however, saw a way out. In California, "persons of opposing races" were not allowed to marry.[47] Yatko's marriage was therefore void, and his "wife" could testify against him. Yatko was found guilty and sentenced to life in prison.

Race and the unwritten law figured in the famous Massie case in Hawaii in the early 1930s. Hawaii, then and now, was home to a mixture of races – and by no means

who had borne him two children. Drennan said she shot Reeves to ward off a second attack. She was acquitted, and the spectators "stood up, shouted and clapped their hands."

38 See Hartog, "Lawyering, Husbands' Rights, and 'the Unwritten Law' in Nineteenth-Century America", p. 75, describing the lawyers in three famous cases.

39 See "West Pardons Aged Farmer," *Los Angeles Times*, Oct. 4, 1912, p. I3.

40 See "Heated Legal Clash Marks Wright Trial," *Los Angeles Times*, Jan. 14, 1938, p. I1.

41 See "Unwritten Law Frees Slayer," *Los Angeles Times*, Sept. 8, 1913, p. II7.

42 See "Pleads Unwritten Law," *Los Angeles Times*, May 7, 1925, p. II2.

43 "Unwritten Law Covers Black as Well as White," *Atlanta Constitution*, Nov. 3, 1911, p. 5.

44 "Protected His Wife, Says Little Negro; Plea Wins Freedom," *Atlanta Constitution*, July 1, 1915, p. 5.

45 "Justice to the Negro," *Atlanta Constitution*, Aug. 12, 1893, p. 1. 46 See "Pleads Unwritten Law."

47 See "Life Term for Filipino Slayer," *Los Angeles Times*, May 9, 1925, p. II2.

a harmonious mixture. Thalia Massie, the white wife of a young naval officer, left a party at night and walked home.[48] Something happened – only Thalia knows what actually occurred – and she turned up later with bruises and a broken jaw. She claimed a gang of Hawaiian men had attacked and raped her. Five men – none of them white – were arrested. Elements of the white community and the press reacted with hysteria. In an editorial, a journalist wrote that even "among the cannibals of New Guinea or the aboriginal blacks of North Australia womanhood is safer than in this enlightened American territory."[49]

The problem at the trial was that there was essentially no evidence at all against the five defendants; Thalia was almost certainly lying, as the defense made quite clear. Still, the prosecution could invoke powerful local emotions. When the case went to the jury – a decidedly mixed-race jury – members of the jury were totally unable to agree. The defendants, of course, had to be released. Lieutenant Massie, together with his mother, Grace Fortescue, a most formidable woman, refused to accept this result. They hatched a plan. The core of the plan was to get one of the defendants to confess. They decided that the most likely defendant was Joe Kahahawai. They kidnapped him, the plan went awry, and Kahahawai ended up shot to death. A second trial now took place. Massie and his mother, among others, went on trial for killing the young Hawaiian.[50] Clarence Darrow appeared for the defense.

This too was a sensational trial. Darrow later wrote that the "unwritten law" was a crucial factor in the proceedings.[51] If so, it did not quite work out the way it usually did. The jury struggled with the case, and ended up with a guilty verdict – but guilty of manslaughter, with a recommendation of mercy. The defendants were sentenced to ten years in prison, but in fact they did not spend a single day behind bars. Governor Judd announced that, "in view of the recommendations of the jury," he was commuting the sentence to "one hour in custody of the High Sheriff."[52]

PATRIARCHY AND THE UNWRITTEN LAW

What accounts for the development of the unwritten law? In the classic cases, a husband kills a man who has had sexual relations with his wife; the husband goes on trial, but the jury acquits him. Public opinion, as refracted in jury behavior, was clearly on the defendant's side. A woman was at the core of the drama, but in many regards, her role was subordinate. In the nineteenth century, a strong body of opinion defined respectable women as essentially "passionless," that is, as having little or no sexual appetite.[53] Their sphere was in the home.

[48] David E. Stannard, *Honor Killing: Race, Rape, and Clarence Darrow's Spectacular Last Case* (New York: Penguin, 2005).
[49] Ibid., p. 134.   [50] See ibid., p. 376.   [51] Ibid, p. 376.   [52] Ibid., p. 390.
[53] On this question, see Nancy F. Cott, "Passionlessness: An Interpretation of Victorian Sexual Ideology, 1790–1850," *Signs: Journal of Women in Culture and Society* 4: (1978), p. 219.

They lacked a "public role."[54] God and Nature intended them to be wives and mothers. Moreover, respectable women were naïve, weak, innocent, and passive. They lacked the strength and the intellect of men. Nature condemned them to weakness and submission. They could be preyed on by powerful, evil, and seductive men.

Cases of the unwritten law presuppose something like this image of womanhood. In the typical case of the unwritten law, one hears surprisingly little about the woman's role in the affair. Nobody seems to blame her. Nobody seems to ascribe to her what we would now call "agency." All the fault rested on the man. He was a villain, a libertine, he had taken advantage of her, seduced her, led her to betray her husband and to fall into sin and destruction. Defense attorneys in these cases hammered away at the victim's reputation. He had conspired to "ruin" a woman, who was pure and innocent (even if married); his act was "more injurious ... than murder."[55] Jurors, for their part, seemed to agree with this point of view.

Of course, today this seems like nonsense. There is no reason to think that Teresa Sickles, for example, was an innocent victim. These are not cases of rape; there is no reason to think she and other women had been victimized, that they had no role in starting or continuing the affair. But the cases almost never point a finger of blame at the women. It was almost as if the wives were not really unfaithful – that they were unwilling, or unwitting, or otherwise somehow innocent; their male lovers were as a rule entirely to blame.

In some cases, to be sure, one hears a claim that a woman was assaulted, or was drugged, or was "plied with" alcohol before sex.[56] Yet no newspaper ever used the word "rape" or anything similar. The accounts and the cases do not treat the woman as a willing participant, but in a way, they also ignore any notion that she was truly a victim. Or, to put it another way, the accounts more or less leave her out altogether. What the dead man did was an offense against the woman's husband; *his* marriage had been invaded; *he* had been wronged and humiliated; *he* was the injured party, whose very manhood demanded that he take revenge. Hendrik Hartog pointed it out: the "unwritten law" had very little to do with the woman, even though she was a central figure in the drama. Discussion of the unwritten law was by, about, and

---

54 Rosemary Gartner and Jim Phillips, "The Creffield–Mitchell Case, Seattle, 1906: The Unwritten Law in the Pacific Northwest," *Pacific Northwest Quarterly* 94 (2003), pp. 69, 79.
55 See Ireland, "The Libertine Must Die," supra note, at 34 (internal quotation marks omitted).
56 See, e.g., "Unwritten Law Fails to Save Rush Strong," *Atlanta Constitution*, June 2, 1917, p. 10; in this case, the defendant claimed that his victim had "drugged and assaulted" his wife. See also "The Unwritten Law Invoked by Cline," *New York Times*, Oct. 25, 1922, where the defendant claimed his wife had been "plied with liquor"; in "Unwritten Law Is the Keynote of the Defense," *Atlanta Constitution*, June 29, 1907, the victim had supposedly drugged the defendant's daughter during a buggy ride; in "Unwritten Law Plea of Vawter," *Atlanta Constitution*, May 2, 1917, p. 1, the defendant said he found the victim in "a compromising position" with his wife after bringing her "intoxicating liquor."

between men.[57] Women's voices were rarely heard – unless they had to appear in court and testify about their own infidelity.[58]

The cases, then, rested on stereotypes about women, but also, and perhaps more powerfully, on stereotypes about men and what makes a real man. Male jealousy and sexual insecurity lie at the base of the unwritten law. The cases also reinforced, at least symbolically, men's power over the lives and sexual behavior of their women. Killing a sexual trespasser was not only justified, it was the essence of manly behavior. To be cuckolded was emasculating and humiliating.[59] It destroyed the sanctity of the home, poisoned the marriage, and cast doubt on the paternity of children. It was a kind of psychic castration. Defense attorneys, in some prominent cases, argued that their clients "could not have faced their public had they failed to kill the men who had ruined their marriages."[60] A terrible act of violence was the only way to prove and save one's manhood. It was irrelevant, then, whether the woman had been a victim or indeed the source of sexual misbehavior. Ray Kilgore, a twenty-three-year-old Stanford graduate, murdered Francis A. Bartley, a "clandestine lover of the defendant's mother."[61] Kilgore intercepted a love letter from his mother to Bartley. Kilgore then drove to Bartley's home with a shotgun and ambushed him in a pasture of his dairy ranch. Kilgore's lawyer breathlessly told the jury: "In any land where the honor of woman is recognized, where the virtue of a mother is prized and where the sanctity of home and fireside is revered, no jury would convict a man who defends that honor and virtue and sanctity." Apparently, the jury agreed. Kilgore was found not guilty. Whether his mother appreciated what her son had done is another question.

In those cases where women, not men, were the killers, gender stereotypes were also significant. If a woman killed a man who abused or betrayed her, people often felt no blame should be attached to what she did. As an editorial in 1887 put it, "[t]heirs was the impulse of outraged womanhood – their act was the despairing deed of wronged and helpless women, who struck back upon those who had thrown them like weeds upon the world, wrecks in all the humanizing virtues and decencies of

---

[57] See Hartog, "Lawyering, Husbands' Rights, and 'the Unwritten Law' in Nineteenth-Century America", p. 79.
[58] Sometimes, to establish a basis for the defense of the unwritten law, a husband made his wife suffer the public humiliation of going on the stand and admitting her sin in open court. As one newspaper account put it, in a case involving a father and his daughter, it was hypocritical to "defend" the honor of a woman by "putting her on a public witness stand to tell her shame to the world." "'Unwritten Law' Gets Jolt," *Los Angeles Times*, Feb. 16, 1909. Indeed, some men were apparently willing to plead guilty, to avoid the testimony of the woman in question, in order to save them "from the necessity of relating in court the domestic affairs that led up to the slaying." "Pleads Guilty to Save Wife," *Los Angeles Times*, Apr. 2, 1920, p. II1. But such cases were the exception, not the rule.
[59] The wife had, of course, committed adultery, and this was a very serious breach of the social order. This was the age of the double standard: *his* adultery, if he committed this offense, was much less serious.
[60] See Ireland, "The Libertine Must Die," *supra* note, at 33.
[61] "Jury Acquits Ray Kilgore," *Los Angeles Times*, Feb. 21, 1929, p. I14.

life."[62] Ideas about the delicacy of a woman's nervous system pervaded some of these cases, along with myths about women's frailty and subservience. We return to this theme in what follows.

The Rise of the Unwritten Law

Newspaper data suggest that the unwritten law emerged in the mid-nineteenth century, rose sharply in the early twentieth century, and then declined gradually, ending altogether in the 1950s. The success of this defense demonstrates that judges and juries, all across the country, approved of a kind of vigilante justice; they let scores of men and women get away with what might be considered murder.

Daniel Sickles's lawyers were probably not the first to plead what came to be known as the unwritten law. But the Sickles trial of 1859 was the first trial of this type that captured national attention.[63] Sickles's lawyers had few other options. After all, their client shot Key in broad daylight in Lafayette Park, directly across from the White House. And Sickles could hardly deny that he fired the gun that killed Key. At the trial, the defense hammered away at one great theme: Philip Barton Key deserved to die.[64] He was an adulterer, a libertine, an evil home-wrecker. The Good Book itself demanded death for adulterers – death by stoning.

Of course, the Good Book might say what it pleased; no such provision appeared in the District of Columbia code. As far as the formal law was concerned, killing an adulterer was no different from killing anybody else. It was simply murder. So while the lawyers made a powerful *social* argument on behalf of their client, their only *legal* defense was temporary insanity. The news that his wife was unfaithful, they claimed, had unhinged Dan Sickles. He had killed Philip Key in a sort of temporary frenzy. Whether anybody on the jury actually believed this argument is hard to say. Most likely, the more powerful argument was the argument of just deserts: Key got what was coming to him. But temporary insanity gave the jury a legal hook to hang its decision on, a kind of legal fig leaf. In any event, the jury, in short order, and in the teeth of the evidence, set Sickles free.

[62] "Two Women: On Trial for Their Lives for Murder in California," *Los Angeles Times*, Jan. 28, 1887.
[63] Robert Ireland, trying to explain why early American society seemed to lack the unwritten law, has argued that life in the colonial period and early republic simply provided few opportunities for adultery. See Ireland, "The Libertine Must Die," supra note, at 27–28. There was little privacy, and society in small towns was vigilant for signs of moral indiscretion. The fact that the law prescribed rather severe punishments for adultery, at least on the books, may have further deterred the practice. Ireland's argument may be plausible for the seventeenth century but becomes more dubious for the late colonial period and the period of the early republic. In any event, by the time young Philip Key and Teresa Sickles were having their fling, the social conditions for the commission of adultery were quite different.
[64] Hartog, "Lawyering, Husbands' Rights, and 'the Unwritten Law' in Nineteenth-Century America," p. 78.

The insanity defense – or, to be more accurate, temporary insanity – became a staple of the unwritten law.[65] It appears in case after case; it was also a staple of cases in which a woman was on trial, though, as we see in what follows, in a somewhat different form. Did some jurors actually buy into this notion? We have no way of knowing. The doors to the jury room were closed. The jurors in these cases are long since dead, and while they were alive, they rarely said anything outside the court-room. Robert Ireland thinks "temporary insanity" was perhaps something stronger than a fig leaf, that it had real influence (maybe) on outcomes. In some trials, the defense put doctors on the stand to talk about the defendant's state of mind. In one case, the jury heard about the defendant's symptoms, including a "chronically accelerated" pulse. At the trial of George Cole, a surgeon testified that a horse fell on the defendant during the Civil War, injuring his intestines and bladder and making him "nervous and irritable." Cole was "chronically depressed," and suffered from constipation and a "deficiency in the kidneys."[66] In some cases, witnesses testified that defendants behaved strangely, that they were "highly agitated," or "wild-eyed, tearful," or "screaming in agony." Sickles supposedly screamed and tore at his hair when he got the dread news of his wife's immoral behavior.[67]

All well and good; still, it is hard to take "temporary insanity" seriously as a medical category. Rather, if it meant anything at all, it described a kind of emotional state. It meant a kind of sudden and murderous rage – though one that passed quickly, like a summer storm. What really counted was the fact that this kind of rage was, as one author put it, an emotion "to which all good men alike were subject"; it was a "legitimate and appropriate attribute of male identity."[68] Any decent and honorable husband, in other words, would feel the same way if he discovered his wife's betrayal. And an honorable man might well act out as these men did. It was true manhood to behave this way.

During the last half of the nineteenth century, a number of high-profile trials stretched the unwritten law into new territory.[69] In 1867, Major General George Cole, recently returned from the Civil War, caused a sensation in Albany, where New York State was holding a constitutional convention, by killing a prominent delegate, L. Harris Hiscock. This "appalling tragedy" took place in the "public room" of the hotel where Hiscock was boarding. Hiscock was shot through the head.[70] Hiscock had, allegedly, convinced Cole's wife to "submit to his caresses" during the war.[71]

[65] Ibid., p. 83.   [66] "The Cole–Hiscock Trial," *New York Times*, Nov. 21, 1868.
[67] Robert M. Ireland, "Insanity and the Unwritten Law," *American Journal of Legal History* 32 (1988), pp. 157, 160. The concept of "irresistible impulse" was also useful in these cases, bolstering the claim of "temporary insanity."
[68] Ibid., p. 84.
[69] Hartog, "Lawyering, Husbands' Rights, and 'the Unwritten Law' in Nineteenth-Century America," pp. 70–75.
[70] "Murder at Albany," *New York Times*, June 4, 1867.
[71] "The Cole–Hiscock Case – Argument for a Postponement of the Trial – The Cause to Be Tried at a Special Term of the Oyer and Terminer," *New York Times*, Feb. 3, 1868, p. 1.

Cole was yet another defendant who claimed temporary insanity. Insanity, that is, as he pulled the trigger, perfect sanity before and after.[72] The jury went along. The *New York Times* called this "the most extraordinary verdict ever returned by a jury made up of men supposed to be sane themselves."

Extraordinary, perhaps, but hardly unique. And extremely popular, at least with the crowds in the courtroom. In 1869, Daniel McFarland shot and killed Albert Richardson, a well-known journalist.[73] McFarland believed that Richardson had lured away McFarland's wife, an aspiring actress named Abby Sage. Sage had separated from her husband years earlier and had since taken up with Richardson.[74] At the trial it became clear that McFarland was an abusive drunk who resented his ex-wife's success. But the defense attorney deftly painted an image of McFarland as a victim – a victim of Richardson, the sly dog; a victim of shifting social values that encouraged women to abandon their husbands; a victim of modernity itself.[75] The lawyers also brought in medical evidence. One Dr. Hammond visited McFarland in jail and claimed he saw evidence of "cerebral congestion."[76] "[H]is face and head [were] abnormally hot"; the "carotid and temporal arteries" were "throbbing"; and when shown photos of his wife he became "incoherent" and his pulse "rose to 142." Hammond's conclusion was "transitory mania, temporary insanity, and morbid impulse." The jury acquitted him in short order, to the cheers of the crowd in the courtroom; "ladies crowded around McFarland . . . some kissing him."[77]

The unwritten law also figured in the trial of famous photographer Eadweard Muybridge, a protégé of Leland Stanford, founder of Stanford University. Muybridge, among other things, proved through photographs that a horse could have all four of its legs off the ground at once.[78] Earlier in his life, he was on trial for murder. The victim was one Harry Larkyns, who had had an affair with Muybridge's wife, Flora. When Muybridge found this out, he became enraged. "His appearance was that of a madman. He was haggard and pale, his eyes glassy – his lower jaw hung down, showing his teeth – he trembled from head to foot, and gasped for breath." Nonetheless, he was calm enough, and in enough control, to travel to Calistoga, California, where he found Larkyns at the Yellow Jacket Mine. Larkyns realized that Muybridge knew about the affair and sensed that he was in danger. "He turned to run," said Muybridge, "like a guilty craven . . . and I had to shoot him. The only thing I am sorry for is that he died so quickly." The jury acquitted Muybridge, and

[72] "The Cole–Hiscock Murder," *New York Times*, Dec. 9, 1868, p. 6.
[73] See George Cooper, *Lost Love: A True Story of Passion, Murder, and Justice in Old New York* (New York: Pantheon Books, 1994), p. 127.
[74] See Hartog, "Lawyering, Husbands' Rights, and 'the Unwritten Law' in Nineteenth-Century America", pp. 73–74.
[75] See ibid., pp. 73–75. [76] Cooper, *Lost Love*, pp. 191–192. [77] Ibid., p. 225.
[78] Edward Ball, *The Inventor and the Tycoon: A Gilded Age Murder and the Birth of Moving Pictures* (New York: Doubleday, 2013), pp. 56, 122, 162, 166. The Muybridge case is one of the main themes of the book.

when he left the courthouse, "a large crowd in front of the courtroom erupted in cheers and applause, and he was mobbed." A reporter felt that there was "nearly unanimous" agreement that the verdict was just.[79]

These trials, especially those in which the defendants were rich or famous, became national sensations. In the Sickles case, Sickles acted quickly; this made it somewhat easier to argue temporary insanity. The shock of discovery had clouded his judgment. In some later cases, to argue for some kind of frenzy was a bit of a stretch. George Cole, for instance, after learning that he had been betrayed, set about consulting various friends, "procuring a pistol, arranging his plans, writing letters to screen himself and traveling to find his victim."[80] In the McFarland–Richardson case, two full years had passed between the end of McFarland's marriage and the day he killed his rival.[81] And Richardson did not even begin a relationship with Abby Sage until after the dissolution of her marriage.[82] No matter: the unwritten law, tied to the legal fig leaf of temporary insanity, was a powerful magnet for American juries.[83] The victim – this was the strongest argument – deserved what he got. And, as these cases accumulated in American courts, they came to be something more than isolated cases here and there; they came to constitute, as it were, an actual *law*. Killing your rival was (legally) a crime, but a crime without punishment.

The Golden Age of the Unwritten Law

Some of the nineteenth-century cases of the unwritten law were big news. But this happened sporadically. Then, rather suddenly, early in the twentieth century, stories about the unwritten law erupted in the press with greater frequency. In part, this may be a matter of journalistic habits: databases are wonderful things, but you need a way to plumb their depths, and if a newspaper report failed to use the magic phrase "unwritten law," an item was likely to be overlooked, even if the facts of the case fit the typical pattern. The phrase clearly became more common in the early twentieth century.[84] Also, in the age of yellow journalism, newspapers understood that sensational trials – full of sex, violence, and scandal – were wonderful tools for selling newspapers. And cases of the "unwritten law" had the capacity, like few others, to dish up doses of sex, violence, and scandal. Still, one particular trial in 1907 seemed to play a part in this journalistic boom. This was the sensational trial of Harry K. Thaw, one of the most famous in American history.

[79] Ibid., p. 279 (internal quotation marks omitted).   [80] "The Cole–Hiscock Murder."
[81] Hartog, "Lawyering, Husbands' Rights, and 'the Unwritten Law' in Nineteenth-Century America," p. 74.
[82] See ibid.
[83] Professor Hartog has a fascinating account of these three trials, and how the defense attorney at each new trial built on precedents to extend the unwritten law. See generally ibid., pp. 69–96.
[84] Only a small number of cases before 1900 used the term "unwritten law." But many stories written afterward referred back to some of these, and applied the term retroactively, as it were.

Like the other trials in this category, Thaw's grew out of a love triangle, though a rather odd one. The victim here was Stanford White, one of the country's leading architects. White had designed Madison Square Garden in New York City, and many other notable buildings.[85] He was also a notorious womanizer. Harry Thaw, the defendant, was a wild, wealthy, and erratic young man; he had once been a student at Harvard, but was expelled for misbehavior. And in many ways the star of the show was Thaw's wife, Evelyn Nesbit Thaw, a ravishingly beautiful and famous woman. Evelyn Shaw had had a career on the stage since she was quite young; she was one of the "Floradora" girls on Broadway. There she caught the practiced eye of Stanford White; he invited her to visit his studio, where she sat in his red velvet swing. And, when she was only sixteen, White took her to his apartment and (according to her account) drugged and raped her. He gave her, she said, a drink of champagne that was "bitter and funny-tasting."[86] Then (she said), "[e]verything went black" and she passed out.[87] When she woke up, she was naked, and there were "blotches of blood on the sheets." White brought her a kimono and said, "It's all over." He had (she said) accomplished her "ruin." Afterward, according to her account, he asked her to tell no one what had happened.

But she did tell someone, and this turned out to be a kind of death warrant for Stanford White. She told Harry K. Thaw, who, like many other men, fell in love with this beautiful woman. He asked Evelyn to marry him; she said it was impossible. He asked her why. She told him how Stanford White had "ruined her." Thaw (she claimed) burst into tears. But she did marry Thaw after all. Thaw was not exactly the picture of mental health, and at some point, he decided to kill White as payback (he said) for despoiling the woman he loved, the woman he had married. He found White and shot him to death – in public. Ironically, the incident took place in Madison Square Garden, White's own creation, at 11 o'clock at night, "just as the first performance of the musical comedy 'Mamzelle Champagne' was drawing to a close." As the body tumbled over, a character on stage was "singing a song entitled 'I Could Love a Million Girls.'"[88]

Thaw was arrested and put on trial. The trial, which began in January 1907, was a total sensation; it had everything: sex, celebrities, drama, human interest. Huge crowds gathered every morning, trying to catch a glimpse of the cast of characters, especially Evelyn Nesbit Thaw. A special telegraph office was set up to feed the

[85] Umphrey, "The Dialogics of Legal Meaning," pp. 399, 401, 414–415. Scholars have published a sizeable literature on this notorious case. See Michael M. Mooney, *Evelyn Nesbit and Stanford White: Love and Death in the Gilded Age* (New York: Morrow, 1976); Gerald Langford, *The Murder of Stanford White* (Indianapolis, IN: Bobbs-Merrill, 1962).

[86] Deborah Dorian Paul, *Tragic Beauty: The Lost 1914 Memoirs of Evelyn Nesbit* (Morrisville: Lulu, 2006), p. 46; see Lawrence M. Friedman, *The Big Trial: Law as Public Spectacle* (Lawrence: University Press of Kansas, 2015), pp. 72–74.

[87] Paul, *Tragic Beauty*, p. 46.

[88] "Thaw Murders Stanford White: Shoots Him on the Madison Square Garden Roof," *New York Times*, June 26, 1906.

hunger of the press (and the hunger of the public). The jury was sequestered for two and a half months. The climax of the trial came when Evelyn herself took the stand. She had the "grace of a fawn ... a mouth made out of rumpled rose petals."[89] The defense painted White in dark colors: a vicious debaucher, a libertine, a seducer. Evelyn, on the other hand, was a helpless, hapless victim, an innocent dove.[90] The district attorney ridiculed this idea. Evelyn was no "angel child ... reared chastely and purely ... [d]rugged and despoiled." That story was "nonsense." Evelyn was not exactly brought up in a convent. She had become a showgirl at a very young age, as part of the "Florodora chorus." She had gone with many men. It was absurd to claim she had been dragged into a "den of vice and drugged."

The unwritten law figured in the Thaw trial, but this was hardly a typical case. White had "ruined" young Evelyn long before she met and married Harry Thaw. In the usual case, the seduction or adultery was recent, often ongoing, and the male ego had suffered a raw, open wound. In the Thaw case, Stanford White's actions were long gone, and the facts were probably a lot more murky than Evelyn Nesbit painted them. Thaw himself was a dubious character, a rich boy with wild, profligate, and somewhat pathological habits. In this case, the insanity defense (not "temporary" insanity, but real honest-to-goodness insanity) was not inappropriate. Thaw was tried twice. The first trial ended in a hung jury. In the second trial, the verdict was not guilty by reason of insanity; Thaw was sent off to an asylum.

Hardly any trial in American history created such a storm of excitement. A movie, *The Unwritten Law: A Thrilling Drama Based on the Thaw White Case*, appeared on the nation's screens soon afterward (and ran into a good deal of censorship trouble). A fine of $100 was imposed on a nickelodeon for showing the film, which was "imperiling the morals of young boys."[91] And a play by Edwin Milton Royle, *The Unwritten Law*, opened on Broadway in 1913.[92] In the play, a husband is accused of killing a man who was paying too much attention to the killer's wife. In the play, as in real life, the verdict was "not guilty."[93]

---

[89]   Irvin S. Cobb, *Exit Laughing* (Garden City, NY: Garden City Publishing Company, 1942), pp. 198–199.

[90]   Umphrey, "The Dialogics of Legal Meaning," pp. 414–415, 419.

[91]   Daniel Czitrom, "The Politics of Performance: Theater Licensing and the Origins of Movie Censorship in New York," in Francis G. Couvares, ed., *Movie Censorship and American Culture* (Washington, DC: Smithsonian Institute Press, 1996), pp. 16, 22; see also Lee Grieveson, *Policing Cinema: Movies and Censorship in Early Twentieth-Century America* (Berkeley: University of California Press, 2004), p. 37. Another movie, *The Girl in the Red Velvet Swing*, which also dealt with this affair, appeared in 1955.

[92]   "Royle's New Play," *New York Times*, Feb. 8, 1913, p. 13.

[93]   A review of the play appeared in the *New York Times* on February 8, 1913. In the play (according to the review), Kate Wilson, a married woman, is seduced by a blackguard. She plans to divorce her husband and marry her seducer, but he refuses her and she kills him. Her husband, who was drunk at the time of the killing, takes the blame, but the foreman of the grand jury whispers to the prosecutor that the unwritten law will prevail and the husband will go free. The *Times* reviewer did not think much of the play and its "almost unrelieved gloom." There were some scenes of "considerable power," wrote the critic, but there was "little freshness in the inspiration."

After the Thaw trial, cases that invoked the unwritten law increased in number. In all likelihood, some of this was fallout from the case. Before the trial, the three sampled newspapers reported less than one trial per year. But in 1907 alone the three newspapers reported on twenty-three trials in which the unwritten law played a role; these trials took place in every region of the country. That year, the writer of a St. Louis editorial (reprinted in the *Atlanta Constitution*) commented that "precedents are almost unanimous in favor of the assertion that any man has a right to kill the betrayer of his wife, his sister or his daughter."[94] It would be "almost fair to say that the 'unwritten law' has become the law of the land." And at a meeting of the American Bar Association in St. Paul, Minnesota, in the same period, a Louisiana lawyer, tongue in cheek, proposed codifying the law: "Any man who commits a criminal indiscretion may be put to death with impunity by the injured husband, who shall have the right to determine the mode of execution, be it never so cowardly."[95] Between 1905 and 1909, the unwritten law contributed nearly fifty reported trials to the newspapers. The Thaw trial, no doubt, had been a consciousness raiser.

Many of these cases followed a timeworn script. The defense attorney would argue that the victim, using "wiles" and tricks and devices, insinuated himself into a married woman's affection, duping the woman into betraying her husband. The husband eventually found out; the wife tearfully confessed. In some cases, the wife testified at the trial, with the idea of absolving her husband from blame. In others, the husband tried to excuse himself on the basis of self-defense. After finding out about the betrayal, the husband went out in search of the scoundrel. He carried a weapon – for self-protection, of course. The two men met – often in some public place. The husband denounced the villain; the villain reached for his weapon. In self-defense (and, of course, in a temporary frenzy), the husband fired the fatal shot.[96] The jury now had two legal excuses for acquittal: temporary insanity and self-defense. Both were probably bogus. "Insanity" was quite convenient, since it seemed to evaporate once the defendant pulled the trigger. An "insanity" that lasted only until that point was certainly a convenient form of "insanity." If the victim had reached for a gun (which probably rarely happened), it made sense to kill him first. After all, the husband's life was in mortal danger, and defending himself might have been *his* only hope.[97] Still, what really moved juries was probably not self-defense or temporary insanity; what moved juries was the unwritten law.

94 "Freed by the Unwritten Law," *St. Louis Globe-Democrat*, reprinted in the *Atlanta Constitution*, Aug. 26, 1907, p. 4.
95 Ibid.
96 This happened during the trial of C. Walter Jones for the murder of Sloan Rowan in Montgomery, Alabama. Jones claimed that Rowan had made "evil charges" against his wife and boasted "of a personal liaison." Jones confronted Rowan at a train station and shot Rowan after Rowan attempted to draw his gun. See "Unwritten Law and Self-Defense," *Atlanta Constitution*, Aug. 1, 1912, p. 16.
97 The three newspapers reported only one case in which the home-wrecking lover succeeded in killing the husband during a fight, rather than the other way around. Not surprisingly, the killer's attempt in this case to plead a sort of reverse unwritten law was unsuccessful. See "'Unwritten Law' Plea Fails to Acquit Butt," *Atlanta Constitution*, Oct. 1, 1916, p. B13.

Betrayed husbands were not the only men protected by the unwritten law. The defense shielded fathers, brothers, and sons as well. In 1907, two brothers, James and Philip Strother, went on trial for killing William Bywaters. The Strothers were prominent people; one of the brothers was serving as a representative in the West Virginia legislature. William Bywaters was "a clubman, horseman, politician, and general 'good fellow' about town."[98] He was also, when he died, married to Viola, sister of the Strothers brothers.[99] Bywaters's marriage was both brief and reluctant. It seems that he had gotten Viola pregnant. She had had an abortion in Washington, DC; the operation left her ill and in pain. When her brothers heard about these matters, they told Bywaters he had to marry Viola. A shotgun wedding followed, but soon after the ceremony, the new bridegroom tried to get away – first down a back stairway, and then through a window. At that point, the brothers killed him.

The high point of the trial was the testimony of the widowed bride, Viola Bywaters. Her sister wheeled her into court "in an invalid's chair." "Pale and wan, her face showing traces of illness and suffering," she told her tale of woe. The judge, in his charge, did not specifically mention the unwritten law, but he did tell the jury about "emotional insanity," which was, as usual, the main *legal* defense.[100] The outcome was never much in doubt: a verdict of not guilty.[101] Cheers broke out in the courtroom. The judge himself told the jurors they had done the right thing: in Virginia, "no man tried for defending the sanctity of his home should be found guilty." In the Kilgore case already mentioned, the victim had been the lover of the defendant's mother.

Most newspaper accounts of the unwritten law described actual trials. These were cases, in other words, where the prosecution at least *tried* to get the killer punished.[102] But sometimes the case never got as far as trial by jury. In San Francisco, in 1907, Charles Hess, a barber, found his wife alone in a room with one Charles Gaskell, a "teacher of advertising."[103] The barber chased Gaskell for twelve blocks, shooting at him; Gaskell was wounded slightly. Gaskell was lucky to get out of this situation alive. This may have helped the judge who, invoking the unwritten law, simply dismissed the charge of attempted murder. And in Richmond in 1926, a grand jury, "recognizing the 'unwritten law,'" refused to indict James C. Moore, a railroad

[98] "Unwritten Law Again," *Oshkosh Daily Northwestern*, Feb. 21, 1907, p. 11.
[99] See "Widowed Bride Tells Her Pathetic Story to Save Her Brothers," *Atlanta Constitution*, Feb. 28, 1907, p. 1.
[100] "Unwritten Law in His Charge," *Atlanta Constitution*, Mar. 6, 1907, p. 5. On the testimony (on both sides of the issue) relating to the "emotional insanity" of the brothers, see "Made Insane by the Wrong Done Sister," *Atlanta Constitution*, Mar. 3, 1907, p. B1.
[101] "Strother Boys Freed and Judge Approves Verdict of the Jury," *Atlanta Constitution*, Mar. 8, 1907, p. 1.
[102] It would have been difficult to ignore these episodes completely; after all, a dead body is hard to overlook, and the killing often took place in daylight and in public.
[103] "Judge Admits Unwritten Law," *San Francisco Chronicle*, July 3, 1907, p. 10.

flagman who killed W. Lee Gordon "when he found him seated in an automobile with Mrs. Moore in front of the Moore home."[104]

The unwritten law sometimes made its mark even after a jury verdict. Letha Purdue killed the widower of her deceased sister, after the man "paid attentions to her" and then left her for another woman.[105] She was found guilty, but the judge fined her $71, a laughable punishment. A few years earlier, in Washington State, Bert Taylor had emptied a revolver into W. F. Wibie; Taylor's unmarried sister had died giving birth to Wibie's child. Taylor's punishment: a $500 fine.[106] Apparently, this was far too severe for Taylor. He filed a motion for a new trial; presumably, he felt he deserved no punishment at all by virtue of the unwritten law. In 1924, F. C. Gossett, in Tennessee, coming home early and unexpectedly from work, found a man in his wife's room. Gossett dropped a piece of gas pipe on the man's head. He was fined $5 for this crime.[107] In a moment of refreshing candor, the sentencing judge told him: "You are guilty, technically, but I would have done the same thing."

These may be extreme instances. In those cases where the jury did in fact find the defendant guilty, the judge would usually impose some jail or prison time. Sentences, however, could be quite short. In 1898, Mrs. M. I. McGuirt got off with a sentence of two years after killing her husband in what she claimed was self-defense.[108] The headline in the *Atlanta Constitution* read "Another Woman Who Will Not Hang." A Georgia man, Rush Irwin, killed John George Moody, a boarder in his home; he claimed he caught Moody creeping into his wife's room.[109] He was sentenced to one year in prison; this seemed too harsh, and he asked for clemency.[110] In 1930, Shelton W. Herrin shot and wounded John A. Quickel after climbing through a window in his home to find Quickel in bed with his wife.[111] The jury convicted him, but of simple assault, rather than attempted murder. The judge clearly sympathized with Herrin. He sentenced him to serve a single day in prison.[112]

The unwritten law, in short, operated at every stage of the process of criminal justice. It seeped in at every pore of the system. Thus, even if the jury convicted, and the judge imposed a meaningful sentence, the state governor could intervene with his pardoning power. Pardons were common in the South, and appeared particularly common in Alabama. In 1907, the governor of Alabama, B. B. Comer, pardoned W. E. Shill, convicted for killing the man who "betrayed" his youngest daughter.[113] The governor explained that "a man had the right to protect his own

---

[104] "Slayer Is Cleared by 'Unwritten Law,'" *Washington Post*, Feb. 3, 1926, p. 2.
[105] "Fined $71 for Killing Her Brother-in-Law," *Atlanta Constitution*, Nov. 18, 1913, p. 1.
[106] "Meets Luck, Eyes Shut," *Los Angeles Times*, Apr. 17, 1909, p. I3.
[107] "'Unwritten Law' Made to Let Man Preserve Home," *Atlanta Constitution*, Mar. 9, 1924, p. C3.
[108] "Another Woman Who Will Not Hang," *Atlanta Constitution*, Oct. 12, 1898, p. 3.
[109] "Trial of Rush Irwin Will Begin Tomorrow," *Atlanta Constitution*, Nov. 4, 1919, p. 11.
[110] See "Irwin Will Ask for Clemency," *Atlanta Constitution*, Jan. 10, 1920, p. 1.
[111] "Unwritten Law Fails to Acquit," *Los Angeles Times*, Aug. 2, 1930, p. II3.
[112] See "Husband Who Wounded Rival Punished Lightly," *Los Angeles Times*, Aug. 6, 1930, at II8.
[113] "Unwritten Law Up to Governor," *Atlanta Constitution*, Mar. 23, 1907, p. 4.

home." Later that year, the same Alabama governor pardoned J. D. Williams, who killed a man who had "invaded" his home.[114] Alabama governors had a particularly strong reason to favor the unwritten law. John Anthony Winston, a governor of Alabama in the nineteenth century, had himself been acquitted under the unwritten law; in 1847 he had killed Sidney S. Perry, a physician who had "wrecked his home."[115]

Equal Opportunity: Women and the Unwritten Law

An important variant of the unwritten law acted to protect women who were on trial for murdering a husband or lover. Carolyn Ramsey's research has shown that judges and juries, in the late nineteenth and early twentieth centuries, were deeply sympathetic to women who did away with abusive husbands or who killed men who had "ruined" them and then refused to make amends by marrying them.[116] In our sample, thirty-eight cases appeared in which a female defendant invoked the unwritten law. This defense was for the most part extremely successful.

A "guiltless" woman, according to an 1887 editorial in the *Los Angeles Times*, should be able to invoke the unwritten law, if, "in the desperation of her sorrow, or in the face of a dishonored life," she "sheds the blood of her betrayer."[117] This principle was on full display in the trial of Clara Falmer, prosecuted for murder in Oakland, California, in the 1890s.[118] Clara was fifteen years old and pregnant. She met her boyfriend, Charles LaDue, at a Grant Street restaurant in San Francisco and begged him for help. He laughed at her and she shot him. At the trial, the defense pictured Clara as a poor, innocent victim, seduced and abandoned by a heartless rogue who deserved to die. There was also the usual claim of temporary insanity; Clara had acted (it was said) during a "state of emotional insanity"; she was "unhinged … brooding about her delicate condition." There was also evidence about insanity, which, allegedly, ran in her family. Meanwhile, Clara's lawyers stage-managed Clara with great skill. She came to court dressed demurely in blue, with a veil over her young face; she wore a blue hat and gloves, and clutched in her hand

[114] "Comer Favors Unwritten Law: Governor Pardons Man Who Killed Invader of Home," *Atlanta Constitution*, Aug. 28, 1907, p. 3.
[115] See "Freed by the Unwritten Law"; John Anthony Winston, Encyclopedia of Alabama, Aug. 4, 2008, www.encyclopediaofalabama.org/face/Article.jsp?id=h-1621.
[116] See Carolyn Ramsey, "Domestic Violence and State Intervention in the American West and Australia, 1860–1930," *Indiana Law Journal* 86:185 (2011), pp. 236–254; Carolyn Ramsey, "Intimate Homicide: Gender and Crime Control, 1880–1920," *University of Colorado Law Review* 77:101 (2006), pp. 118–140.
[117] See Ramsey, "Domestic Violence," p. 250 (quoting "Two Women: On Trial for Their Lives for Murder in California," *Los Angeles Times*, Jan. 28, 1887, p. 10).
[118] Lawrence M. Friedman and Robert V. Percival, *The Roots of Justice: Crime and Punishment in Alameda County, California, 1870–1910* (Chapel Hill: University of North Carolina Press, 1981), pp. 239, 241.

a bouquet of violets. A "morbid crowd" filled the courtroom, eager to see and to hear the proceedings.

The prosecution warned of dire consequences if Clara got off. Acquittal might encourage "disreputable women" to point guns at men and "demand to be made their wives." The prosecutors also hinted strongly that Clara was not quite so innocent as the defense made her out. These arguments fell on deaf ears. The jury clearly felt that the victim, the late Charles LaDue, got exactly what he deserved. On the first ballot, the jury voted eleven to one for acquittal; on the second ballot, the vote was unanimous. Clara went free.[119]

On December 18, 1899, Katie Cook went on trial in Santa Ana, California.[120] Cook had killed her husband, Tom. She shot him in the brain while he was sleeping. The defendant took the stand on December 22. Her husband, she said, led an "unspeakable life"; he brought young girls into the home and "accomplished their ruin." He wrote and read vile poetry. He made a German servant girl appear in the nude, in front of Katie. He "openly boasted ... of his degradation." The last straw was when Mabel Moody, a hired girl, came on the scene. Tom Cook talked "dirty" to her and trimmed her fingernails. Katie Cook begged her husband to change his ways; he refused. What happened after that? Her mind, she said, was "a blank." At the trial, she "burst into tears, sobbing bitterly." The jury needed only fifteen minutes to reach a verdict: not guilty. The crowd in the courtroom "arose as one person, filling the corridors with deafening applause."

The unwritten law (women's version) seemed more frequent after 1900. In 1902, a judge in Chicago made news by declaring that "it is the duty of a wife to shoot her husband when he beats her."[121] Four years later, a few women seem to have taken the judge's counsel to heart. Acquittals were common enough to appall one prosecutor; he warned, in 1906, that if women were free to shoot husbands who attacked or beat them, "there won't be many husbands left in Chicago six months from now" – a sorry commentary on Chicago husbands.[122] Normally, self-defense is a strong argument; it is a valid excuse for killing a person, if that person is in the process of attacking you. But this was not the situation these women faced. These were, for the most part, cases of premeditation; she killed, not because she was in actual danger at the

[119] Ibid., p. 244. See also Ireland, *supra* note for a discussion of the case of Mary Harris, who was acquitted in 1865 for murdering her former fiancé; the jury seemed to think (it was said) that "any woman who considers herself aggrieved in any way by a member of the other sex, may kill him with impunity."

[120] Gordon Morris Bakken, "The Limits of Patriarchy: The 'Unwritten Law' in California Legal History," in Gordon Morris Bakken, ed., *California History: A Topical Approach* (Wheeling, IL: Harlan Davidson, Inc., 2003), pp. 84, 99–102.

[121] "'Shoot Him on the Spot!'" *Atlanta Constitution*, May 1, 1902, p. 6.

[122] Jeffrey S. Adler, "'I Loved Joe, But I Had to Shoot Him': Homicide by Women in Turn-of-the-Century Chicago," *Journal of Criminal Law & Criminology* 92 (2002), pp. 867, 883 (quoting "Finds Mrs. Trope Guilty of Murder; Gives Her 14 Years," *Chicago Inter-Ocean*, Jan. 10, 1906, p. 1). On the "unwritten law" for women in Chicago, see Jeffrey S. Adler, *First in Violence, Deepest in Dirt: Homicide in Chicago, 1875–1920* (Cambridge, MA: Harvard University Press, 2006), pp. 108–119.

moment the deed was done, but because she was attached to a violent, abusive man, and she chose this way out of a tough situation. Most juries seemed to sympathize. A man who savagely beat his wife was breaking the rules. This was not manly behavior. Juries seemed to feel that he acted badly enough to forfeit the right to stay alive.[123]

Not all of these were cases of physical abuse. Some were cases of sexual betrayal or acts that dishonored the woman. In 1906, Angie Birdsong, a Mississippi woman, killed one Dr. Butler, who had disparaged her character. She was convicted of manslaughter and sentenced to five years in prison.[124] This sentence was not particularly harsh, yet a writer for the *Atlanta Constitution* wrote bitter words of criticism. "A woman and a southerner, and a senator's niece at that, confronted with a jail term of possibly five years for avenging her honor in the conventional way! Is southern chivalry declining and is the weaker sex denied man's refuge in the 'unwritten law'?" Almost immediately, Governor Vardaman pardoned Birdsong; she never saw the inside of a jail cell.[125] In 1907, Estelle Corwell was tried for killing George Bennett, her unmarried lover, "after she had been threatened with the exposure of her six years of shame."[126] The trial was quite a sensation – in part because Wyatt Earp, the famous gunslinger, appeared as a witness for the defense.[127] She was found not guilty by reason of insanity.[128]

The 1918 trial of Gabrielle Darley was another variant; it was also a testimony to the power of clever lawyering. Gabrielle was, to be blunt, a prostitute, who shot and killed her pimp and lover, Leonard Tropp, in Los Angeles.[129] Gabrielle claimed the gun went off accidentally. Gabrielle's lawyer, Earl Rogers, did a magnificent job in defense; at the trial, he managed to convey a sympathetic image of Gabrielle. She was simply a "pitiful young woman," a "soul-starved little waitress," who, until Tropp

[123]   The results in these cases, along with the research by Carolyn B. Ramsey cited here, seem inconsistent with the common belief that before fairly recent times, and in particular before the modern feminist movement, the criminal justice system did not take domestic violence seriously at all. Ramsey's research – and, indeed, most of the cases in this chapter – stem from the late nineteenth century and the early years of the twentieth. Is it possible that in the years between, say, the 1920s and more recent times, the criminal justice system *did* ignore domestic violence – a change from its earlier attitude? Ramsey herself speculates that this is possible: as women got the vote, as they were more prominent in the workforce, as divorce became easier, the system might have less often seen abused wives "as frail beings who needed protection against their violent husbands"; there was rather a "false sense" that women could easily exit these marriages. Carolyn B. Ramsey, "The Exit Myth: Family Law, Gender Roles, and Changing Attitudes toward Female Victims of Domestic Violence," *Michigan Journal of Gender & Law* 20:1 (2013). Whether this is in fact true has to wait for more complete and rigorous research on this interim period.
[124]   "Chivalry and 'Unwritten Law,'" *Atlanta Constitution*, Dec. 23, 1906, p. B8.
[125]   "Mrs. Birdsong Is Pardoned," *Los Angeles Times*, July 19, 1907, p. II11.
[126]   "Held by Jury for Murder," *Los Angeles Times*, July 25, 1907, p. II3.
[127]   "Gun Fighter for Defense," *Los Angeles Times*, Jan. 23, 1908, p. II1.
[128]   "Mrs. Corwell Clear of Murder Charge," *Los Angeles Times*, Feb. 22, 1908, p. II1.
[129]   Alfred Cohn and Joe Chisholm, *Take the Witness* (Garden City, NY: Garden City Publishing Company, 1934), pp. 259–260, 262–264.

entered the picture, was "as pure as the snow atop Mount Wilson." This was almost total fantasy, but it worked. The jury acquitted her.[130]

Clever lawyering also helped Mae Talbot, a singer who killed her husband, Al, in her lawyer's office in Reno, Nevada, in 1909.[131] Husband and wife started quarreling, then the quarrel turned physical; Mae shot her husband with a gun she had hidden in her fur muff. At her trial, she accused Al of being a wife-beater. The prosecution tried – unsuccessfully – to paint her as immoral; she appeared in court dressed in deep black mourning and projected the image of a good girl seduced by a vicious, violent gambler twice her age. Al Talbot had in fact been physically abusive, and the jury acquitted her. A few months later, she was back on stage in Chicago, in a musical comedy called *Get Busy with Emily*.

Good lawyering – and the women of Los Angeles – also helped Hattie Woolsteen, who shot to death a dentist, Charles Harlan, in 1887; his charred body was found in a barn that had been (deliberately) set on fire.[132] Hattie and the dentist had been lovers; the dentist, however, was a married man. Apparently, he was unwilling to divorce his wife and marry Hattie. Hattie Woolsteen seemed unable to tell a consistent story about what actually happened. Early coverage labeled her a "she-devil," but by the time the trial took place, she (and her lawyers) had concocted a story that aroused public sympathy. She was painted as a poor, weak woman, raped and brutalized by a man who refused to marry her. She had, in other words, transformed herself into a woman with the right to invoke the unwritten law. The jury took a mere ten minutes to declare her not guilty, and the courtroom erupted with applause. Each of the jurors shook Hattie's hand. As she left the courtroom, people outside cheered.

In 1919, Mrs. Emma Simpson shot her husband to death.[133] They had separated and were wrangling over money. Emma told a newspaper reporter that she would win, because of the "new unwritten law, which does not permit a married man to love another woman." She said, "I will tell my whole story to the jury, and they will free me." She was wrong about that; the jury convicted her. But she had a point about the unwritten law in Chicago. Records compiled by Marianne Constable

---

[130] Ibid., p. 265. The book is about the career of Earl Rogers. Gabrielle later made legal history by suing the makers of a movie, *The Red Kimono*, which told the story of her life (somewhat fictionalized), including the trial, and used her actual name. The movie was highly favorable to Gabrielle, but she brought suit nonetheless; she claimed the movie makers had invaded her privacy. In this case, she also succeeded in bamboozling a California court into thinking she was a reformed woman, though in fact she remained a prostitute and madam for most of her life. The case is *Melvin v. Reid*, 112 Cal. App. 285 (1931), a leading case on the right to privacy in California.

[131] On this case, see Carolyn B. Ramsey, "A Diva Defends Herself: Gender and Domestic Violence in an Early Twentieth-Century Headline Trial," *Saint Louis University Law Journal* 55 (2011), p. 3547.

[132] A full account of the trial, in context, can be found in Cara Anzilotti, *She-Devil in the City of Angels: Gender, Violence, and the Hattie Woolsteen Murder Case in Victorian Era Los Angeles* (Santa Barbara, CA: Praeger, 2016).

[133] Marianne Constable, "Chicago Husband-Killing and the 'New Unwritten Law,'" *TriQuarterly Review* 124 (2006), p. 85.

show that 265 women killed a husband or lover between 1870 and 1930; only twenty-four were convicted, and very few ever went to prison.[134]

In a few cases, a woman killed another woman. In 1904, Nancy May was tried for the murder of Alice Smith; Smith, she claimed, "was her rival for her husband's affections."[135] A jury convicted her; she was sentenced to ten years in prison, but the governor of Kentucky pardoned her before she served any jail time. Four years later, a coroner's jury in Kentucky excused Mrs. Nancy Murrill, who had killed Mrs. Mary Terry; Terry "had stolen Mrs. Murrill's husband's affections."[136] And in the 1940s, Gwendolyn Wallis was tried for killing Ruby Clark, after Clark (she claimed) had taken away from her a husband's love.[137] Her first trial ended in a hung jury.[138] In the second trial, the judge dismissed the case; "by the written letter of the law," he said, Gwendolyn was "guilty of murder, but we would be no more successful in a retrial than we were in the first." As usual, courtroom spectators applauded wildly.

Thus our figures show that women, like men, could invoke the "unwritten law." They were successful, though perhaps not quite as successful as men. In one sensational case, in 1870, Laura Fair, who was thirty-three, boarded the *El Capitan*, a ferry that ran between San Francisco and Oakland.[139] Her lover, Alexander Crittenden, was also on the *El Capitan*, along with his wife and three of his children. Laura pulled out a gun and shot him. She was tried for murder – twice, in fact. In the first case, the jury found her guilty and she was sentenced to death. Clearly, that jury was unsympathetic. Laura had been married a number of times, and had lived with a married man for seven years. The prosecution called her a scarlet woman, a woman addicted to "free love," and an "affront to ... femininity." The defense painted Crittenden as a heartless cad and also brought in testimony about "female hysteria," a condition caused by "organic female problems," and one that could lead to "extremely violent insanity."[140] A nurse testified that, two days after the murder, Laura was "in a perfect state of unconsciousness."[141]

Despite the jury verdict, Laura Fair was not doomed to die at the hands of the state. The Supreme Court of California reversed her conviction and ordered a new trial;[142] moreover, the court tied the hands of the prosecution. Evidence of Laura Fair's reputation and sexual history was not relevant, according to the court, and was not to be admitted into evidence. At the second trial, the defense focused exclusively on temporary insanity. The jury heard testimony about her "prolapsed" womb, and

[134]   Ibid. Juries, Constable thinks, were applying their notions of what later came to be called the battered woman syndrome, or, perhaps, an expanded notion of self-defense, which a woman could use if she were locked into an abusive relationship. See ibid., pp. 89–92. Exactly what juries were actually thinking is of course a closed book; and see also Jeffrey Adler, op. cit. supra, on the situation in Chicago.

[135]   "Pardon for Murderess," *New York Times*, July 8, 1904, p. 1.

[136]   "Woman Freed by 'Unwritten Law,'" *Atlanta Constitution*, June 11, 1908, p. 2.

[137]   "Unwritten Law Plea Made in Wallis Trial," *Los Angeles Times*, Mar. 7, 1946, p. A2.

[138]   "Wallis Murder Case Dismissed," *Los Angeles Times*, Mar. 12, 1946, p. II2.

[139]   Haber, *The Trials of Laura Fair*.   [140]   Ibid., pp. 51, 99.   [141]   Ibid., p. 81.

[142]   *State* v. *Fair*, 43 Cal. 137 (1872).

the "disordered condition of her menstrual functions."[143] The second trial ended up with an acquittal. Laura Fair walked out of the courtroom, a free woman.

Robert Ireland studied a small group of cases – one of them was the case of Laura Fair – and came to the conclusion that the system did forgive "female avengers," but "more reluctantly, less consistently" than it forgave men, and it forgave women "in ways that enhanced the already negative stereotype of nineteenth-century women."[144] Women defendants, according to Ireland, used the old chestnut of "temporary insanity"; but also added to it, or replaced it, with an image of women as "feeble" and "prone to hysteria." They brought in testimony about such things as "suppressed and irregular menstruation," which might have had the woman in its grip when she did the bloody deed. This kind of evidence, Ireland argues, cannot be dismissed as simply an invention to be used in this type of trial. Rather, it was part of a package of stereotypes and beliefs about the "general emotional disorder that afflicted most women," not only during their menstrual periods, but all the time.[145]

The insanity defense, in other words, appears in these cases, but the precise form it took was not the same as in the cases where men stood trial. In 1865, Mary Harris "stepped out from behind the floor-to-ceiling grandfather clock" on the second floor of the Treasury Building, in Washington, DC, and shot to death Adoniram J. Burroughs as he was leaving work.[146] She explained, "[t]earfully ... that he had promised to marry her, ruined her, and then married someone else." Her chief defense was insanity. Doctors testified about "severe congestive dysmenorrhea" and "paroxysmal insanity"; her own lawyer took the stand and stated that she was "insane from moral causes aggravated by disease of the body." He asked the jury to let this "poor, blighted, afflicted, ruined, and persecuted girl go." The district attorney, facing disaster, told the jury, "If you acquit her upon the ground of insanity, it will be a pretext only ... if you wish to acquit her, do it because you want to, but do not render yourselves ridiculous by listening to this nonsense of insane impulse." The jury took up the challenge. After a few minutes, the foreman announced the verdict: "not guilty," plain and simple, rather than "not guilty by reason of insanity." The courtroom audience cheered. Ironically, this was a case in which the defendant perhaps *was* insane. In 1867, she was admitted to the Government Hospital for the Insane in the District of Columbia, diagnosed with "periodic homicidal mania." From then on, she spent many years in and out of the institution.

---

[143] Ibid., p. 157.

[144] Robert M. Ireland, "Frenzied and Fallen Females: Women and Sexual Dishonor in the Nineteenth-Century United States," *Journal of Women's History* 3 (1992), pp. 95, 97.

[145] Ibid., p. 104. Ireland also argues that some of these notorious cases, which invoked the unwritten law, "focused public attention on the alleged inadequacy of the common and statutory law as it related to libertinism" and were a factor in the passage of laws against "seduction." Ibid., p. 108.

[146] This account of Mary Harris's case is taken from Allen D. Spiegel, "Temporary Insanity and Premenstrual Syndrome: Medical Testimony in an 1865 Murder Trial," *New York Journal of Medicine* 88 (1988), p. 482. In 1883, Mary Harris, who was then forty or so, married her chief defense lawyer, Joseph H. Bradley Sr., who was in his eighties. He died four years later. Ibid., p. 490.

The trial of Lastencia Abarta was probably somewhat more typical. Abarta was a beautiful young woman, eighteen years old; she shot dead her forty-year-old lover, Francisco Forster, on the streets of Los Angeles, at 4 o'clock in the afternoon of March 16, 1881.[147] On trial, she took the stand and told a "love story with numerous promises of marriage and entreaties for sex prior to the ceremony." She and Forster did have sex; but, alas, no marriage took place. Abarta's lawyers provided the jury with a whole menu of defenses. One was that the gun went off "accidentally." More significant was that old faithful, the insanity defense. Abarta, it was said, "remembers nothing of what occurred." Moreover, she was "subject to hysteria at certain times of the month." A Dr. Joseph Kurtz told the jury that "any virtuous woman when deprived of her virtue would go mad undoubtedly." Another doctor talked about dysmenorrhea "accompanied by hysterical spasms." Still another doctor voiced the opinion that at the time of the shooting "her brain was undoubtedly congested with blood." The prosecution dragged out its own cluster of doctors, whose testimony tried to refute and contradict the testimony of the defense doctors. Abarta's lawyer, summing up, claimed that Lastencia was "a mere child who had been wronged." Forster "met his just deserts." The jury took less than an hour to bring in a verdict of not guilty "on the ground of insanity." As often happened, the courtroom crowd cheered lustily.

Another woman who said her mind was blank was Ada Werner of San Francisco. In April 1894, she killed her husband, a local butcher. They had been married for only seven months. After a quarrel, George went to sleep. His wife took a revolver, pressed it to the temple of the sleeping man, and fired. "I killed him after he told me he was going to get a divorce," she said, as she cried "wildly."[148] At the trial, where she appeared "with veiled face and dressed in deep mourning," she testified that she found notes in George's pocket from "girls"; she said her husband cursed her and after that her mind "was a blank." She "remembered nothing of the shooting."[149] The jury was sympathetic. She was found guilty of "murder in the second degree," with a strong recommendation for mercy. The judge was having none of it. He gave her a "scathing" dressing down. He said this was murder if anything was, and premeditated at that; he usually followed the jury recommendation, but in this case he would not. He sentenced her to life imprisonment, the most severe punishment he could give her.[150] But in 1905, the governor "assented to the parole" of Ada Werner. The prison director had recommended the parole, and it was endorsed, oddly enough, by the Butchers' Association of San Francisco, of which the murdered man had been a member.[151]

Katie Cook, whose trial was described earlier, also claimed her mind was a blank when she did the deed. Four physicians for the defense testified that she was insane

[147] On this trial, see Bakken, "The Limits of Patriarchy," pp. 95–99.
[148] "Shot while Asleep," *San Francisco Chronicle*, Apr. 12, 1894, p. 12.
[149] "Her Mind a Blank," *San Francisco Chronicle*, Sept. 27, 1894, p. 7.
[150] "To Prison for Life," *San Francisco Chronicle*, Dec. 13, 1894, p. 8.
[151] "Shortens Terms of Convicts," *San Francisco Chronicle*, Aug. 15, 1905, p. 3.

at the time she pulled the trigger. The jury, as mentioned before, acquitted her. And in her case, the verdict (like Mary Harris's) was not guilty, plain and simple (in Abarta's case, the verdict had been not guilty by reason of insanity).[152] And when a judge released Margaret Finn, who killed her absconding fiancé on a crowded Los Angeles street, he stated that she was "hysterical at the time of the killing," in a "peculiar nervous state," and "probably did not know what she was doing."[153] Clara Falmer too had the benefit (if that is the right word) of testimony about her mental state, a state brought about by her "delicate condition," among other things. In Chicago, in 1928, Victoria Yonan was arraigned before a magistrate; she had beaten Elsie Maye McKibbin of Oak Park. Yonan "pleaded the unwritten law"; McKibbin had "lured my husband away from me." Yonan's punishment? A peace bond of $500 and a warning to stay out of Oak Park.[154]

Juries, as we saw, were quite sympathetic to women they considered wounded doves, and some judges shared this opinion. Nonetheless, the double standard was at work in these cases. There was a difference between the male and female versions of the unwritten law. Juries did not seem to care whether, say, Sickles or the other men who were on trial were themselves pure at heart and faithful to their wives. Character and sexual behavior were more lively issues if the defendant was a woman. The two trials of Laura Fair formed a kind of natural experiment. Juries who heard about her sinful life voted for conviction; juries who heard nothing about her sex life acquitted her. Polite society could be cruel to a woman whose morals fell below Victorian standards – though, as we see later, there were exceptions to this tendency.[155] A woman who seemed decent and respectable, on the other hand, got the benefit of the doubt; any sins were laid at the door of the man who compromised her.

Take the case of Clara Falmer, who shot her boyfriend and was acquitted. The defense worked hard to paint her as innocent, vulnerable, naïve – even somewhat mentally unstable. The prosecution had a different image in mind: a shameless young woman, drenched in sin. Today, I suppose, we would simply call her a sexually active teenager. But this was not, in the late nineteenth century, an acceptable image for a girl like Clara Falmer. She was either a blameless victim or a fallen woman. Basically, there was nothing in between – at least nothing that worked with a jury.

The Unwritten Law: Success and Failure

Courts and juries, in general, followed the unwritten law. Defendants in cases that fit the pattern were overwhelmingly successful. In the 201 cases sampled, almost two-thirds (64 percent) of the defendants got off scot-free. In another 14 percent (twenty-

[152] Bakken, "The Limits of Patriarchy."
[153] "Margaret Finn Is Acquitted" (internal quotation marks omitted).
[154] "Unwritten Law Saves Wife Who Beat Up Woman," *Chicago Tribune*, Oct. 20, 1928, p. 1.
[155] I refer here to the leniency shown toward women who killed newborn – and illegitimate – babies. See Chapter 3.

eight cases), the penalty was light: a fine, a sentence of eight years or less, or a pardon. In only 15 percent (thirty cases) did defendants end up with substantial punishment: more than eight years in prison. Even so, the normal punishment for murder, life imprisonment or the death sentence, was extremely rare in the sample. Did the cases sampled show some kind of selection bias? The cases came, after all, from newspaper accounts. Acquittals are rarer than convictions in criminal cases, hence perhaps more newsworthy. A different sort of bias was probably more important: social class. Important people, people with money or position, were overrepresented among the defendants. They were, after all, men and women who had enough money to hire good lawyers. Good lawyers surely made a difference. Good lawyers knew how to work the unwritten law, not to mention how to work the insanity defense. Sometimes – Clara Falmer again comes to mind – prominent lawyers probably took on a case for a small fee or no fee at all, because the case was notorious and therefore good for business. Clara Falmer made headlines in Oakland. This could be seen as free and valuable advertising for her lawyers.

Nonetheless, the success rate of the unwritten law is a striking fact. Juries in these cases simply did not very often convict. This was so, whether the defendant was a man avenging his family honor, or a woman telling a story of brutality or betrayal.

If we tried to codify the unwritten law, we might phrase it (or at least the male version) more or less this way: a man who discovers that some other man has had dishonorable relations with a wife or female relative, or has a reasonable belief that such a thing has occurred, has the right to kill the person in question. In 1907, a former Virginia judge, William Loving, was tried for shooting and killing Theodore Estes.[156] Estes, according to Loving, had taken Loving's daughter riding, gotten her drunk, and assaulted her when she was unconscious. At least this was the story she told her father. It "tore" all his "heartstrings," he said, to "know that she had been . . . defiled." He ordered his buggy, "intending to seek this man and put him to death." But was Miss Loving telling the truth? The prosecution wanted to cast doubt on her story.[157] The judge refused to admit any evidence along these lines. According to the judge, it was "not material whether her story was true or not."[158]

Loving's team of lawyers put forward the usual (legal) defense, temporary insanity, but (no surprise) the main argument rested on the unwritten law.[159] Why should Loving be condemned to death? "[F]or what? I do not undervalue life," said a defense lawyer, "but there is something sweeter to all Virginians – the purity of our women." Loving's daughter was "his pride. He admired her beauty and her purity." Another defense lawyer begged the jury not to "let it go out to the world that

[156] "Miss Loving Tells of Estes's Wrong," *New York Times*, June 26, 1907, p. 1.
[157] "Jerome Gives Aid to Loving Judge," *New York Times*, June 28, 1907, p. 1.
[158] Ibid. The headline of the story refers to the fact that William Travers Jerome, the New York district attorney, had sent a telegram to the judge, citing legal authorities on the question whether evidence could be admitted to show if the daughter's story was true.
[159] "Unwritten Law for Loving," *New York Times*, June 29, 1907, p. 2.

a jury of Virginia gentlemen put the felon's stripes on a Virginia gentleman."[160] Still another argued that the "gift of God" was the "purity and the dignity of our homes."

The prosecution wanted the judge to tell the jury that no one had "a right to be the avenger of his own wrongs ... The unwritten law ... has no place in the criminal jurisprudence of Virginia."[161] The judge refused to give any such charge. The result, by this time, seemed foreordained. The jury spent less than an hour in the jury room – by one account, thirty minutes.[162] On the very first ballot, the vote for acquittal was unanimous, presumably on the (legal) grounds of insanity.[163] After the trial, the foreman (a merchant and farmer) said he thought "Judge Loving was out of his mind" when he killed young Estes: "The stress ... had been brought on by the story told him by his daughter." Whether he and the rest of the jury really believed this is something we will never know. The verdict was clearly popular. Tears streamed down Judge Loving's face, and his friends gathered around to congratulate him.

In a Kentucky case, R. E. Culley went on trial for killing W. E. Proctor, a prominent politician.[164] Culley's wife felt unloved. To make her husband jealous, she told him that Proctor had "assaulted" her. Hearing this, Culley went out and shot Proctor. At his trial, Culley claimed that the killing was justified – even though the affair might have been nothing but a figment of his wife's imagination. Culley was acquitted. The jury was willing to apply the unwritten law, even though it was likely that Culley's belief was just plain wrong and Proctor had not, in fact, betrayed him. Poor Mr. Proctor was simply collateral damage. At least in this case, for a change, the community (according to a journalist) found the verdict astonishing.[165]

In cases of the unwritten law, juries sometimes acted with lightning speed – spending no time at all in discussion and debate; the result they were going to reach was clear to them from the outset. In 1908, in Oklahoma, one Dr. E. W. Dakan slit the throat of his wife's lover.[166] The jury deliberated all of ten minutes before announcing a verdict: not guilty. A jury in Richmond, Virginia, beat this record in 1900: the defendant, William J. Rhodes, "shot down Frank Barnett for having destroyed his home." Acquittal took seven minutes.[167] In Alameda County, California, in 1912, the jury acquitted Harry F. Prescott, who had killed Ralph Thompson, "the despoiler of his home."[168] This jury took two hours, but much of

---

[160] "Judge Loving Is Acquitted in 30 Minutes," *Atlanta Constitution*, June 30, 1907, p. 1.

[161] "Unwritten Law Is the Keynote of the Defense" (internal quotation marks omitted).

[162] "Judge Loving Is Acquitted in 30 Minutes." The *New York Times*, reporting on the acquittal, said that the jury was out for an hour. See "Unwritten Law for Loving." In either case, it was a very short period of deliberation.

[163] "Judge Loving Is Acquitted in 30 Minutes."

[164] "Stands Pat on Worn Excuse," *Los Angeles Times*, Apr. 1, 1910, p. 15.   [165] Ibid.

[166] "Saved by Unwritten Law," *Atlanta Constitution*, Jan. 19, 1908, p. B1.

[167] "Unwritten Law Saves," *Washington Post*, May 13, 1900, p. 11. The wife was a "woman of refinement and considerable beauty." Her testimony, "substantiating the defense in every detail at the cost of her own good name," was apparently a crucial factor.

[168] "Unwritten Law Applied in H. F. Prescott Case," *San Francisco Chronicle*, May 30, 1912, p. 8.

that was taken up by lunch. The verdict, according to the local press, was a "direct application of the 'unwritten law.'"

The unwritten law was even more successful for women in our sample than for men. In 97% of the cases where we know the outcome (33 out of 34), women defendants were acquitted or won light sentences. By contrast, men were either not convicted or sentenced lightly in 80 percent of the cases where we know the outcome (122 out of 152). It is possible that newspapers were more apt to report acquittals for women than for men. And the sample size is small. It is clear, though, that women who killed betrayers or abusers often found protection under the wings of the unwritten law.

Clearly, juries responded to the unwritten law. But there were judges too who were as willing as their jurors to ignore formal law. After a Pennsylvania jury acquitted James Nutt of killing a home-wrecker,[169] the judge said the dead man was a "villain" who had suffered "proper retribution." And, he added, "I could scarcely have done less as a private [citizen] myself."[170] When J. L. Gibson, a former Georgia sheriff, was tried for killing Elgin Stewart (Gibson had discovered love letters between Stewart and his wife),[171] the judge directed a verdict of acquittal.[172] Homicide, he explained, was justifiable in two situations: self-defense and "the protection of ... honor as a husband and father."

Other judges, whether sincerely or not, sternly warned the jury not to follow the unwritten law or told juries their duty was to follow the written law in every regard. This preaching usually fell on deaf ears. In 1934, a California jury acquitted Judson Doke of murder.[173] Doke was a milk inspector from San Leandro. His wife was a poetry buff; in the course of her "poetry activities" she met Lamar Hollingshead, a student at the University of California.[174] The two of them published poetry and shared ideas. One thing led to another. A neighbor tipped off Doke and gave him incriminating love letters. Doke took the letters and a pistol and confronted Hollingshead "in the bunk house of a ranch where the young poet had been working." Doke wanted Hollingshead to write a letter, ending the affair once and for all. Hollingshead refused, "and the fatal shot rang out." The judge told the jury murder was not the way to handle this kind of problem; the law "provides ample redress" for men with unfaithful wives. No matter. Doke went free – a result that was, as often, popular with the courtroom crowd. In 1922, George Cline and two accomplices killed "handsome" Jack Bergin, a film actor; Bergin had apparently plied Cline's wife with liquor and then "attacked" her.[175] The judge told the jury no evidence

[169] "Young Nutt Acquitted," *Atlanta Constitution*, Jan. 24, 1884, p. 1.
[170] "What the Judge Said," *Atlanta Constitution*, Jan. 25, 1884, p. 1 (internal quotation marks omitted).
[171] "Love Letters Will Play Part in Trial of Deputy Sheriff," *Atlanta Constitution*, Aug. 11, 1918, p. 1.
[172] "Gibson Acquitted of Murder Charge," *Atlanta Constitution*, Aug. 17, 1918, p. 7.
[173] "Jury Frees Doke in Murder of Poet," *New York Times*, Dec. 16, 1934, p. 22.
[174] Ibid. This was Doke's second trial. The first jury was deadlocked. After Doke was set free, his attorneys said he planned to file suit for a divorce from his wife.
[175] "The Unwritten Law Invoked by Cline," *New York Times*, Oct. 25, 1922, p. 2.

could possibly sustain an acquittal.[176] The jury ignored him. All three defendants were acquitted. "One juror said, 'I have a wife and daughter,' which apparently swayed him to acquit." In one of the rare cases that went up on appeal, the Kansas Supreme Court (1930) stated plainly that the unwritten law had no legal standing in Kansas.[177] But statements of this sort rarely had any effect on juries.

The unwritten law was astonishingly successful, as we have seen, but there were cases where it apparently did not work. Why did this happen? In some instances, perhaps, the jury was simply not convinced by the defendant's story. If a jury came to the conclusion that the defendant was telling a lie, the jury might well convict. In Mississippi, in 1910, John T. Carter went on trial for killing Dr. R. P. Wendell.[178] Carter claimed Wendell had "drugged" his wife "with cocktails." He said he "heard the bed springs creaking" in his wife's room; he barged in and found the pair in bed together, his wife wearing "a pink kimono." But Carter's wife took the stand and denounced her husband as an outright liar. The jury found Carter guilty. He was sentenced to twenty years in prison.[179]

Similarly, a year earlier, a Mississippi millionaire named Smith was on trial for homicide; the victim (Smith said) was the man who had "ruined" his daughter. But the daughter refused to back up the story.[180] Smith was convicted and sentenced to life in prison.[181] In a 1914 case, Walter B. Brooks, of Savannah, Georgia, had killed Charles Barbour. Barbour, Brooks said, had been paying unwanted attention to Brooks's wife. He was acquitted. Later, in divorce proceedings, the wife insisted that she had never even met Barbour and that her husband resorted to the unwritten law "to save his own skin."[182]

Sam Aiken, an unemployed painter in Georgia, was a bootlegger during Prohibition.[183] In 1929, he shot and killed his wife and his neighbor. He defended himself on the grounds that his "home had been wrecked," but the jury apparently thought he was lying.[184] He and his neighbor had been partners in their bootlegging business; the two quarreled over a liquor deal, and this business dispute was apparently the real reason Aiken killed his partner. He then killed his wife, so that he could invoke the unwritten law. At least this is what the jury seemed to

[176] "All Three Acquitted in Bergin Tragedy," *New York Times*, Oct. 26, 1922, p. 1.
[177] *State* v. *Kelly*, 291 P. 945, 947 (Kan. 1930); "'Unwritten Law' Is Barred as Defense by Kansas Court," *New York Times*, Oct. 12, 1930, p. 3.
[178] "Husband's Hope Shattered by Testimony of His Wife," *Los Angeles Times*, Apr. 2, 1910, p. 18
[179] "Jury Turns Down Unwritten Law," *Atlanta Constitution*, Apr. 6, 1910, p. 3.
[180] "'Unwritten Law' Gets Jolt," p. II4.
[181] A writer for the *Los Angeles Times*, commenting on this case, sneered at the unwritten law. Men who claimed this defense, he said, were usually acting out of "homicidal mania, jealousy or some other equally contemptible motive." Ibid.
[182] "Wife Brands as Fake Unwritten Law Plea Which Saved Husband," *Atlanta Constitution*, Nov. 18, 1914, p. 5.
[183] "Liquor-Selling Feud Seen in Double Killing," *Atlanta Constitution*, June 19, 1929, p. 1.
[184] "Sam F. Aiken Found Guilty of Murder of His Wife," *Atlanta Constitution*, July 4, 1929, p. 1.

believe. He was convicted and sentenced to death (later commuted to life imprisonment).[185]

Aiken's case was hurt by the fact that he had killed the wife as well as the (supposed) lover.[186] This was an unusual and unmanly act, which probably pre-judiced both judge and jury. Carolyn Ramsey's data strongly suggest that judges, juries, and law enforcement officers in the nineteenth and early twentieth centuries condemned and punished violence against women – at least extreme violence.[187] Ramsey's data come from Western states, especially Colorado, from New York, and from Australia.[188] But they are likely to hold more generally.

In any event, Sam Aiken, who killed his wife, found no sympathy from a jury. Neither did Walter Harris, tried in Philadelphia in 1933. Harris made the mistake of coming home earlier than expected. He found his wife, Betty, "in the midst of a tryst" with his neighbor, Matthew Lindsay. Harris killed his wife and wounded his neighbor, who lost the sight of an eye. The judge denounced the idea of an unwritten law and the jury found Harris guilty of murder in the first degree; he was sentenced to life imprisonment.[189] And in 1927, in New York, Earl Battice, a cook on a schooner, got a ten-year sentence for murdering his wife, slashing her throat with a razor "because she accepted the attentions of another member of the ship's crew."[190]

Nor was there sympathy for Joseph L. Steinmetz, whose trial caused quite a stir in 1929.[191] This was a bizarre and pitiful story. Steinmetz, a young divinity student, was on his honeymoon in New York City; he had been married all of sixteen days.[192] After an all-night drinking party, he claimed he found his bride in bed with a Catholic priest in the Knights of Columbus Hotel.[193] Drunk and furious, he killed them both on the spot. He was tried for double homicide, but the killing of his wife dominated the proceedings. His defense attorney boldly invoked the unwritten law: when Steinmetz found his wife in bed with the priest, the discovery threw a "monkey

---

[185]   Aiken escaped from prison, but was caught years later living in Texas with a new wife. See "Sam Aiken Flees from Chain Gang," *Atlanta Constitution*, Apr. 17, 1937, p. 1. It was this wife's pleas that apparently moved the governor to commute Aiken's sentence. See "Embarrassing Quiz Faces Sam Aiken," *Atlanta Constitution*, Dec. 4, 1937, p. 7. But Aiken escaped again. He then turned up in Texas once more – again with a new wife.

[186]   In one bizarre 1925 case in Illinois, Warren J. Lincoln, a lawyer, tried to use the "unwritten law," but this hardly seemed to fit the crime: he killed his wife and her brother and sealed their heads in a cement block ("Warren Lincoln Takes Charge of His Defense," *Chicago Tribune*, Jan. 25, 1925, p. 19). He was sentenced to life imprisonment and died in 1941 ("Warren J. Lincoln, Killer of Two, Dies in Joliet Hospital," *Chicago Daily Tribune*, Aug. 12, 1941, p. 8).

[187]   Ramsey, "Intimate Homicide," pp. 179–180, 187–189.

[188]   See Ramsey, "Domestic Violence," pp. 222–231; Ramsey, "Intimate Homicide."

[189]   Randy Dixon, "Walter Harris 'Honor Slayer' Is Given Life," *Philadelphia Tribune*, Sept. 28, 1933, p. 1.

[190]   "Battice Gets Ten Years," *Philadelphia Tribune*, Aug. 25, 1927, p. 1. The jury had found him guilty of second-degree murder.

[191]   See "'Unwritten Law' Cited by Steinmetz Aid," *Atlanta Constitution*, May 28, 1935, p. 3.

[192]   "Unwritten Law Plea Hinted in Priest Slaying," *Chicago Daily Tribune*, Nov. 28, 1934, p. 7.

[193]   See "Steinmetz Weeps as His Trial Opens," *New York Times*, May 17, 1935, p. 14.

wrench" into his "mental machinery, robbing him of his stability of mind." Steinmetz merely "did what any red-blooded man with a spoonful of manhood would have done under the circumstances." But the jury seemed to feel that "red-blooded" men did not kill their wives. Steinmetz was convicted of first-degree manslaughter and sentenced to eight to sixteen years in Sing Sing.[194] He was not retried for killing the priest. Killing his rival was apparently defensible; it was wife murder that went a step too far.

Though not always. There were, as usual, exceptions. In a California case, Paul A. Wright was tried for "empty[ing] [a] weapon's nine bullets" into his wife and his best friend, John B. Kimmel, after finding them "in a passionate embrace" in his home.[195] The newspapers called the affair the "White Flame" killing – apparently because Wright supposedly acted in a "'white flame' of jealous frenzy."[196] The prosecutor told the jury that "there is no such defense as the 'unwritten law.'"[197] Nevertheless, the jury let Wright go free. He was acquitted on the grounds of temporary insanity.[198] More than forty years earlier, Nellie Gordon's husband had found her in bed with the son of Governor Brown of Kentucky.[199] The husband killed them both on the spot. A grand jury refused to indict him. In an astonishing testament to the power of the unwritten law, Governor Brown, father of a victim, claimed that he would have pardoned the killer of his son, if the man had been convicted.

The unwritten law was apparently a coast-to-coast affair. It seemed to embrace all social classes, although, as we pointed out, a good defense cost money, and our sample probably overrepresents prominent people. Particularly in the North, the unwritten law may have been the province of the well-to do; these were men who could pay a legal team to pull off this defense.[200] In the South and West, the unwritten law may have been more routine. The defendants were not just the rich and famous; they were, rather, something of a cross-section of (white) society – farmers,[201] airport workers,[202] miners,[203] immigrants.[204]

The sample of 201 American cases includes trials in thirty-one states and the District of Columbia. New England is missing from the sample, however. Evidence does suggest that the unwritten law had its biggest impact in the South and West. Contemporaries certainly thought so, as we saw in the case of Mary Ertell (1901).

[194] "Steinmetz Gets 8 to 16 Years in Hotel Slaying of Young Wife," *New York Herald Tribune*, June 15, 1935, p. 28.
[195] "Heated Legal Clash Marks Wright Trial," p. I1.
[196] "'White Flame' Wife Slayer Goes on Trial," *Atlanta Constitution*, Jan. 14, 1938, p. 1.
[197] "Wright Seen in Triangle," *Los Angeles Times*, Jan. 15, 1938, p. II1.
[198] "Jury Declares Wright Insane," *Los Angeles Times*, Feb. 17, 1938, p. I1.
[199] "Freed by the Unwritten Law."
[200] See Hartog, "Lawyering, Husbands' Rights, and 'the Unwritten Law' in Nineteenth-Century America," p. 75, describing the pedigree of the lawyers in three famous cases.
[201] See "West Pardons Aged Farmer," *Los Angeles Times*, Oct. 4, 1912, p. I3.
[202] See "Heated Legal Clash Marks Wright Trial."   [203] See "Unwritten Law Frees Slayer."
[204] See "Pleads Unwritten Law," p. II2.

And we noted expressions of pride in Texas with regard to the unwritten law. Still, some famous instances of the unwritten law were centered outside the South and West. George Cole and Harry Thaw were both tried in New York. And while Congressman Sickles was tried in the District of Columbia, he himself was a New Yorker. In 1913, a jury in St. Paul, Minnesota, acquitted Professor Oscar Olson in the murder of Clyde N. Darling, "alleged wrecker of the Olson home," on the basis of the unwritten law.[205] In 1938, Rudolph Sikora, a dispatcher's clerk in Chicago, killed Edward Solomon, described as the "rival for his wife's love."[206] A jury of "eleven husbands and one bachelor" heard the case. The prosecutor asked for the death penalty. The jury was out for two hours and then announced a verdict of not guilty. A crowd of some 200 in the courtroom, "most of them women," screamed and cried in delight; many "burst into wild tears." "Above the noise came the piercing hallelujah of a tall woman in black, who cried 'Bless his sweet heart … !'" Sikora himself cried, "[i]t's swell," before he was rushed from the courtroom.[207]

Our examples have come only from the United States. But there is no reason to think this was an example of so-called American exceptionalism; something specific to American culture, with a certain flavor of the Wild West or Wild West attitudes. Newspapers occasionally pointed out foreign instances, all of them resulting in acquittals.[208] And the unwritten law was certainly alive and well in England. In 1881, one James Johnson tried to kill a man after finding him in bed with Johnson's wife; Johnson struck him with a cleaver and wounded him so badly the man spent weeks in the hospital. The judge, despite a jury verdict against the defendant, let him go: there was no greater provocation for a man, and Johnson did not deserve to be punished.[209] Other judges and jurists in the United Kingdom were not so keen on the unwritten law and expressed great hostility to the very idea.[210] A Scottish newspaper thought decisions like those in Harry Thaw's case would result in a kind of "anarchy," and could "bring the law into contempt and convert society into chaos."[211]

English juries apparently thought otherwise. In one well-known case, in 1917, defense counsel Sir John Simon referred to the unwritten law as a noxious doctrine from "another country" – presumably the United States. The judge too warned against the baneful influence of this invasive species. The accused in the case, Lt. Douglas Malcolm, shot to death a "scoundrel" named Anton Baumberg. Malcolm found him in a room with Malcolm's wife. The defense was a rather shaky and flimsy claim of self-defense. Despite the judge's lecture, the jury behaved much like an

[205] "Prof Olson Freed by Jury."   [206] Winn, "Sikora Free in Love Murder."
[207] Ibid. See note 39.   [208] See "Unwritten Law Wins in Paris."
[209] Martin J. Wiener, *Men of Blood: Violence, Manliness and Criminal Justice in Victorian England* (New York: Cambridge University Press, 2004), p. 203.
[210] "Acquittal of Lieut. Malcolm," *Manchester Guardian*, Sept. 12, 1917, p. 5.
[211] "Unwritten Law Will Be Theme of Hains' New Novel," *Evening Telegraph and Post* (Dundee, Scotland), Jan. 18, 1909, p. 4.

American jury. They took less than half an hour to find Lt. Malcolm not guilty. A "roar of joy" burst out in the courtroom, and a group of women "shouted with exultation."[212] In 1931, Andrew Frederick Neely, a ship's electrician, murdered Wilfred Powley, a sometime lodger in his house; Neely thought Powley was trying to seduce his wife.[213] The jury was told specifically that the unwritten law had no basis in English law, but the jurors were also told that the victim was a scoundrel who had insinuated his way into the house, "corrupted the mind of the wife," and destroyed the happiness of Neely's home. The verdict: guilty but insane.

The Fall of the Unwritten Law

The spectacular career of the unwritten law did not last forever. After a golden age in the early twentieth century, the unwritten law faded away gradually. By the 1950s, it all but disappeared from the newspapers. More than sixty cases were reported during the five-year period from 1910 to 1914. By 1920–1924, this figure dropped to just over twenty. In the 1930s, cases invoking the unwritten law were even rarer.[214] And during the 1950s, only two lonely cases cropped up.

Were there fewer love triangles than in the past? Fewer betrayed husbands? Fewer wives with lovers? This seems exceedingly unlikely, especially in the age of the sexual revolution. Were betrayed husbands less likely to kill? This is certainly possible. And probably few brothers would take it on themselves to kill someone who had sex with their sister. But above all, the old arguments simply seemed less persuasive. Surely, if lawyers thought such arguments would work, they would trot them out. But this did not happen.

Of course, the unwritten law had always been controversial, had always been contested. Some judges nagged at juries, warning them to disregard any such idea. Juries, as we saw, routinely disregarded these instructions. At a 1906 meeting of the American Bar Association, the unwritten law was roundly denounced.[215] Newspaper

---

[212] "Acquittal of Lieut. Malcolm." The American newspapers occasionally referred to miscellaneous continental European cases; there were four instances of this, from England, France, Belgium, and Germany. South Africa and Canada also contributed one instance each. In all six cases, the trials resulted in acquittals. See, e.g., "Unwritten Law Wins in Paris," *Atlanta Constitution*, May 12, 1907, at 1.

[213] "Woman's Husband Found Insane," *Manchester Guardian*, Dec. 8, 1931, p. 6.

[214] In 1932, Manuel Fontes, a farmer of East Falmouth, pleaded guilty to manslaughter; he had shot to death his wife and her lover ("Gets Five Years for Two Love Slayings," *Boston Globe*, Oct. 27, 1932, p. 4). He was sentenced to five years in prison. The district attorney remarked that Massachusetts, of course, "does not subscribe to any unwritten law," but nonetheless he asked the court to take into account "the background" and the circumstances, especially Fontes's children and their welfare. The punishment – for a double murder – was certainly light, but it did involve a jolt in the penitentiary, which many other defendants did not get.

[215] See "Unwritten Laws Govern Everywhere," *Atlanta Constitution*, Aug. 31, 1906, p. 2.

stories and editorials were also often critical. Some writers called the unwritten law barbaric. One op-ed, from the *Atlanta Constitution* in 1907, warned that the "safeguards of civilization" were "emphatically imperilled by the mawkish sentimentality which seeks to screen downright crime under the guise of the 'higher law.'"[216] In one case, in St. Louis, a judge simply refused to let lawyers for James E. Clark invoke this defense. Clark was on trial for killing a telegraph operator, Joseph Flood; Flood, presumably, had had a relationship with Clark's estranged wife. "There is no such thing as an unwritten law in Missouri," the judge said; "no statements based on such an assumption will be tolerated in this court."[217] A writer for the *Los Angeles Times*, in 1922, called the unwritten law a "wraith of the past when every man was a law unto himself."[218]

These criticisms seemed to become more persuasive with the passage of time. They may have had an impact on the occasional case. In 1908, Captain Peter C. Hains Jr., with help from his brother Thornton, killed William E. Annis; Hains's wife had confessed to "improper relations" with Annis.[219] Thornton was tried first, and was promptly acquitted, surely because of the unwritten law.[220] The result was widely criticized. A magistrate called the result a "gross miscarriage of justice."[221] A former judge called the trial and verdict "monstrous." An editorial in the *Atlanta Constitution* warned that the unwritten law was being "stretched to cover unmeritorious cases."[222] The bad press apparently hurt Peter Hains's chances of getting off. He went on trial later that year. Unlike his brother, the jury found him guilty. He was sentenced to a long term in prison (up to twenty years).[223] One juror explained this result: yes, the jurors all agreed that the victim "deserved his fate," but the jurors felt they should not consider the unwritten law.

In the end the steamroller of social and cultural change undid the unwritten law. Gender images – and the reality of gender relations – had altered immeasurably since the nineteenth century. Old assumptions about the nature of women and the role and duty of men fell into decay. Women more and more entered the workforce. They won the right to vote, to serve on juries, to hold public office. By the 1950s, there was a strong feminist movement, and the "sexual revolution" was in full flow. Marriage was rapidly losing its monopoly over legitimate sexual relations. Companionate marriage had replaced traditional marriage. Women were independent actors, much more than before; they had largely escaped from the traditional role that had once been their prison. They were no longer merely an appendage of men. Divorce rates were high; divorce was consequently much less stigmatic.

[216] "Warning from a Capable Source," *Atlanta Constitution*, Dec. 3, 1907, p. 6.
[217] "Unwritten Law Barred in Clark Murder Defense," *St. Louis Post-Dispatch*, Apr. 21, 1909.
[218] "The Unwritten Law," *Los Angeles Times*, Sept. 26, 1922, p. II4.
[219] "Jury Convicted Captain Hains," *Atlanta Constitution*, May 12, 1909, p. 3.
[220] "I'd Do It Again, Declares Hains," *Atlanta Constitution*, Jan. 17, 1909, p. C7.
[221] "Serious Menace in the Unwritten Law," *New York Times*, Jan. 17, 1909, p. 2 (internal quotation marks omitted).
[222] "The Elasticity of the 'Unwritten Law.'"   [223] "Jury Convicted Captain Hains."

Women (and men) had a much clearer way to get rid of an intolerable marriage.[224] Violence in defense of male honor was harder to justify.

The official image of the respectable woman, in the nineteenth century and beyond, pictured her as innocent, weak, naïve, passive – and essentially sexless. This image faded over time. The unwritten law treated women as chaste and subservient; their men (husbands, brothers) had a kind of dominion over them. The true man had the right, if not the duty, to avenge slights to his sexual and family honor. Reality was always surely more complex – maybe the golden age of patriarchy never really existed in its pure and unadulterated form; but in any event, by 1950, the past was dead or dying, and new forms of social order were emerging.[225]

Lawyers in the middle of the twentieth century still tried, once in a while, to stir up a jury by appealing to unwritten law. But the magic was gone. In 1949, Robert C. Rutledge, a pediatrician in St. Louis, twenty-nine years old, "handsome," and young, went on trial for killing Byron Hattman, an aircraft engineer.[226] Hattman had supposedly seduced Dr. Rutledge's "tall, statuesque wife," Sydney Goodrich Rutledge, after a drinking party. The doctor followed Hattman to Cedar Rapids, Iowa, confronted him in a hotel room, and stabbed him to death. Rutledge claimed self-defense; he said that Hattman had attacked him. His lawyers brought up the old story of the unwritten law: Dr. Rutledge was "defending the sanctity of his home" against "a venomous viper." This time, however, the jury did not take the bait. Rutledge was convicted and sentenced to seventy years in prison.[227] The Iowa Supreme Court affirmed his conviction in 1951.[228]

Oddly, the two last gasps of the unwritten law both involved dentists. In 1954, Dr. Kenneth B. Small, a Michigan dentist, shot and killed Jules H. Lack, president of the Majestic Air Conditioning Company, a "playboy industrialist," in New York.[229] Dr. Small's wife said she was in love with Lack and wanted a divorce; Dr. Small tried to talk her out of it. Mrs. Small had left town, ostensibly to visit friends. But her husband found out that she had gone away with Lack; the couple was at a weekend

---

[224] On the rise of divorce, see generally Joanna L. Grossman and Lawrence M. Friedman, *Inside the Castle* (Princeton, NJ: Princeton University Press, 2011); William L. O'Neill, *Divorce in the Progressive Era* (New Haven, CT: Yale University Press, 1967).

[225] Unwritten law killings were almost always committed with a revolver. At least one newspaper suggested that easy access to firearms was partly to blame for the frequency of these impulsive, vengeful killings. See "Blood Flowed in a Crimson Stream during Year 1912," *Atlanta Constitution*, Jan. 1, 1913, p. 1. And when asked whether he would continue to carry a handgun after his acquittal for murder, Thornton Hains responded: "Certainly, I'll carry a gun ... A man can't tell when he might have to use it" ("I'd Do It Again, Declares Hains").

[226] "Unwritten Law Appeal Fails for Rutledge," *Chicago Daily Tribune*, Apr. 5, 1951, p. 3.

[227] "Rutledge Given 70 Years in Love Triangle Killing," *Los Angeles Times*, Aug. 9, 1949, p, I2.

[228] *State* v. *Rutledge*, 47 N.W.2d 251, 258 (Iowa 1951). The issues on appeal, of course, had nothing to do with the unwritten law; they concerned (as usual) jury instructions, admission of evidence, and the like (ibid., pp. 260–264).

[229] "Expect Love Rival Killer to Plead 'Unwritten Law,'" *Chicago Daily Tribune*, May 31, 1954, p. B17; "Dentist Is Cleared," *New York Times*, July 17, 1954, p. 28; "Industrialist Is Slain," *New York Times*, May 31, 1954, p. 27.

getaway. Dr. Small drove to where they were staying, burst in, "shot his rival, and waited quietly for the police." He was acquitted on grounds of temporary insanity; he was, however, required to report to a state mental facility.[230] Four years later, Bobby Gene Hunter was found not guilty of attempted murder; he had stabbed Dr. John Henry Glascock. Hunter's wife worked as an assistant to Dr. Glascock in his dental office; she admitted to her husband that she and the dentist had "engaged in an office romance." Hence the stabbing. The dentist survived; this may have made it easier for the jury to acquit Bobby Gene.[231] After these two dental eruptions, the rest is silence.

There was, however, a dim echo, in 1974, when Inez Garcia, a woman from Monterey, California, went on trial.[232] Garcia had been raped, and she killed a man who she claimed had acted as an accomplice. (This was the rare case that accused the dead man of involvement in an actual rape.) Garcia argued that a raped woman had "the right to kill back" – a claim that made her a hero in some circles. But the jury disagreed; she was convicted of second-degree murder. And the old rules were little or no help to Jean Harris, former headmistress of an elite girls' high school in Virginia and the jilted lover of Dr. Herman Tarnower, the "Scarsdale Diet Doctor."[233] After years of mistreating Harris and dallying with younger women, Tarnower planned to leave her; she shot him to death. Nobody so much as mentioned the unwritten law at her trial in 1981; she was convicted and given a prison sentence of fifteen years to life.

In the early twentieth century, these would have been classic cases of the unwritten law. Indeed, Inez Garcia was very much like Carrie Davis, a Canadian woman who, sixty years earlier, lay in wait and killed Bert Massey, who "mistreated her" after a dinner party.[234] And it is hard to distinguish Jean Harris's case from the case of Olivia Stone, also sixty years earlier. Olivia was the "common law wife" of Ellis Kinkead; she killed him when he planned to abandon her, after they had lived together for years.[235] What changed between these sets of cases was not the basic situation, but the social norms that were applied.

Today, the unwritten law is a distant memory. Of course, love, sex, and marriage still evoke the very strongest of emotions. But virginity, chastity, male honor, "true manhood," marital fidelity: these have very different meanings today, at least in developed countries. Men no doubt still kill rivals and the women who cheat on them, or who give them their walking papers, but it is harder to justify these acts and

[230] "Dentist Is Cleared."
[231] Art Ryon, "Husband Cleared in Knifing Dentist in Row over Wife," *Los Angeles Times*, June 12, 1958, p. 12.
[232] Lacy Fosburgh, "Assertion of Rape and 'Unwritten Law' Form a Coast Woman's Murder Defense," *New York Times*, Aug. 31, 1974, p. 32.
[233] See Joseph Berger, "Headmistress, Jilted Lover, Killer, Then a Force for Good in Jail," *New York Times*, Dec. 29, 2012, p. 1.
[234] "Unwritten Law in Canada," *New York Times*, Feb. 28, 1915, p. 1.
[235] "Jury Frees Nurse at Murder Trial," *Atlanta Constitution*, Apr. 7, 1922, p. 1.

the unwritten law simply cannot be used as such. The classic unwritten law is never invoked. To be sure, killing within the family is apparently not punished as often or as severely as the killing of strangers. In Texas, in 1969, the "degree of intimacy between killer and victim" had an inverse correlation with the penalty. In the Texas sample (the data are from Houston), 61 percent of the killers of relatives were not punished at all, as opposed to 36 percent of the killers of strangers.[236]

Women who kill abusive husbands or lovers still often go free, but courts justify this result in a different way. The battered woman syndrome, a kind of mutation of self-defense, can be used; the defense can introduce material on this syndrome into evidence in court.[237] The basic idea is that an abusive relationship can form a kind of steel trap for a woman, a trap from which she can escape only through violence. This is not the old, traditional (male) idea of self-defense, but a new and subtler version. It is a version for women who live in fear, who feel helpless, unable to break free. This strikes some scholars as something dramatically new. As such, yes, it is new: but the unwritten law (female version) was in a way an older mutation of self-defense; and it was in a way the functional equivalent of the battered woman syndrome. The new version is a more subtle, more contemporary, more contextual under-standing of the pitiless dramas of domestic violence.

---

[236] Henry P. Lundsgaarde, *Murder in Space City: A Cultural Analysis of Houston Homicide Patterns* (New York: Oxford University Press, 1977), p. 16.

[237] See, e.g., *Smith v. State*, 277 S.E.2d 678 (Ga. 1981). Josephine Smith was charged with "murdering her live-in boyfriend." The boyfriend was physically extremely abusive, and Smith said she shot him "in fear of her life." The issue in the case was whether the court should have allowed expert testimony on the battered woman syndrome. Smith had been convicted, but the Supreme Court of Georgia reversed, holding that the "expert's opinion . . . was improperly excluded."

3

Dead on Arrival

A minor story – one paragraph long – appeared in the *New York Times* in 1886, reporting the arrest of a "German girl of 24," Cecilia Ringold. Cecilia had been working for two months as a domestic servant in the house of the Pfarr family, in Newark, New Jersey. Cecilia was accused of killing her newborn child. Its body was "found in an outhouse." Cecilia refused to tell the name of the father.[1]

In Brockton, Alabama, in 1900, Mrs. J. W. Garrett and her stepdaughter were arrested and charged with infanticide. Miss Garrett, it was claimed, had "killed and burned her illegitimate child," to "hide her shame." Allegedly, her stepmother had helped her kill the child. The newspaper described the family as "very prominent" in their home area and said that the arrest "created considerable excitement."[2]

According to a story in the *Los Angeles Times*, in 1887,[3] a telegraph operator in Chicago, "hardly more than a child," had given birth to a baby; she wandered through the streets "starving, desperate, half-crazed, and freezing." The situation had affected her mind; in her weakened mental condition, she left the baby to die in the cold.

These are three accounts of women accused of infanticide, or, to be more accurate, neonaticide – the killing of a baby, usually during its first day of life, just after the mother gave birth. Mothers also have once in a while killed older children – for example, Andrea Yates, a Houston mother, who drowned her children in 2001.[4] This kind of child-murder is a rare event, and it is different in important ways from neonaticide. Typically, a mother accused of killing her newborn baby had been hiding the very fact of pregnancy and birth. This is obviously not the case if a mother kills a child of five, or fifteen, or even a one-year-old. Killing a newborn seems to be a special sort of crime, and it has been treated that way, on the whole – not formally, not "legally," but in fact.

---

[1] *New York Times*, Jan. 18, 1886, p. 5.   [2] *Atlanta Constitution*, Jan. 23, 1900, p. 3.
[3] *Los Angeles Times*, Jan. 8, 1887, p. 10.
[4] On this case, and the issue in general, see Elizabeth Rapaport, "Mad Women and Desperate Girls: Infanticide and Child Murder in Law and Myth," *Fordham Urban Law Journal* 33 (2006), p. 527.

Legal and social attitudes toward these mothers have been complex, and have changed greatly over the years. In the nineteenth century, and into the twentieth, neonaticide, it seems, was another one of our crimes without punishment. Women accused of this crime were treated with astonishing lenience. Legally, they had committed murder. But here too a kind of unwritten law kicked in. Juries treated these women with understanding, if not downright sympathy.

Neonaticide has occurred in many cultures, in many societies, and in many historical periods. There is a sizeable literature on the subject.[5] Legally speaking, however, penal codes rarely had anything special to say about neonaticide. There was infanticide in England in the early modern period, and also in the American colonies: both the killing of newborns and the killing of older children.[6] But at all times, in this country, it was just as much murder to kill a newborn baby as to kill anybody else. Killing was killing.[7]

I have written elsewhere about neonaticide in England in the Victorian period and the early twentieth century.[8] In England, juries were astonishingly lenient toward women defendants. The records of the Old Bailey (the central criminal court of London) show this with remarkable consistency. In this chapter, however, my main focus is on the United States, and roughly the same period, that is, the nineteenth century and the first part of the twentieth, with a coda on contemporary times.

Most (though not all) of those accused of this crime have been women. We can distinguish three main reasons why a woman might want to kill her newborn child; the three cases noted at the beginning of this chapter illustrate these three reasons. The first is sheer economic desperation. This was the dominant motive in nineteenth-century England, as least as far as we can tell from reported cases. A servant girl, working in London or some other city, and who found herself pregnant was in an absolutely desperate situation if, as often happened, she had no way to pressure the father of the child. For some of these women at least, the only way out of this

---

5   See, for example, William L. Langer, "Infanticide: A Historical Survey," *History of Childhood Quarterly* 1 (1974), p. 353; Lita Linzer Schwartz and Natalie K. Isser, *Endangered Children: Neonaticide, Infanticide, and Filicide* (Boca Raton, FL: CRC Press, 2000); Cheryl L. Meyer and Michelle Oberman, *Mothers Who Kill their Children* (New York: New York University Press, 2001); Mark Jackson, ed., *Infanticide: Historical Perspectives on Child Murder and Concealment, 1550–2000* (Aldershot: Ashgate, 2002); P. J. Resnick, "Murder of the Newborn: A Psychiatric Review of Neonaticide," *American Journal of Psychiatry* 126:10 (1970); James Sharpe, *A Fiery and Furious People: A History of Violence in England* (London: RH Books, 2016), ch. 6, "Mothers and Infanticide"; Judith Flanders, *The Invention of Murder* (London: Harper Press, 2011), pp. 223–227. See also Douglas V. Snow, "Infanticide in New Jersey: A Nineteenth-Century Case Study," *New Jersey History* 115:3 (1997).

6   Peter C. Hoffer and N. E. H. Hull, *Murdering Mothers: Infanticide in England and New England, 1558–1803* (New York: New York University Press, 1981).

7   As we see in what follows, statutes now try to treat neonaticide as a special or separate crime. See also Margaret Ryznar, "A Crime of Its Own? A Proposal for Achieving Greater Sentencing Consistency in Neonaticide and Infanticide Cases," *University of San Francisco Law Review* 47 (2013), p. 459.

8   Lawrence M. Friedman, "The Misbegotten: Infanticide in Victorian England" (forthcoming).

predicament was to get rid of the child. There were other options, but they cost money. Economic desperation was probably why Cecilia Ringold killed her baby. It was most likely what motivated one Della Clark, seventeen years old and unmarried, who, in North Carolina in 1921, gave birth to twins and who (according to a coroner's jury) promptly put them to death.[9]

In the United States, like in England, many of the women charged with this crime were domestic servants. Johanna Moynahan, accused of choking her newborn child to death in 1885, was a "young and rather good-looking Irish girl," working for a Mrs. Margaret Oakes in Holyoke, Massachusetts. Johanna had been in the United States only three months; the father of the child, she said, was Michael Roach, who had promised to come to the United States and marry her but clearly had not done so.[10] There were many cases of this sort. In the United States, as in England, servants worked for respectable, middle-class families; a servant who was proved (by her pregnancy) that she was not respectable herself, and who therefore was not going to be able to "produce a character reference," would have poor chances of getting another job.[11]

This was the dominant motive in England. In the United States, on the other hand, sheer economic desperation was not always the basic motive. Some cases (it is hard to know how many) had other causes. Some mothers were reported to be from "good families"; they acted as they did because they faced ruin, humiliation, loss of respect, loss of status, shame, dishonor. Their babies died, in other words, to hide the sins of their mothers. Of course, scandal and shame were what made poor women so desperate, economically. But a middle-class woman, pregnant, with no prospect of marriage, was not afraid she might starve on the streets; the English servant girls often faced this awful prospect.

A third motive emerges from the shadows: mental illness. A few women, like the young telegraph operator in Chicago, suffered from what today we would call extreme postpartum depression, or some other form of mental disorder. A few recent, tragic incidents come from what we might call a fourth motive: a teenager gives birth secretly to a baby; she feels totally overwhelmed by the prospect of having a child; she is a child herself, and she kills to preserve her childhood.

The motives overlap; in the twentieth century, we can find examples of all three (or four). A woman today who kills her baby is probably not motivated by sheer economic desperation. Shame and scandal also play much less of a role. Giving birth outside of marriage is definitely not as scandalous as it used to be. Indeed, it happens in the best of families. Some women deliberately choose to give birth without a male partner. Changing attitudes toward gender, gender roles, and sex have made the difference here, just as in the case of the "unwritten law." The nineteenth century was worlds apart. There are no hard statistics on

9   "Girl of 17 Murders Her Twin Babies," *Chicago Defender*, Aug. 20, 1921.
10 "Arraigned for Infanticide," *Boston Daily Globe*, Apr. 8, 1885, p. 1.
11 Snow, "Infanticide in New Jersey," p. 17.

neonaticide, but scraps of evidence suggest a crime much more common then than now. For the United States, we have to rely for the most part on newspaper accounts; there is no practical way to mine the trial court records. For England, the sources are richer, at least for London. The Old Bailey Papers (records of London's central criminal court) are one of these sources; they are available and searchable online.[12] The volume of cases was never very large – a handful each year. Numbers did, however, increase in the second half of the nineteenth century.[13] And the subject was taken quite seriously in England.

The women in the dock in London, were women like Cecilia Ringold: poor, unmarried women in domestic service. Or perhaps we should put the matter more cautiously. These are the women who stood trial. If a middle or upper-class woman did away with a newborn baby, and surely this happened, it left no trace in the sources.

Prosecuting women for killing newborn babies was never easy. The juries in Victorian England – made up only of men – tended to be quite sympathetic. Many – almost half – of the women who stood trial were acquitted (45 percent of them, to be exact). It was, for one thing, hard to prove that the mother actually killed the infant: defendants often claimed the baby was born dead, which was, after all, hardly a rare occurrence in the nineteenth century. We hear, to be sure, of certain medical "tests" used to figure out if the baby was born dead or alive. In 1877, in New York, the deputy coroner conducted an autopsy on a "fully developed newly-born child" found "on the roof of the malt-house of White's Brewery." The "lungs were subjected to the hydrostatic test," and the conclusion was that "the child had been born alive."[14] Any such tests were probably quite crude, and probably also inconclusive.

It was hard, then, to convict a woman of neonaticide, for various reasons, and there was an alternative – a lesser crime they could be charged with. The English Parliament in the seventeenth century passed a law "to prevent the destroying and murthering of bastard children." Under this law, it was a crime to conceal the birth of a "bastard" child by secretly drowning or burying the child, whether born dead or alive. The punishment in the original statute was death.[15] But this statute was repealed in 1803 and replaced with a milder version. Mere concealment of birth did not raise a presumption of murder. A later amendment, in 1828, made it a crime to dispose of the body of a dead child for the purpose of hiding the fact that it was born at all, whether dead or alive.[16] This kind of statute made it possible to convict the mother of *something*, even if she insisted the child was stillborn or died a natural

---

[12] They are cited here by the name of the defendant and the date.
[13] I am indebted to Malcolm Feeley and to Ashley T. Rubin, a doctoral candidate at Berkeley, for data on the numbers of such cases; see Friedman, "The Misbegotten."
[14] "The Ninth Ward Infanticide," *New York Times*, Oct. 8, 1877, p. 8.
[15] The statute was 21 James I ch. 27, quoted in Hoffer and Hull, *Murdering Mothers*, p. 20.
[16] Offences Against the Person Act 1828, 9 Geo. IV c. 31, § XIV (Eng.); Jackson, *Infanticide*, pp. 6, 7.

death, and the state could not prove otherwise. Under this law, a defendant could be
sentenced to jail for a period up to two years.

Similar statutes, or variants, were common in the United States as well. For
example, a law of Georgia in 1833 made it a crime for a woman to "conceal or
attempt to conceal the death of any issue of her body, which if it were born alive,
would by law be a bastard"; this could be punished "by fine or imprisonment in the
common jail, or both."[17] A Connecticut statute provided that "Every woman who
shall conceal her pregnancy, and shall willingly be delivered in secret by herself of
any bastard child," could be fined and imprisoned for up to three months.[18] Some of
these statutes are still on the books, for example, in Oregon; under the current
statute, a person "commits the crime of concealing the birth of an infant if the person
conceals the corpse of a newborn child with intent to conceal the fact of its birth or to
prevent a determination of whether it was born dead or alive."[19]

In the Old Bailey Papers, there is rich evidence of the use of this type of law. Many
juries took advantage of it. Murder carried the death penalty; conviction under the
concealment statute meant only a fairly short stint behind bars. In 38 percent of the
cases in the Old Bailey files, the defendant was convicted of concealment. For
example, Sarah Freeman, in October 1848, was charged with the "willful murder of
her infant male child." Sarah was a cook in the household of a man who lived in
Eaton Place. The housekeeper, Harriet Nuttall, testified that she had suspected
Sarah was "in the family-way," but Sarah "always denied it." Then Sarah gave birth.
A police inspector found her at home with a dead baby in a basket; the prisoner
claimed the baby lived for only a few minutes. Sarah was, quite understandably,
frightened: she asked, "Oh, sir . . . Do you think I shall be hanged?" She claimed she
was planning to take the body to a "woman in Chelsea, who promised to bury it for
me." The medical evidence was inconclusive. Sarah was not, in fact, hanged;
instead, she was found guilty of concealing the birth of the child and given
a sentence of twelve months.[20]

Even though juries tended to be lenient, newspaper stories show that many people
in England considered this killing of babies a serious problem. A writer in
The Observer, in 1862, talked about a "shocking increase of infanticide," which, in
London, had reached "fearful dimensions." Every week there were "five or six
inquests" on the bodies of newborns, and the coroner's verdict was usually "willful

---

[17] Laws Ga. 1833, ch., sec. 22. The law also provided that the concealment in itself would not be
considered "sufficient or conclusive evidence to convict . . . of . . . murder," without proof that the
child was born alive, or the "circumstances attending it shall be such as shall satisfy the minds of the
jury that the mother did willfully and maliciously destroy and take away the life of such child." Ibid.,
sec. 21.

[18] Gen. Stats. Conn. 1918, sections 6389, 6390.

[19] 2011 ORS sec. 167.820. This crime is a "Class A misdemeanor." In North Carolina, "secretly burying or
otherwise disposing of the dead body of a newborn child" to "conceal the birth of such child" is
actually a felony. No. Car. General Stats. Sec. 14–46.

[20] LCCC, Sarah Freeman, Oct. 23, 1848.

murder," yet not one in 100 of the "culprits" was actually punished.[21] There were those in the United States too who saw neonaticide as a problem, but less so than in England, at least judging from newspaper accounts. In both countries, we are almost totally in the dark about actual numbers.[22]

On the whole, judging from newspaper accounts, many and maybe most of the American instances come out of situations not unlike the English cases. Cecilia Ringold can be taken as typical. Many other examples fit this pattern: an unmarried woman who works as a domestic servant. For example, in 1887, Annie McDaniel, a "servant girl," was arrested in Knoxville, Tennessee, charged with infanticide. She had given birth to "a male child ... and locked it up in a trunk." Annie, we are told, after giving birth, got up "at the usual time and went about discharging her duties."[23] As in England, a young woman working in the United States as a servant who gave birth was almost sure to lose her job. Kate Collins, in New York City (1887), a "domestic," got a place in a "flat house," but when her mistress found out that she "was approaching maternity," the job disappeared and she was told "that she must seek a place elsewhere."[24] Susan Clement, of Paterson, New Jersey, for example, was in service in the home of a bishop. She disappeared, and the body of a child was found on the premises.[25] In the South, judging from reports in the *Atlanta Constitution*, many of the women accused of this crime were African-Americans. So, in Richmond, Virginia, in 1874, Hannah Brown, accused of killing her newborn infant, was described as "a colored servant girl lately employed by a family named Glenn."[26] In 1904, two African-American women in Pelham, Georgia, were arrested and charged with infanticide.[27] Similarly, in Washington, DC, with its large African-American community, some women charged with this offense were identified as African-American, for example, Mary Cyrus, a "colored" woman, charged with killing her newborn baby in 1863.[28] These women in domestic service, like their English counterparts, were extremely poor and were dependent for work on employers who were, of course, middle or upper class.

In the United States, as in England, many cases were doomed to remain unsolved. Two little boys in Atlanta, in 1889, while playing, "discovered the body of a new born negro baby ... Every indication pointed to a case of infanticide, but how and by whom will perhaps forever remain a mystery."[29] In Macon, Georgia, two men, paddling on a river, noticed a bloodstained newspaper lying on the bank of the river; underneath was the body of a baby. "Who placed the little baby there will doubtless forever remain a mystery. It was doubtless illegitimate and to hide the shame its unnatural mother consigned its tiny form to the dark river which refused to

---

[21] "The Increase of Infanticide," *Observer*, May 24, 1962, p. 5.
[22] Nor is there any evidence of the number of mothers whose babies were, in fact, born dead and who disposed of the bodies in violation of the concealment statute.
[23] *New York Times*, June 21, 1887, p. 1.   [24] *New York Times*, Aug. 7, 1887, p. 8.
[25] "Charged with Infanticide," *New York Times*, Apr. 14, 1880, p. 10.
[26] *Atlanta Constitution*, Aug. 30, 1874, p. 7.   [27] *Atlanta Constitution*, Mar. 11, 1904, p. 7.
[28] *Daily National Republican*, Apr. 17, 1863, p. 2.   [29] *Atlanta Constitution*, Aug. 26, 1889, p. 5.

keep the secret."[30] There are reports of small bodies found in remote and hidden places; the authorities, often enough, have no clue as to the identity of the mother. In February 1859, the body of a "healthy male infant" was found in a vacant lot in Chicago. The baby was "wrapped in a piece of cotton batting." The body had been "deposited there lately as no snow had fallen since." Near the spot were "the tracks of a female who wore slippers, and who appears to have carried [the child] … in a pail." The coroner held an inquest, "but without ascertaining any traces of its parentage."[31] In Philadelphia too coroners' inquests in the late nineteenth century had to render a verdict of "death by unknown causes" in cases of "infants found dead in yards, inlets, lots, culverts, on the docks, and under bridges"; it was estimated that every year, hundreds of infants were left to die or deliberately killed.[32] In still other cases, no doubt, the body was disposed of in such a way that no trace of it was ever found, and nobody was ever the wiser.

MEASURING NEONATICIDE

All the sources agree, as we have noted, that it is almost hopeless to try to measure the incidence of neonaticide. For England, the Old Bailey records, which are online, at least allow us to count infanticide cases in this important court in London, the capital of the kingdom. But even for England, this does not tell us much about aggregate figures. Indeed we have to be cautious about interpreting the Old Bailey records: many women claimed they were innocent; many insisted the baby was born dead, and surely some of them were telling the truth. And even this kind of source is unavailable for the United States. One might comb through coroners' records, and police reports, and court files, jurisdiction by jurisdiction, but panning in these turgid streams, without indexes or databases that allow searching by key words, would yield only small and occasional nuggets of fact. For this reason, it has rarely been done.[33]

Newspaper databases are the best source of information, sketchy though this is, about neonaticide in the United States. To get at least a general idea, the online archives of three prominent American newspapers, in three sections of the country, were searched: the *New York Times*, the *Atlanta Constitution*, and the *Los Angeles Times*; newspapers in some other cities, notably San Francisco, Boston, Chicago, and Washington, DC, were looked at in a less systematic way. The period covered was basically the last half of the nineteenth century and the first half of the twentieth. The newspapers cannot be compared directly – after all, Los Angeles in the

[30] "Infanticide in Macon," *Atlanta Constitution*, Dec. 4, 1886, p. 9.
[31] *Chicago Press and Tribune*, Feb. 9, 1859, p. 1.
[32] Sherri Broder, "Child Care or Child Neglect? Baby Farming in Late-Nineteenth Century Philadelphia," *Gender and Society* 2 (1988), pp. 128, 131.
[33] See Kenneth H. Wheeler, "Infanticide in Nineteenth-Century Ohio," *Journal of Social History* (1997).

nineteenth century was a small town, while New York City was huge. The dates overlap, but are not identical: the *Atlanta Constitution* was founded in 1868, later than the *New York Times*. The reports tend to be regional: infanticide was a local crime, and newspapers generally reported only incidents close to home. Any figures that come out of the survey are bound to be rough, but they do shed some light on the subject.

Most frequently, we read about the discovery of bodies of newborn children. People found these in rivers, fields, vacant lots; usually, there was no hint of who or what produced these bodies and who was responsible. Practically speaking, the matter often ended right there. There might be a coroner's inquest, but the inquest would produce some statement about "persons unknown." No arrest and prosecution followed. Other newspaper articles would report that some unfortunate woman had been arrested, accused of killing her baby. Many times, there is little or no follow-up in the press – nothing about a trial, a verdict, or a punishment.

At any rate, in the *New York Times*, for the period 1851 to 1926, 144 articles mentioned a dead newborn, killed or alleged to be killed by its mother; in the *Atlanta Constitution*, between 1869 and 1930, there were 119 such articles, and in the *Los Angeles Times*, between 1885 and 1929, there were 33. In the *New York Times*, the decade of the 1870s produced the highest number of mentions (this was apparently also the case for the *Chicago Tribune*); in the *Atlanta Constitution*, the highest density came a bit later, in the 1880s. In any event, after 1900, newspaper accounts of neonaticide in the cities studied fall off dramatically.

These figures should be taken for what they are; as a quantitative measure, they have to be used with extreme caution. But they tell us a lot about the problem itself, and they shed at least some light on who committed the crime and why. There are regional differences: in Atlanta, sixty-one cases involved African-American babies, or part African-American babies – this accounts for roughly half of the cases where the child's color is mentioned. Very few reports in New York or Los Angeles newspapers mention the (nonwhite) race of the baby or its mother. Maggie Rosas, accused of infanticide in 1885 in Gilroy, California, was said to be of Mexican and Indian descent.[34] The Atlanta accounts of African-American babies always state that the mother (if her identity was known) was herself African-American. There is only one counterexample. The race of the father is usually not known or at least not given. Atlanta had the highest percentage of reports on infanticide in relationship to population; New York had the most mentions, but of course the population of New York City was much higher than the populations of Atlanta or Los Angeles. Articles in, say, the *New York Times* were not necessarily about events that occurred in the city itself – for example, an article in 1869 told about two cases of infanticide in Reading, Pennsylvania. Most reports, however, were local news, or, if not local, then regional.

---

[34] *Daily Alta California*, Mar. 18, 1885, p. 5.

A few scholars have tried to measure neonaticide. One small study looked at two counties in Ohio in the nineteenth century. This study found thirty-five instances of "certain" or "possible" infanticide between 1806 and 1879 in Ross County, Ohio, little bodies found in and around towns in the county. In fifty-nine cases in Philadelphia, in the nineteenth century, only one ended up in a verdict of first-degree murder, and three for second-degree murder. Forty-two defendants were simply declared not guilty, a few were convicted of manslaughter, and four were convicted of "concealment" of a bastard child.[35] In many, if not most cases, there was no clue as to parentage. In a study of Providence, Rhode Island (relying on coroners' inquests), the mothers were identified in only 38 percent of the cases;[36] the percentage in other places was apparently even lower.

An 1884 article in the *Washington Post* claimed that dead babies were to be found almost daily; sixteen such bodies turned up in the first quarter of the year.[37] The same newspaper, in 1905, reported that, in a six-month period, "almost half a hundred infants" were found "dead on lots and in barrels and alleys." In most cases, the "guilty persons," parents who abandoned their children, "have never been located."[38] Another newspaper account claimed that, in Philadelphia, between January and February 1904, twenty-seven babies, most of them newborns, were found on the streets; in the six months prior, the count was ninety. "Many more" were probably disposed of by cremation.[39] Coroners' inquests, arrests, and trials certainly took place and are reported in the newspapers. But an accurate body count is not to be had.

In 1895, Helen Campbell and coauthors, writing about New York City, claimed that neonaticide had once been common in that city. Some twenty years before, almost every morning, the "daily journals" noted "that the body of a new-born babe

[35] The Philadelphia figures are from Roger Lane, *Violent Death in the City: Suicide, Accident and Murder in 19th Century Philadelphia* (Cambridge, MA: Harvard University Press, 1979), p. 98; the Ohio figures are from Wheeler, "Infanticide in Nineteenth-Century Ohio"; see also Ian C. Pilarczyk, "'So Foul A Deed': Infanticide in Montreal, 1825–1850," *Law & History Review* 30 (2012), p. 575; for Canada, see also Judith A. Osborne, "The Crime of Infanticide: Throwing Out the Baby with the Bathwater," *Canadian Journal of Family Law* 6:47 (1987). In Chicago, it was "not uncommon" to find dead babies "in alleys and gutters, in trash heaps and privies, along desolate roads," and in bodies of water. From 1906 on, the police department reports listed the number of such bodies. Cases of infanticide were "routinely overlooked," though after about 1910, somewhat more attention was paid. Jeffrey S. Adler, *First in Violence, Deepest in Dirt: Homicide in Chicago, 1875–1920* (Cambridge, MA: Harvard University Press, 2006), pp. 227–231.
[36] Simone Caron, "'Killed by Its Mother': Infanticide in Providence County, Rhode Island, 1870 to 1938," *Journal of Social History* (2010), pp. 213, 217.
[37] "Is Infanticide Increasing?" *Washington Post*, Mar. 31, 1884, p. 4. Apparently, the count was forty-one for all of 1883 and forty-seven for 1880. A health officer of the District claimed that not all of the bodies were the product of infanticide; he also hinted that one root cause of the deaths was the "large colored population," especially the large class of African-Americans who were "indigent, huddled together in by-ways and alleys, subject to diseases bred among themselves," and who thereby increased the "mortality list of the city."
[38] "Charged with Infanticide," *Washington Post*, Aug. 4, 1905, p. 12.
[39] "Finds Evidence of Infanticide," *San Francisco Chronicle*, Feb. 17, 1904.

had been found floating near the docks, buried in an ash-barrel, or flung into some lonely area."[40] Apparently, the incidence of neonaticide declined toward the end of the nineteenth century. Fewer notices appeared in the newspapers. But the practice surely continued – at some level. In 1914, Dr. George B. Ewing, a professor at the Cornell Medical School, complained about the work of New York's coroners. They had made, he said, "little or no attempt to detect and punish persons guilty of infanticide." Dr. Ewing had been told that only one case was reported in 1913. And yet, in Dr. Ewing's opinion, there had to be many more. Since the coroners paid no attention, "infanticide might be carried on with impunity in New York."[41]

Dr. Ewing was, of course, simply guessing. But his guess seems correct – surely there were more than one instance of neonaticide a year in New York City. We can draw two conclusions from his remarks. First, the crime was not taken very seriously in the United States; apparently, people did not judge these mothers as harshly as the formal law might suggest. We see more evidence of this later. Second, the practice may well have abated, at least somewhat. It is certainly possible that, compared to England, fewer new mothers had ever killed their babies in the United States; and that the numbers continued to decline. Far fewer women in the United States were in domestic service and their situation was (for white women at least) much less desperate. Moreover, it was probably easier in the United States for a woman to give birth unmarried, but then move to another town and pass herself off as a widow. Americans were rolling stones; this was less true for women than for men, but a new life in a new place was a possible option. Moving on was, of course, hardest for African-Americans in the South (and elsewhere, no doubt); this, along with the sheer poverty of these women and their lack of skills and education, may account for the data from the *Atlanta Constitution*; accounts of neonaticide in this newspaper were heavily canted toward African-American babies.

Still, even if we concede that American women, even women in service, were less desperate than their English sisters, unmarried pregnancy was nonetheless a serious problem for such women. Their options were limited. Moving on with a baby was not easy. It meant tearing up roots and leaving family and home. Another option was to give the child to a "baby farm." This was, in England, basically a kind of slow infanticide. The new mother would hand her baby to the baby farmer, paying some small amount of money and promising to pay more later; in return, the baby farmer promised to take care of the child. Very often, no more payments were made. The baby would be neglected, perhaps even starved; it would almost invariably wither away and die. Indeed, this was fairly deliberate. Nobody wanted these babies. An English woman named Margaret Waters, put on trial in 1870, had drugged and starved more than a dozen infants; she wrapped up the bodies and tossed them onto

---

[40] Mrs. Helen Campbell, Col. Thomas W. Knox, and Supt. Thomas Byrnes, *Darkness and Daylight: Or Lights and Shadows of New York Life* (1895), p. 384.
[41] "Ignore Infanticide in Coroners' Work," *New York Times*, Nov. 12, 1914, p. 9.

the streets.[42] Society – or at least the men who served on juries – had a lot of sympathy for mothers who killed their babies, but very little for baby farmers. They were legally and socially condemned. Margaret Waters, in fact, was convicted, and on October 11, 1870, she met her death on the gallows.

Baby farming was known to exist in the United States as well. In Jacob Riis's book *How the Other Half Lives* (1890), his classic exposé of slum life in New York, he refers to baby farming as a "fiendish plan of child murder."[43] The name, he adds, "put into plain English, means starving babies to death." This was almost surely correct. To be sure, some "baby farms" were legitimate, even caring, businesses. For some women in Philadelphia, for example, it was a "legitimate occupation that merely formalized the informal child-care networks of single mothers and other laboring women."[44] And baby farms could be a source of children for adoption; in one story, out of Philadelphia (1904), we hear about babies "sold at auction at $50 each" and about babies "palmed off on families who needed an heir."[45] These babies were the lucky ones. In other instances, baby farming was as cruel and deadly as it was in England. An 1874 article in the *New York Times* suggested that thousands of children were turned over to baby farmers; the point was to dispose of these babies by hook or by crook. Many illegitimate and "pauper" children were born every year in New York City, and the "wretched parents" were eager "to be rid of their unwelcome offspring."[46] In 1873, a woman named Mrs. Ellen Roberts was charged with running a baby farm in New York City, one of "numerous infantile nurseries for 'love-children.'" The alleged toll was thirty children starved or left to die.[47] An 1875 article in a Chicago newspaper refers to a baby farm run by a Mrs. Richer; here young women from "respectable" families (and, in one case at least, from a wealthy family) could come and leave their unwanted and illegitimate babies, presumably to die, which many of them promptly did.[48] In 1889, police reported a "cruel case of baby farming" in St. Louis, Missouri. They arrested a woman named Jennie Seiffert, and found "two dead babies in a room"; the coroner concluded that they had been "starved to death. Four live children, in various stages of decline, were

---

[42]   George K. Behlmer, *Child Abuse and Moral Reform in England, 1870–1908* (Stanford, CA: Stanford University Press, 1982), p. 29.

[43]   Jacob Riis, *How the Other Half Lives* (New York: C. Scribner's Sons, 1890), ch. xvi.

[44]   Broder, "Child Care or Child Neglect?"

[45]   "Babies Sold at Auction," *Chicago Daily Tribune*, Apr. 1, 1904, p. 3. This was a report on investigations run by the coroner in Philadelphia, which revealed such "horrors" as "babies put to sleep with dogs, babies starved and passed the rounds of baby farms seeking purchasers, and babies maltreated, killed and thrown into sewers or abandoned in churches and alleys."

[46]   "Baby-Farming: How Little Children Are Disposed Of," *New York Times*, July 30, 1874, p. 2.

[47]   *New York Times*, Oct. 7, 1873, p. 2. Mrs. Roberts claimed that she had given up the trade of baby farming, and that she was herself the mother of five children.

[48]   *Chicago Daily Tribune*, Aug. 29, 1875, p. 5. Writing about a somewhat later period in Chicago, Jeffrey Adler, in *First in Violence, Deepest in Dirt*, at 228, suggests that the authorities "preferred to look away" rather than prosecute those who ran baby farms.

found toddling around the apartment."[49] A 1907 item in the *Los Angeles Times* referred to a baby farm in Des Moines, Iowa, run by a Mrs. Fred West. Mrs. West was charged with murder for poisoning a baby with laudanum. It was alleged that she burned the corpses of other babies in her furnace.[50]

For some women, giving a child over to a baby farmer was less distasteful than neonaticide, because somebody else did the dirty work of letting the baby die. But even the most miserable of the baby farmers charged money. That might put it out of the reach of the poorest mothers. Perhaps, too, it was not always easy to find a baby farmer. Another way out of an unwanted pregnancy was, of course, abortion. This was an option for married women as well, if, for whatever reason, they did not want to carry the child to term. Abortion was expensive, however, and often quite dangerous. The legal history of abortion is quite complicated, but whether legal or illegal, abortionists were never in good odor. In New York City, the most famous, or infamous, abortionist was a woman who called herself Madame Restell.[51] Madame Restell (her real name was Ann Lohman) made a fortune off rich women who wanted abortions. Her practice flourished for years. She made enough money to build herself a lavish mansion on Fifth Avenue; its fifty-two windows were "hung with satin and French lace curtains," and there were "three immense dining-rooms, furnished in bronze and gold" and decked out with "imported furniture." Madame Restell provided "certain recipes for producing abortions" for her customers; she also sold contraceptive devices. Her clientele came from the "wealthy classes," women and families who could afford her "exorbitant" charges.[52] She had, in the course of her career, frequent run-ins with the law. Finally, in 1878, hounded by Anthony Comstock, facing arrest and the destruction of her business, Madame Restell gave up. Out on bail, and wearing "a diamond-studded nightgown," she cut her throat in the bathroom of her mansion.[53]

The services of Madame Restell, of course, were miles beyond the reach of the urban poor. Cheaper abortions were certainly available, but they were extremely risky; hundreds of women died as a consequence of botched abortions. But even a back-alley abortion cost money. Self-induced abortions, which many

---

[49] "Baby Farming in St. Louis," *New York Times*, Jan. 15, 1889. The mothers were "poor working girls" who paid from $6 to $8 a month. "They did not know the children were being killed off," or at least so they said, and, at any rate, one woman whose child had died "had not been notified ... and continued to pay."

[50] *Los Angeles Times*, June 4, 1907, p. 13.

[51] On Madam Restell, see Clifford Browder, *The Wickedest Woman in New York: Madame Restell, the Abortionist* (Hamden, CT: Archon, 1988); the description of her mansion is from James D. McCabe Jr., *Lights and Shadows of New York Life* (New York: Farrar, Straus and Giroux, 1872), p. 627; he does not mention her name, but is clearly referring to Madame Restell.

[52] George W. Walling, *Recollections of a New York Chief of Police* (New York: Caxton, 1887).

[53] Andrea Tone, *Devices and Desires: A History of Contraceptives in America* (New York: Hill & Wang, 2001), pp. 33–34. Tone's book shows that conceptive devices, though legally dubious, were readily available. But they too cost money.

poor women resorted to, were even more dangerous, and accounted for many tragic deaths.[54]

A middle-class woman, pregnant but unmarried, had certain other options. In some states, she could try to invoke the action of seduction; under the law, it was a crime to seduce and have sex with an unmarried woman of "previously chaste character."[55] This was not much use for poor women or minorities, or for a woman who had been sexually active. If a woman gave birth, knew the father, and could argue that he had deceived her, she could sue for breach of promise of marriage. This was a well-recognized cause of action in the nineteenth century. When a man and woman became engaged, legally speaking they had entered into a binding contract, as valid and enforceable as an agreement to buy and sell a horse. If one party broke off the engagement without a good reason, the jilted party had the right to sue for damages. In theory, this was available both to men and women; but in practice, the plaintiffs were virtually always women.[56] In theory, the man was liable in damages, even if all he did was break off the engagement. Usually, however, the lawsuit claimed something more: that she, the plaintiff, had given in to him sexually; as a consequence she was now "ruined" goods. In many cases, she was not only "ruined" but pregnant, which was of course an even more serious predicament. Juries in these lawsuits in the nineteenth century sometimes awarded extremely hefty damages. Many men, no doubt, faced with a possible lawsuit, opted instead for a "shotgun" marriage.

Breach of promise was a pretty blunt weapon. There had to be a promise, implicit or explicit; defendants often simply denied that they had ever agreed to marry the woman. A woman who sued for breach of promise, moreover, was airing her dirty linen in public; clearly, this was unpleasant and undesirable, at least for respectable women. Yet only respectable women had much of a chance to win their case.

Plaintiffs in breach of promise lawsuits were usually not poor women, and almost never minority women. They were, however, often poorer (and lower in status) than the men they were suing. Indeed, some quite well-known men, men of substance,

[54]   See Leslie J. Reagan, *When Abortion Was a Crime: Women, Medicine, and Law in the United States, 1867–1973* (Berkeley: University of California Press, 1997).

[55]   Lawrence M. Friedman, *Guarding Life's Dark Secrets: Legal and Social Controls over Reputation, Propriety, and Privacy* (Stanford, CA: Stanford University Press, 2007), pp. 99–106; Estelle B. Freedman, *Redefining Rape: Sexual Violence in the Era of Suffrage and Segregation* (Cambridge, MA: Harvard University Press, 2013), pp. 33–52; Stephen Robertson, "Seduction, Sexual Violence, and Marriage in New York City, 1886–1955," Law & History Review 24 (2006), p. 331.

[56]   On breach of promise, see Friedman, *Guarding Life's Dark Secrets*, pp. 111–117; Ginger S. Frost, "'I Shall Not Sit Down and Crie': Women, Class and Breach of Promise Marriage Plaintiffs in England, 1850–1900," Gender and History 6 (1994), p. 224; Joanna L. Grossman and Lawrence M. Friedman, *Inside the Castle: Law and the Family in 20th Century America* (Princeton, NJ: Princeton University Press, 2011), pp. 90–95, on the demise of this cause of action in the twentieth century.

elite men, were forced to defend themselves against a suit for breach of promise. Almost from the start, breach of promise lawsuits were controversial, and, in many circles, in bad odor. Gilbert and Sullivan sneered at breach of promise in *Trial by Jury*. Many condemned this cause of action as a crude tool used by unscrupulous gold diggers; and, indeed, as an open door to blackmail. Most of the states ultimately abolished breach of promise.

There was, in big cities, another place for desperate women to turn to: special homes for unwanted children. In New York, Catholic nuns established and ran a foundling asylum. A mother could bring her baby to the home and leave it in the care of the sisters. This was an alternative to dumping the baby in a river or letting it die on the streets. At the end of the first year of its existence, the asylum was caring for more than eighty children.[57] Chicago too had a foundling home, established in 1871.[58] And in San Francisco, the "Female Hospital," established in 1868, promised to take in sick and poor women; one of its aims was to check the "progress of the crimes of foeticide and infanticide."[59]

Not everyone approved of these homes. The very idea of a foundling hospital, arguably, put a "premium on vice and shiftlessness."[60] A woman was more likely to sin (so the argument went) if she knew she could safely and secretly get rid of the child of that sin. But this was probably a minority view, and psychologically implausible. As one writer put it, the "experience of mankind in all countries ... is that children will be born to unmarried persons and to persons too poor to care for them," whatever the "moralists" might think.[61] Then, too, however one judged the mothers, surely it was wrong to let the innocent babies die.

The foundling homes never lacked for customers. And many of them, certainly, were benign – safe, caring places, often run by religious orders. But there were egregious exceptions. A report of 1893 claimed that the San Francisco Foundling Asylum was a scandal that would "outrage an Esquimau or a Hottentot." There were ten babies in the place; the "stench" was unbearable; the children were lying in "indescribable dirt, and the mattresses were literally rotten with filth." The children's faces were "black" with fly marks; they were dressed in "rags."[62] If this report was correct, then the San Francisco institution was no better than a baby farm: a method of slow infanticide. But even well-run homes could not solve the problem of neonaticide, which continued to occur.

---

[57] Martin Gottlieb, *The Foundling: The Story of the New York Foundling Hospital* (New York: Norfleet Press, 2001), p. 12.

[58] "Chicago Foundling Home: Twenty-Fifth Anniversary of Its Founding," *Chicago Tribune*, Jan. 19, 1896, p. 40.

[59] "The San Francisco Female Hospital," *San Francisco Daily Morning Chronicle*, Mar. 4, 1869, p. 3.

[60] "Chicago Foundling Home," *Chicago Tribune*, Jan. 19, 1896, p. 40.

[61] "Foundling Asylums," *Chicago Tribune*, Aug. 9, 1874, p. 8.

[62] "Caring for Babies," *San Francisco Chronicle*, Oct. 7, 1893, p. 16. The management of the asylum vigorously denied the charges.

INFANTICIDE: THE AMERICAN SCENE

For a number of women, then, pregnant, in trouble, desperate, unmarried, there was, in their minds, no other way out, no way to salvage their lives, except to rid themselves of the unwelcome guest in their womb. This was true, as mentioned, both in England and in the United States. There were differences in the demographics of neonaticide, however, between the two countries. All of the Old Bailey defendants, as far as we can tell, were women; all of them were poor, all of them were unmarried, and if their occupation was mentioned at all, it was domestic service. Newspaper accounts from other parts of England suggest that this was true outside of London as well.[63] In the United States, the English pattern was also common: Cecilia Ringold, noted at the beginning of this chapter, faced a similar dilemma. And poor African-American women, in the accounts noted in the Atlanta newspaper, must have been often driven by poverty and desperation to commit this crime.

But not all of the poor, friendless women in American cases were women in domestic service. In Oakland, California, in 1911, Mrs. C. W. Welshorn, married to a railway conductor, tossed her baby from a train. She was arrested and charged with murder. She said she was separated from her husband, and "had no income"; she asked "what else was I to do?" Rather than be a burden to her brother, "I got rid of the baby shortly after it was born."[64] But what most strikingly separates American from English cases were those instances where economic desperation was not a factor at all. Rather, the root motive was fear of scandal and loss of reputation. These mothers came from respectable, even prominent families. This was true of Alice Errett, "daughter of a prominent Methodist minister," in Pottsville, Pennsylvania. Alice had been "receiving the attentions of a young man ... by whom she was betrayed." When she gave birth in 1884, she "strangled the child" and "dug a grave" with her own hands; then she buried the child. Alice became "dangerously ill"; the sheriff was sent to arrest her, if possible, "on a charge of infanticide."[65]

In San Jose, California, in 1876, the body of a "pretty female infant" was found in an orchard. The coroner's jury found that the child had been born alive. The local rumor mill had it that the mother was a fifteen-year-old girl, "a student in the State Normal School," and the "daughter of a prominent family."[66] A 1896 report in the *Atlanta Constitution* mentioned a woman from a good family (her name is not given), who was strongly suspected of giving birth and then killing her child.[67] And the *New York Times* reported an unusual case of "double infanticide" at Amityville, Long Island; the perpetrators were apparently two young women, who each "gave

[63] See Friedman, "The Misbegotten."
[64] "Will Charge Infanticide," *Los Angeles Times*, Dec. 28, 1911, p. 16. Mrs. Welshorn was traveling with her brother, John Rutledge, a "mining man of Cortez, Placer county." Rutledge claimed to have no "knowledge of the act of his sister."
[65] *New York Times*, Aug. 15, 1884, p. 1.
[66] "Evil in Eden," *San Francisco Chronicle*, Dec. 29, 1876, p. 3.
[67] *Atlanta Constitution*, Sept. 10, 1873, p. 3.

birth to an illegitimate child within a period of two months"; the women were "daughters of a very respectable Irish farmer of Amityville."[68]

In the Old Bailey cases, the mothers seemed to be pitifully and desperately alone. In almost no case in the Old Bailey records is a man mentioned – either as a kind of accomplice or otherwise. Indeed, there was virtually never mention of anybody else, male or female, relatives or friends, with a role in the matter, only the mother herself. This was also true for the most part in the American cases. But in some instances, families aided and abetted the mother, probably to help cover up her disgrace. In Cleveland, Tennessee, in 1896, Mary Browder of Cleveland, and her aunt, Mrs. McDade of Chattanooga, were indicted "on the charge of infanticide." Workmen repairing a house "came across the badly decomposed remains of a white infant buried under a brick hearth." The two women had occupied the house; Miss Browder had been "in a delicate condition" when she moved in, but "when she left all evidences were gone." Mary Browder was described as a "well known young woman at Cleveland," who had "recently ... been led astray," and Mrs. McDade was "well connected" too. The case was "exciting much interest because of the standing of all parties."[69]

Occasionally, a family member was accused of the crime itself. This might be the mother's husband, or a man who had fathered the child. In Middletown, Connecticut, in 1904, Thomas Bransfield was charged with murdering Minnie Kenanen's infant child; both he and Minnie were acquitted.[70] In 1892, in Cincinnati, one James Dubois was arrested, together with a woman "said to be his wife." They had taken rooms in a boarding house, and the woman gave birth to a boy. Dubois told the landlady he was taking the baby to a niece who would take care of it. But the body of the child was found in the river the next morning. Dubois "broke down and confessed ... [H]e had thrown the babe into the river because he was not able to support it."[71] In 1883, Frank Bowker of Port Byron, Illinois, "inhumanly" disposed of his own baby, burying it in a stable, under "frozen earth and barnyard refuse." Bowker had married Cassie Reese; when she gave birth, only four months after the marriage, Bowker (according to the newspaper) was anxious "to hide the evidence of ante-marital intimacy."[72] The *National Police Gazette* in 1879 reported a "Shocking Case of Infanticide," from Lynn, Massachusetts. John Biddle and Carrie Proctor were arrested. Biddle, according to the account, had "seduced Carrie, who is a good-looking girl of twenty, and of good family." The result was the birth of a baby girl, quickly strangled.[73] In 1866, the *Chicago Tribune* reported the arrest of one Charles Schultz, suspected of killing his two

68 "Shocking Child Murders," *New York Times*, May 29, 1876, p. 8.
69 *Atlanta Constitution*, Jan. 19, 1896, p. 13.
70 "Acquitted of Infanticide Charge," *Boston Daily Globe*, May 7, 1904, p. 11.
71 *Los Angeles Times*, Mar. 6, 1892, p. 4. The paper reported that the man's "real name" was William A. Boyce of Portland, Indiana; his wife was "said to be a daughter of F. J. Settle of Muncie, Indiana."
72 "A Case of Infanticide," *Chicago Daily Tribune*, Mar. 13, 1883, p. 3.
73 *National Police Gazette*, June 7, 1879, p. 4.

newborn babies – apparently twins. The bodies, partially decomposed, were "buried in a woodshed under the kitchen of Schultz's house." Schultz denied guilt and claimed that his wife had drowned the babies at birth. But the jury found him guilty of infanticide.[74]

In other cases, members of the mother's family were involved or actually did the killing. Maggie Rosas, mentioned earlier, was the dead baby's grandmother. Rosas's daughter had given birth to an "illegitimate child"; the "supposed father of the child" was also complicit. An autopsy found the baby's "vital organs" to be healthy; there was evidence that it was born alive and then strangled.[75] In 1912, in Quitman, Mississippi, an eighty-year-old man, H. B. Elfring, his wife, son, and daughter Kate were "charged with the murder" of Kate's daughter.[76] And in Hoboken, New Jersey, in 1878, three people – the mother of the baby, the father of the baby, and another woman, probably a midwife, were charged with getting rid of a newborn baby. The midwife claimed the baby died a natural death.[77] In 1886, in Dover, New Hampshire, Mina and Jane Farnham, sisters, were arrested and jailed; Mina was charged with infanticide, and Jane was accused of acting as an accessory. A "square box in a clump of bushes" had been discovered in a river; inside the box was the dead body of an infant "together with some old clothes and a brick intended to sink the box."[78] In 1859, Margaret Perry, granddaughter of a former governor of Illinois, was accused along with her mother of murdering her infant child.[79] And in 1881, Susan Leek was charged with killing her granddaughter; she had (she said) too many mouths to feed without adding another one, so she buried the child alive.[80]

Information on the outcome of the cases is hard to come by, as we noted. Newspaper accounts often talk about arrests; sometimes they report that the mother has been charged with murder or some other crime.[81] But very few of the accounts tell us about the actual trials (if trials took place), and there is almost never anything about the punishment, if any, imposed on the defendant. Many cases were apparently not prosecuted. There is no way of knowing how many women or their accomplices were actually convicted of murder – or of any crime. Death sentences must have been exceedingly rare. In a way, this is not surprising. Most defendants were women, and women, in general, were rarely sentenced to

74 "The Schultz Infanticide," *Chicago Tribune*, May 24, 1866.
75 "A Girl's Shame," *Los Angeles Times*, Mar. 18, 1885. Maggie Rosas was described as a "coarse old woman, part Mexican and part Indian," who sat "immovable" at her hearing, "with the demeanor of a stoic. Evidently her conscience, if she has one, is troubling her but little."
76 *Atlanta Constitution*, Feb. 1, 1912, p. 9.
77 "The Murder of an Infant," *New York Times*, Nov. 14, 1878.
78 "A Pair of Them Implicated," *Boston Globe*, May 13, 1886, p. 3.
79 "Infanticide in Illinois," *New York Times*, Nov. 27, 1869, p. 3.
80 "Infanticide at Flushing," *New York Times*, Apr. 1, 1881.
81 For example, a small paragraph in the *Chicago Tribune*, Jan. 11, 1877, p. 5: a woman in Fort Wayne, Indiana, found the body of "a male infant wrapped in a cloth" inside a trunk. A servant girl, twenty years old, who owned the trunk, was arrested and charged with murder.

death.[82] In England, the defendants were treated with surprising leniency; this was also the case in other places where scholars have investigated this issue. Pilarczyk, who studied infanticide in Montreal in the first half of the nineteenth century, concluded that there was "strong sympathy" for mothers of dead babies, trapped as they were in "untenable situations." The mothers were "rarely identified, seldom brought to trial, and more infrequently convicted"; if they were convicted at all, it was usually for "concealment" rather than "infanticide."[83] And Constance Backhouse, who studied Ontario records between 1840 and 1900, found that in eighteen instances (two-thirds of her cases), the mother went free; in six cases, the jury found the woman guilty of concealment; in only two cases was the verdict guilty as charged.[84]

Lenience was almost certainly the case in the United States as well. The tendency in Ross County, Ohio, for example, was simply not to prosecute the mothers.[85] In some instances, young mothers were objects of pity, not horror or indignation. In a case from San José, California, in 1876, the *San Francisco Chronicle* reported "pity" as the "prevailing feeling with regard to the young girl implicated."[86] In San Francisco, in 1869, a woman named Mary Regan also evoked sympathy instead of condemnation. Mary Regan worked on Clay Street as a servant. The family she worked for found the body of a "full-sized male child, wrapped in a sheet," lying in the bottom of an outhouse. Mary admitted the birth, but claimed the child was born dead. She was arrested. She told her sad story to the coroner's jury; she was a divorced woman from Brooklyn with two children. She claimed her husband was the father of the child. But the coroner's jury found her responsible for the death of the child. This was on December 17. However, a week later, on December 24, a brief newspaper account noted that the police court judge dismissed the case of Mary Regan, "alleged to have murdered her child"; what is more, "Officer Woodruff immediately went to work and made up a purse of $50 for her relief"; the onlookers were full of "sympathy" for her after hearing the "recital" of her story.[87]

Dolly Pritchett, in Georgia, lost her case in court in 1901, but was ultimately pardoned. Dolly was sixteen and lived in Cherokee County, Georgia. A dead baby was found about half a mile from the home of Dolly's older sister, Mrs. Peek. Dolly was arrested and charged with infanticide; she said she had never even been pregnant. A jury convicted her and she was sentenced to life imprisonment.

[82] See David V. Baker, "A Descriptive Profile and Socio-historical Analysis of Female Executions in the United States: 1632–1997," *Women & Criminal Justice* 10 (1999), pp. 57, 61–62. Only three women, apparently, were executed for concealing the birth of a child; this must have occurred in the early years, since this was not a capital offense in the postcolonial period.

[83] Pilarczyk, "'So Foul a Deed,'" pp. 631–632.

[84] Constance Backhouse, "Desperate Women and Compassionate Courts: Infanticide in Nineteenth-Century Canada," *University of Toronto Law Journal* 34 (1984), pp. 477, 458–459, 461–462.

[85] Wheeler, "Infanticide in Nineteenth-Century Ohio," p. 411.

[86] "Evil in Eden," *San Francisco Chronicle*, Dec. 29, 1876, p. 3.

[87] *San Francisco Chronicle*, Dec. 4, 1869, p. 3; Dec. 17, 1869, p. 1; Dec. 24, 1869, p. 3.

Women's clubs in Georgia begged the governor to grant her a pardon because of her age and her "pitiable" story. Local officials, members of the jury, county officers, and even the judge in her case asked for "executive clemency." In 1902, a new governor, Joseph Terrell, did grant Dolly a pardon and she went free.[88]

In 1875 or so, a young woman, Lizzie Sullivan, came to Boston from Marblehead and worked various jobs; after a couple of years, she found work as a cook at the Island Lodge House in Saco, Maine. Here she met another cook, John Fairlove, who "with his honeyed words and numerous promises, accomplished her ruin." She begged him to marry her, but he deserted her and took off for parts unknown. She got another job; her new employer had no idea she was pregnant. She gave birth, but strangled the child. The coroner's inquest found, accordingly, that Lizzie Sullivan bore full responsibility for the death of this baby.

The heading of the story in the *Boston Globe* was: "Deliberate Infanticide," but the subheading included the phrase "The Old, Old Story of Woman's Trustfulness and Man's Deception"; the whole account is framed in tones of sympathy for this "nineteen-year-old girl."[89] In court, Lizzie pleaded guilty to manslaughter. The prosecutor explained why he accepted the plea (rather than try Lizzie for murder). The prisoner was young, and never had the "advantages of ... moral or educational training." Society had a duty to help women like Lizzie Sullivan. Her lawyer added that this was "one of those unfortunate cases where society looked with pity rather than with severity upon the girl." She was sentenced to five years in the House of Correction.[90] In 1869, in Petersburg, Virginia, a woman was charged with infanticide. The court suggested a "physical examination"; her attorney resisted, and the crowd cheered. Finally, the court yielded "to the clamors of the mob" and released her.[91] In a case in the District of Columbia (1863), mentioned earlier, Mary Cyrus, a "colored" woman, was accused of killing her baby; she was simply acquitted.[92]

Later examples are even more extreme: in 1932, the district attorney of Middlesex County (Massachusetts) dismissed a murder charge against an "unwed girl" who had killed her newborn. The girl (her name is not given in the newspaper) was weak, sick, and friendless. District Attorney Warren L. Bishop called her a "pitiful figure, alone, forlorn, penitent, bewildered"; she was "desperately trying to shield her shame

88 The story was covered in detail in the *Atlanta Constitution*. See L. Graham Crozier, "Dolly Pritchett's Case Possesses Elements that Make Guilt Seem a Debatable Question," *Atlanta Constitution*, Jan. 6, 1901, p. A3; E. W. Coleman, "Pitiable Story of Dolly Pritchett; Flimsy Evidence that Convicted Her," *Atlanta Constitution*, Jan. 6, 1901, p. A3; "Pardon for Dolly Pritchett Urged," *Atlanta Constitution*, Mar. 9, 1901, p. 9; "Mountain Girl Gets a Pardon," *Atlanta Constitution*, 1902, p. 12.

89 "Deliberate Infanticide," *Boston Globe*, June 28, 1877, p. 5.

90 "Five Year's Imprisonment," *Boston Globe*, Dec. 19, 1877, p. 5. Both attorneys asked the judge to send Lizzie Sullivan to the Reformatory Prison for Women. The judge, however, explained that he had no such discretion in cases of manslaughter, and sent her to the House of Corrections, from which the Commissioners of Prisons might "remove her hereafter" to the Reformatory, "if they should deem it for her improvement so to do."

91 *Atlanta Constitution*, Aug. 11, 1869, p. 2.   92 *Daily National Republican*, Apr. 17, 1863, p. 2.

from her people and from the world." Society, he said, "will be the better if this unfortunate girl goes back home tonight."[93] Bishop expected to be criticized for what he said and did, but what he got instead was praise. Letters poured in, commending him for his courage; one woman called his action "heavenly," and a Baptist minister told him "you did the Christian thing in this distressing matter."[94]

MODERN TIMES

Victorian sources, as we mentioned, talked about two chief motives for neonaticide: "pressure of circumstances," that is, economic desperation, and "depravity" (immoral conduct – sex outside of marriage). In England, quite clearly, desperation was the leading motive, although to be sure, the code of traditional morality, which condemned sex outside of marriage, explains why the woman was so desperate in the first place. In the United States, there were plenty of cases of desperation, but in others, avoidance of scandal was the main, perhaps the only, motive.

In our times, both of these motives have much less bite than in the past. Illegitimacy no longer carries a heavy load of stigma and shame. Cohabitation is as common as dirt; hundreds of thousands of couples cohabit, and many of these couples produce children without bothering to get married. And illegitimate children, for the most part, have the same rights as legitimate children and suffer much less stigma than in the past.[95] A poor, unmarried woman who gives birth might, even today, find herself in an unhappy situation. But she is not going to starve: she will be eligible for some kind of welfare and certain social services, she is less likely to scandalize people, and she will find it easier simply to give the child up for adoption if she wishes. A psychiatrist, writing in 1970, thought neonaticide had declined drastically. He suggested some reasons: more effective birth control, more access to abortion, welfare payments that prevent destitution, and easier placement of unwanted children.[96] This sounds right. Contraceptives are now totally legal and quite available. New methods and devices were developed in the twentieth century, very notably "the pill." Contraception helps prevent unwanted pregnancy – and neonaticide occurs only for unwanted pregnancies. Abortion too is legal and much safer and easier to get than was true in the nineteenth century (despite continuing controversy, and state laws that nibble away at the right). When Margaret Sanger opened the first family-planning clinic in 1916, her advertising circular said (among other things): "Do not kill, do not take life, but prevent."[97] Cultural change has been a powerful force: new attitudes toward sex, marriage, and childbirth. Thus, technology and culture, working hand in hand, have changed the social context; fewer and fewer women feel the desperate need to get rid of a newborn baby.

93 "Frees Unwed Girl in Infant's Death," *Boston Globe*, Feb. 4, 1932, p. 9.
94 "Freeing of Unwed Mother Is Praised," *Boston Globe*, Feb. 10, 1932, p. 15.
95 See Grossman and Friedman, *Inside the Castle*, pp. 238–239.
96 Resnick, "Murder of the Newborn," pp. 141, 149.   97 Tone, *Devices and Desires*, p. 119.

The Old Bailey records, covering basically the Victorian period, show surprising leniency in cases of neonaticide. Many women were simply acquitted; those who were convicted were convicted, not of murder, but of concealing the birth of a child. Prison sentences, when they existed, were short. Figures for Great Britain for the years 1923 to 1945 showed even greater leniency: the percentage of women who served any time at all declined from 49 percent to 33 percent; probation went from 5 percent to 22.7 percent. The figures for the 1960s are still more striking: a little more than two-thirds of the women charged with neonaticide were put on probation; only one woman (out of seventy-two charged between 1961 and 1965) went to prison, and that woman went to prison for six months or less.[98] In England, and most likely also in the United States, killing a newborn baby was essentially a crime without (much) punishment.

Neonaticide still occurs, however. Why would a woman, in our times, do such a terrible thing? Because of mental illness, perhaps. A severe case of postpartum depression, for example. There were cases in the nineteenth century, too, where the mother was said to be disturbed, irrational, clinically depressed. Medical sources mentioned "puerperal insanity"; as early as 1829, one medical writer on women's diseases claimed that a woman's mind could easily become "disordered" in the period when "the sexual organs of the human female are employed in forming, lodging, expelling, and lastly feeding the offspring." The psychological problem was especially acute right after delivery and for the following several months.[99]

In England, the Infanticide Act of 1922[100] reduced the punishment for infanticide to manslaughter if the mother's mind was disturbed at the time she did away with her child. In October of that year, a young woman, Emma Temple, pleaded guilty at Lincoln Assizes to "murdering her newly-born child, adding that at the time she did not know what she was doing." The plea was accepted; she was sentenced to four months in jail. The judge remarked that the law was "most wise and humane"; he said he felt "great pity for the prisoner," who had "suffered punishment enough."[101] In another case, in 1926, Elizabeth Jones drowned her baby (it was fourteen days old); she was unmarried, but lived with a motorbus driver. She testified that she was ill, unable to sleep, and that the baby "was crying and seemed to be in great pain." She "did not realize what she did" and was sorry – she wished she could have the baby back. The jury acquitted her of murder, but found her "guilty of infanticide" under the 1922 law. The judge took into consideration her statement that her "mind was unbalanced"; he was also impressed with her "good character," and he

[98] These figures are quoted in Catherine Demme, "Infanticide: The Worth of an Infant under Law," *Medical History* 22:1 (1978), p. 16.

[99] Quoted in Hilary Marland, "Getting Away with Murder? Puerperal Insanity, Infanticide and the Defense Plea," in Mark Jackson, ed., *Infanticide: Historical Perspectives on Child Murder and Concealment, 1550–2000* (Aldershot: Ashgate, 2002), pp. 168, 172.

[100] 12 & 13 Geo. 5 c. 18. (Eng.).

[101] "First Case under 'Wise and Humane' Act," *Manchester Guardian*, Oct. 11, 1922.

essentially imposed no punishment.[102] The Infanticide Act of 1938[103] gave the mother a defense in cases where her mind was "disturbed by reason of her not having fully recovered from the effect of giving birth to the child or by reason of the effect of lactation consequent upon the birth of the child."

In the United States,[104] a study of forty women who had committed neonaticide (the study was published in 2008) found that most of the offenders were young. They were trying to hide their sexual behavior from their parents. The idea that in middle- and upper-class circles it was a scandal to have a baby out of wedlock "compounded" their fear and sense of shame. [105]

Neonaticide cases are sad, even tragic. Fortunately, they are fairly rare. A study in North Carolina of killed or discarded babies, published in 2003, found only thirty-four cases in a sixteen-year period. This was about two a year, out of around 100,000 yearly births.[106] The public finds these cases shocking, perhaps precisely because they *are* rare. And the young mothers are very different from the classic Victorian mothers. Poverty is not a driving factor. In some cases, teenage girls, totally unable to face motherhood and ashamed or afraid to tell their families, look for a way to escape from their troubles; they are so overwhelmed that they can think of no way out, except to get rid of the baby. Sometimes these girls are able to hide their pregnancy (or may even be, at some psychological level, unaware of it). A college student in Ohio was living with her grandparents and "didn't want them to know that I messed up." A young woman who smothered her baby in New York State said, "I just thought my parents wouldn't find out that way."[107]

A woman who kills a newborn baby, according to Cheryl Meyer and Michelle Oberman, tends to be "in her teenage years"; she is likely to feel totally unable to cope with pregnancy, "let alone [to deal] with the prospect of choosing a course for resolving the pregnancy."[108] The delivery of the baby may take this young mother by surprise; possibly she is "shocked" when the baby cries; she has a "natural reaction" to stifle the crying; from here to "suffocation" is only a small step. The main reason given for the act is this: "I don't want the baby."[109]

---

[102] *Manchester Guardian*, July 28, 1926.   [103] 1 & 2 Geo. 6 c. 36. (Eng.).

[104] See Resnick, "Murder of the Newborn." Dr. Philip Resnick, a psychiatrist, analyzed thirty-five cases of neonaticide, apparently from a number of different countries. Resnick says he drew his sample from a survey of the relevant literature, past and present, in thirteen different languages. Almost all of the mothers were under twenty-five, and twenty-nine out of the thirty-five simply wanted to get rid of the child; no psychoses was involved – which was not true of mothers who killed older children.

[105] Kristen Beyer, Shannon McAuliffe Mack, and Joy Lynn Shelton, "Investigative Analysis of Neonaticide: An Exploratory Study," *Criminal Justice and Behavior* 35 (2008), pp. 522, 530.

[106] Marcia E. Herman-Giddens et al., "Newborns Killed or Left to Die by a Parent: A Population-Based Study," *JAMA* 289 (2003), p. 1425.

[107] Julie Wheelwright, "Nothing in Between: Modern Cases of Infanticide," in Jackson, *Infanticide*, pp. 270, 272.

[108] Cheryl L. Meyer and Michelle Oberman, *Mothers Who Kill Their Children* (2001), p. 43.

[109] Everett Dulit, "Girls Who Deny a Pregnancy: Girls Who Kill the Neonate," *Adolescent Psychiatry* 25 (2000), pp. 219, 225.

In one well-known case, Melissa Drexler gave birth to a baby boy in a bathroom stall at her high school prom. She put it in a bag with some bloody towels, and deposited baby and towels in a bathroom trashcan. She touched up her lipstick and went back out to the dance floor. She was charged with murder; later, however, she agreed to plead guilty to manslaughter. She was sentenced to prison, but released after a few years.[110] Nicole Boyer, of Elizabethtown, Pennsylvania, was fourteen years old when she gave birth to a daughter in her parents' bathroom; she put the baby in a plastic bag and hid it in a drawer in the basement.[111] In another case reported in the press, two college freshmen, Amy S. Grossberg and Brian C. Peterson Jr., "who had been sweethearts in a Bergen County [New Jersey] high school," were accused in 1996 of killing their newborn child, "delivered in a motel in Delaware."[112] They were indicted for murder, pleaded guilty to manslaughter, and went to prison. Amy Grossberg served twenty-two months and was released.[113] And in 2002, a seventeen-year-old senior at Stamford High School in Connecticut, hid her pregnancy and birth from her parents; the baby was buried in the backyard of her boyfriend.[114]

Some of these incidents were highly publicized; they led to a call for some sort of action. In response, states began to pass "safe haven" or "Baby Moses" laws; Texas was the first in 1999. Today every state has some version of a "safe haven" law. The idea is to give mothers a decent alternative to murder. There were to be no more babies thrown into dumpsters and rivers or left to die on streets or in fields. The rush to pass these laws suggests that they have a broad appeal. A number of quite different constituencies back them. Of course, nobody is in favor of abandoning or killing babies. But if you are strongly "pro-life," a Baby Moses law seems particularly urgent. Without such a law, a woman who feels she cannot or will not raise the child might otherwise want an abortion – or, in the worst case, resort to infanticide.[115]

[110]   Robert Hanley, "Woman Gets 15 Years in Death of Newborn at Prom," *New York Times*, Oct. 30, 1998, p. B1; Lynne Marie Kohm and Thomas Scott Liverman, "Prom Mom Killers: The Impact of Blame Shift and Distorted Statistics on Punishment for Neonaticide," *William and Mary Journal of Women and the Law* 9 (2002), p. 43.

[111]   Kohm and Liverman, "Prom Mom Killers," p. 45.

[112]   Jan Hoffman, "Teen-Agers Indicted for Murder in Newborn's Death," *New York Times*, Dec. 10, 1996, p. B1.

[113]   Robert Hanley, "Woman Who Killed Her Baby Returns Home from Prison," *New York Times*, May 11, 2000, p. B8. But after her release, she was obligated to "serve two years on parole and do community service."

[114]   David M. Herszenhorn, "Police Await Autopsy Results in Stamford Newborn's Death," *New York Times*, Dec. 20, 2002, p. B6. The story also mentioned an "18-year-old employee at the Red Colony Diner in Brookfield, Conn.," who "gave birth in the restaurant's bathroom, and the baby was found in the trash." The baby survived and the mother was charged with "abandonment" and "concealing delivery."

[115]   There is a "National Safe Haven Alliance," an organization that "works to publicize safe haven laws so at-risk women know that this compassionate alternative exists for them and their newborns." www .nationalsafehavenalliance.org/about.php, visited Aug. 29, 2013.

Baby Moses laws differ in details, but they all agree on setting up "safe-surrender sites."[116] If the parent of a newborn "voluntarily surrenders physical custody ... at a safe-surrender site," the parent cannot be prosecuted for child neglect or abandonment.[117] And her privacy will be totally protected. In California, the child to be surrendered has to be seventy-two hours old or less; in Florida, the baby can be up to seven days old; in Indiana, up to forty-five days old. The "safe-surrender" sites usually include hospitals; in Michigan, the baby must be left with an "emergency service provider," defined as a "uniformed or otherwise identified employee ... of a fire department, hospital, or police station."[118] Under the Texas law, the baby must be one "who appears to be 60 days old or younger." The person who takes the child "has no legal duty to detain or pursue the parent and may not do so unless the child appears to have been abused or neglected"; the "parent may remain anonymous," although there can be "voluntary disclosure of the child's medical facts and history."[119]

The law was aimed at newborns, at "dumpster babies," but the legislature of one state, Nebraska, somehow neglected or forgot to limit the law to tiny babies. A month after it went into effect, it was reported that parents had taken advantage of the law to get rid of some seventeen Nebraska kids, preteens, or teenagers – and not a single newborn. And someone (unidentified) from Council Bluffs, Iowa, crossed over the line into Omaha, Nebraska, specifically to get rid of a twelve-year-old girl.[120] The state quickly amended its law to make it impossible for parents to use the law to get rid of prickly or delinquent adolescents; now only babies in their first month of life qualify for Nebraska's Baby Moses law.[121]

Have these laws been successful? There are mixed reports. In Florida,[122] between 2000 and 2013, 190 newborns were left at "safe havens," as opposed to 52 who were "abandoned in unsafe places." Most of the babies were delivered to hospitals (129), or to emergency medical stations or fire stations (56). A story from Alaska (2013), on the other hand, reported that nobody had ever used the law in the five years since it went into effect.[123] Of course, compared to Florida, Alaska has a tiny population, rattling

---

[116] See, for example, Cal. Health and Safety Code sec. 1255.7.   [117] Cal. Penal Code sec. 271.5.

[118] Mich. Laws, sec. 712.1 (e). The Michigan law is quite elaborate. The baby has to be accepted, but the parent has twenty-eight days to change her mind. She is encouraged to "provide any relevant family or medical information." She is also told that the "state is required to make a reasonable attempt to identify the other parent" (ibid., sec. 712.3 [2] [a] and [e]). Michigan also has a "Safe Delivery Program" (712.20).

[119] Texas Statutes, sec. 262.302 (b).

[120] Eric Eckholm, "Law's Effect: An Iowa Girl Is Abandoned in Nebraska," *New York Times*, Oct. 9, 2008, p. A21.

[121] Nebraska Rev. Stat. § 29–121.

[122] Information from https://asafehavenfornewborns.com/index/php?option, visited Apr. 21, 2013.

[123] Michelle Therialt Boots, "Alaska Law Allowing Surrender of Newborns Unused," www.adn.com /2013/10/28/3147245/alaska-law-that-allows-for-safe.html, visited Apr. 4, 2014. The story concerns an unmarried, twenty-four-year-old woman, Ashley Ard, who was arraigned on second-degree murder charges after wrapping a newborn in a towel and hiding it under a bush, where a dog walker found it.

around in a vast area, but the real problem, no doubt, was lack of awareness of the law. This was perhaps a problem elsewhere as well. An article in the *New York Times* in 2007 called the law a failure in New York City. According to the article, six dead newborn babies had been found abandoned in New York City in 2006; the safe haven laws "do not reach the women who need them most."[124]

Some states make an effort to publicize these laws. Even in New York City, they may have some impact. These laws, of course, cannot stop the rare but disturbing actions of truly psychopathic mothers. In April 2014, a woman in Utah was arrested after the remains of seven infants were found in cardboard boxes in her garage; the mother, Megan Huntsman, claimed one of them was stillborn; the others, she said, she had strangled or smothered when they entered the world.[125]

Moreover, not everybody approves of these "safe haven" laws, effective or not. One strident opponent is "Bastard Nation," an organization that stands up for the rights of adopted children. A safe haven law, in their view, "strips the infant of all genetic, medical and social history"; it ignores the right of birth parents to change their minds; denies "birth fathers due process"; and discourages women from getting prenatal and postnatal counseling.[126] As this organization points out, Baby Moses laws run counter to a strong trend in the law and practice of adoption. The Baby Moses laws exalt secrecy, while adoption law and practice are moving dramatically in the direction of full knowledge and disclosure. But safe haven laws probably do save the lives of at least a few babies.

A CONCLUDING WORD

What do we learn from this brief dip into one small, dark, depressing corner of American social and legal life? It is, to begin with, a data point, a bit of corroborative evidence, for one feature of social history. Nineteenth-century America professed a rigid code of sexual behavior that bore down most heavily on women. Some forms of sex before marriage were downright illegal; in any event, respectable circles strongly condemned premarital sex and it was risky business indeed for middle-class women. If a man "ruined" a woman of this class, she suffered greatly in the marriage market. For the poor, the scandal factor was perhaps less pronounced. But the risk of economic disaster was greater, especially for the working poor, and most especially for women in domestic service and for minority women. Slowly, over the course of the twentieth century, the Victorian sexual code was weakened, then dismantled. By the dawn of the twenty-first century, it had almost gone the way of the dodo and the dinosaurs.

[124] Cara Buckley, "Safe-Haven Laws Fail to End Discarding of Babies," *New York Times*, Jan. 13, 2007, p. B1.
[125] "Utah Garage Cleaning Turns Up Boxes of Suffocated Infants," *New York Times*, Apr. 15, 2014, p. A11.
[126] The quotes are from the website of Bastard Nation, www.bastards.org/bytes-legalized-baby-abandfonment, visited Apr. 4, 2014.

This is the surface story. But reality is always messy, always hard to sum up in a single lapidary formula. The Victorian social code was much more complicated in practice than in theory. Technically, of course, killing a newborn child was murder. Unmarried mothers had committed a grave sin, which they compounded by putting their baby to death. In England, this should have meant the death penalty. But these women were virtually never sentenced to death. Juries acquitted them or convicted them of a minor crime. The record in the United States is harder to read, but the evidence strongly suggests that here too the norm was great leniency, as we have seen. At times, American criminal justice could be incredibly harsh. A young African-American woman, Caroline Shipp, in North Carolina, was hanged for infanticide in 1892, but her baby, though an infant, was not newborn.[127] We find occasional instances of long sentences, even life imprisonment. Still, on balance, leniency seems to predominate – forgiveness, understanding, even a measure of public sympathy. The few empirical studies confirm that women who killed newborn babies rarely suffered the consequences prescribed by the formal law. At least that was true in the past. Neonaticide, in other words, was another crime without punishment, another case of an unwritten law – not as clear-cut an example as the classic unwritten law, but close enough.

As we noted, unlike England, some of the American instances involved middle-class women (and their families). But most of the defendants were quite poor. Americans cherish the myth that this is a classless society, with a single code of morality and law which applies to everybody. This sounds both just and democratic, but is of course profoundly misleading. It may be that democracy itself has the odd result of making the system of criminal justice quite harsh. Beaumont and De Tocqueville, discussing the American prison system, make an argument somewhat along these lines.[128] An aristocratic society can afford to be, in a way, more indulgent toward the lower classes; it oppresses them, but at the same time, it does not hold them to the same standard as their betters. The United States, on the other hand, had embarked on an experiment in democracy, a system where ordinary people (or at least ordinary white males) had political power. Men voted, they ruled the country, but this also meant that more was expected of them. More was expected too of respectable women. Men and women who misbehaved, who were vice-ridden, who offended against moral standards: these people were unworthy; they betrayed, in a sense, the American experiment in popular government. They deserved to be

---

[127] "Choked to Death by Law," *Gastonia Gazette* (Gastonia, North Carolina), Jan. 22, 1892, p. 1. The subtitle of the article was: "A Young Colored Woman, Is Hanged by the Neck in the Presence of 3,000 Spectators." Shipp claimed she was innocent and blamed a man for the crime.

[128] Gustave de Beaumont and Alexis de Tocqueville, *On the Penitentiary System in the United States and Its Application in France* (Carbondale: Southern Illinois University Press, 1964; originally published in 1833), p. 69: "While society in the United States gives the example of the most extended liberty, the prisons of the same country offer the spectacle of the most complete despotism. The citizens subject to the law are protected by it; they only cease to be free when they become wicked."

treated harshly. The harshness was never consistently applied; it was an in-and-out thing, but it reflected an ideology that underlay many nineteenth-century rules.

England was by no means as democratic as the United States. But in the nineteenth century, a kind of ethical democracy developed. That is, the ethical and religious standards of the middle class were generalized to the population as a whole. Everybody was supposed to follow the rules. Poor women, chained to a life of drudgery as domestic servants, were subject to the stern moral standards of their employers, who were middle-class and above. Some women in the United States – African-American women, very notably – were in a similar situation. Many people, in England especially, called for harsh punishment. They called neonaticide murder most foul, a slaughter of innocent lives. They saw leniency and forgiveness as a sign of moral dry rot. But the *working* legal system sent an entirely different message. Judges and juries – and even prosecutors, at times – expressed genuine sympathy and understanding. This was apparently also the case in the United States.

Gender was also a factor in these cases. Respectable women – white, middle-class women – were supposed to be naïve, sexless creatures; they were easily seduced, easily preyed upon by men. Men, on the other hand, had strong sex drives, difficult to control. Women in short were born victims. Lustful men were able to prey on them. Women who gave birth out of wedlock were subject to stigma and shame, but stereotypes about gender acted as a kind of counterpoint offsetting the stigma and shame. It was easy to see these women as victims, rather than bare-faced sinners. And law was supposed to protect victims, not send them to the gallows. Just as the unwritten law allowed juries and others to forgive women who killed abusive men – those women were victims, after all – another kind of unwritten law forgave women who killed babies born in sin. These women too had been victimized by men.

And, of course, here too, the situation in the twenty-first century is dramatically different. Chastity is no longer a paramount value for women. Illegitimacy is no longer a paramount disgrace. In the age of the welfare state and the sexual revolution, social and economic desperation is no longer a major reason for neonaticide – nor an excuse for it. And the crime is now rarer than it was a century ago, in all likelihood. The few contemporary cases mostly involved young, scared, unready girls, and a handful of women genuinely afflicted with mental illness.

Officially, it is still a crime to kill a newborn baby. It is also a crime to neglect or abandon a child. But the very existence of "Baby Moses" laws is a sign that society refuses to measure a mother's behavior by the formal standards of the penal code. The point, of course, is to protect the babies. But the mother too is protected. She has more options than in the past. She can give the baby up for adoption, for example. Or, if she wishes, she could take advantage of the "Baby Moses" laws. Punishing the mother, it is felt, would do no good; protecting the baby's life – and future – is more important.

Abortion is a major political issue; it was an issue before *Roe* v. *Wade*, and is still very much a political and social issue. Many states have passed laws trying to shut down abortion clinics. Political figures on the right threaten to close down or at least defund Planned Parenthood or even drive it out of business. A few extremists even take violent action against doctors who perform abortions. More moderate "pro-lifers" try to persuade and cajole pregnant women to keep their babies or give them up for adoption. Technically, to "pro-lifers," women who get abortions are themselves guilty of murder, or are at the very least accomplices. Yet nobody really vents their anger at the pregnant women. Donald Trump, at one point in his campaign for the presidency, suggested punishing the mothers. This set off a firestorm of criticism, and he soon retracted. Even for the most avid pro-lifer, abortion is (for the mother) a crime without punishment.

4

The Quality of Mercy

Mercy killing is a rather oxymoronic name, first used apparently in the 1920s, to describe a type of killing that has often been thought of as morally justified. Shai Lavi has defined it as a kind of euthanasia, but performed by a layperson, rather than a doctor.[1] The term, though, is often used more broadly. Sometimes the angel of death *is* the doctor, helping a dying patient into another world. So long as the doctor's motives are benign or in accordance with what the family or the patient wants, this can also be called a mercy killing. It may be the most common form. In this chapter, I use the term broadly, to cover "mercy killing" both by doctors and laypeople.

The formal law, of course, has never accepted benign motives as an excuse for putting someone to death. Even if a "victim" is willing, if not eager to die, or even begs to die, and is in excruciating pain, this does not justify murder. That at any rate is the (formal) law. Consent can validate a lot of things, but killing, no. The penal codes are (mostly) stone deaf to the question of mercy. But in the real world, many people seem to feel that mercy killers should not be punished, that they deserve mercy themselves. Mercy killing amounts, at most, to manslaughter – an act committed under extreme emotional distress. At times, it has even been treated as yet another crime without punishment. And, quite recently, a few states have come to allow assisted suicide – a practice closely allied to classical mercy killing.

Mercy killing has a fairly complicated history. Both theory and practice have changed over time. The history of the practice is, naturally, almost impossible to capture. A lot of it hides in the shadows: it is done secretly or disguised in some way. We learn something from court records and from newspaper coverage; but the size of the "dark figure" will always escape us. Newspaper coverage, quite naturally, is canted toward incidents that are graphic, tragic, or sensational. Incidents that never come to light or are successfully covered up go unreported. Doctors or family members take steps to speed up the process of dying, but nobody is the wiser.

---

[1] Shai J. Lavi, *The Modern Art of Dying: A History of Euthanasia in the United States* (Princeton, NJ: Princeton University Press, 2005), p. 144.

Shai Lavi asks, in his book on euthanasia, how could a fairly widespread practice go on, even though it is "condemned by religion, medicine and law?"[2] One answer is, of course, that the practice was not in fact "condemned," not in reality by medicine, and often, in a real sense, not by law. This chapter looks at some aspects of "mercy killing," in its rather tortuous history.

Despite somewhat skimpy evidence, we can roughly identify three stages in the history of mercy killing in the past century or so in the United States. Or perhaps it would be better to talk about three types of mercy killing. In a few early cases, the victims were severely handicapped members of a family. There was at least a tinge of eugenic thinking in the practice. After all, in the heyday of eugenic theory, American states passed laws permitting the unfit to be sterilized. Nazi Germany later took the practice to the extreme. Thousands of the "unfit" were put to death. Mercy killing turned into merciless murder.

After the Second World War, mercy killing shows up in a more familiar form. Mercy killing means ending the suffering of men and women dying in great pain. Family members or doctors act to end the suffering of these patients. Doctors either do this on their own, or at the request of patients or their families. They do this secretly, for the most part. A few doctors have been willing to talk openly about this practice. How often doctors indulged in "lethal dosing" is of course hard to measure. And the practice has always been controversial. Finally, in recent years, assisted suicide has risen to prominence on the social agenda. A few states (and countries) have actually legalized a form of assisted suicide. Assisted suicide, of course, is not "mercy killing" at all, but it performs a similar function.

In "eugenic" killing, a victim would neither ask for nor want to be put to death. In standard mercy killing, the victim wants to die, but the actual killing is done by somebody else. In a state that allows assisted suicide, victims not only choose to die, but are allowed to do the act themselves (the process is, however, hemmed in by fairly strict regulations). Before this, mercy killing and "lethal dosing" were, technically speaking, murder. Yet, on the whole, these were crimes without punishment.

THE DAWN OF MERCY KILLING

The term "mercy killing," as far as we can tell, does not go back further than the 1920s. No doubt there were earlier examples, but they were not given this name. In 1935, an interesting article in the *New York Times* told the story of a "mercy killing" in the late nineteenth century. Dr. M. A. Warriner of Bridgeport, Connecticut, "espoused 'mercy killings' of incurable patients" and "confessed" that he done this himself, with a clear conscience, in 1887. The victim was a rabbit hunter, a "big, strapping Frenchman, a barber," who discharged his gun accidentally, "almost blowing his face off"; some of the pellets "penetrated his brain." He was doomed,

---

[2] Ibid., p. 129.

or, if he lived, might have become "a dangerous maniac." Dr. Warriner talked it over with another doctor, who gave at least tacit support. The patient, at home, was "maniacal"; the family told the doctor to "do what . . . was right." Dr. Warriner gave him "an extra dose of morphine" and the man promptly died. Dr. Warriner never did anything like this again, but in his opinion, "mercy killings" were justified "for victims of incurable forms of cancer, congenital idiots and mangled automobile victims." But doctors, he thought, should never do this entirely on their own; they should consult the family, other doctors, and, if possible, the patient.[3]

This was probably not a unique case. Interestingly, the doctor approved of mercy killing, not only for people who were dying, but also for "congenital idiots," and his own "mangled" victim, who, if he survived, would have been (in the doctor's opinion) "maniacal." Dr. Warriner said his conscience was clear, and his secret stayed within the bosom of the victim's family. No legal action of any sort followed. The doctor said nothing about any legal issues, and apparently thought there were none; he was, in fact, arguably confessing to a murder.

Another article in the *New York Times*, in March 1925, claimed that recent incidents of mercy killing had occurred, both in the United States and in Europe.[4] There were no legal consequences, but one of the killers committed suicide and another attempted it. The article used these cases as a platform to push for legalizing euthanasia, which was, in the writer's opinion, a modern and merciful way to avoid such tragedies. The ancient Romans apparently engaged in this enlightened practice; the article seemed to favor bringing back this practice in the modern world.

Shai Lavi, using records drawn from newspaper accounts and the archives of a euthanasia society, drew up a list of mercy killings between the 1920s and the 1960s.[5] Mention mercy killing today, and people think of old, sick people, or people with terminal diseases, suffering, wracked with pain. Dr. Warriner, as we saw, had a more expansive vision. Indeed, in some early instances, the victim was not elderly at all or terminally ill, but instead severely handicapped. This was the case of Dr. Harold E. Blazer, a physician, who killed his daughter Hazel, thirty-two years old, a "malformed imbecile." He "did not want her to face possible mistreatment after his own death."[6] The trial, which took place in Colorado, attracted national attention. Hazel, one of Dr. Blazer's two daughters, had developed "cerebral spinal

---

[3] "Bridgeport Doctor Tells of 'Mercy Killing': Ended Life of a Wounded Hunter in 1887," *New York Times*, Nov. 20, 1935, p. 25.

[4] W. G. Tinckom-Fernandez, "Euthanasia Doctrine Still Has Advocates," *New York Times*, Mar. 22, 1925.

[5] Lavi, *The Modern Art of Dying*, pp. 173–180. The list of instances given in an appendix to the book is not always accurate. The first item on his list is "Dr. Howard Ellmer Blazer," and the date given is 1926; the third item is "Dr. Harold Blazer," 1927. Both of these, however, refer to the same case – Dr. Harold Blazer, who was tried in 1925, not 1927. This case is discussed in the text. There are other obvious problems with Lavi's list, but the book is in general a valuable and insightful account of the euthanasia movement.

[6] "Dr. Blazer Is Freed, Jury Disagreeing," *New York Times*, Nov. 13, 1925.

meningitis" at the age of six weeks; as a result, she "became a hopeless invalid . . . Absolutely helpless. She could neither walk nor talk, feed herself or do anything. She could get around a little by rolling on the floor."[7]

At the trial, the prosecutor insisted this was murder, plain and simple. The defense was temporary insanity. This medically dubious concept was, as we saw earlier, a staple of the "unwritten law." The defendant (so the argument went) had faced such a dire situation that his mind had snapped. The killing occurred during a blank period of consciousness; this, however, was only a temporary condition. The defendant's mind quickly snapped back to normalcy. Whether anybody really believed this is open to question, as was true in other instances of unwritten law. Temporary insanity does give the jury a legal hook on which to hang an acquittal. In Dr. Blazer's case, the jury came close to acquittal. In fact, after fourteen hours of deliberation, the vote was stuck at eleven to one for acquittal. The judge asked the prosecution and defense counsel "if they were willing to accept a disagreement and have the jury discharged." They agreed. The prosecutor moved to dismiss the indictment against Dr. Blazer and said "he would not try the case again." Dr. Blazer went free, and (according to the newspapers) nearly everybody in the community was "happy at the outcome."[8]

Community sentiment was, apparently, on the side of the defendant in a number of these cases, and juries reflected this sentiment. In a 1930 case, Andrew Beers, who was seventy-seven, killed his daughter, who was twenty-four and mentally ill. Beers was a widower. He was afraid that his daughter would be put into an institution after he died. This was his motive for killing her. The community, we are told, rallied around Beers.[9] The daughter, one notes, had never consented to this act. In 1939, Louis Greenfield chloroformed his son, who was (supposedly) violent and antisocial: this was also done, of course, without consent.[10] In 1938, a jury acquitted a man, charged with murder, who had strangled to death his "imbecilic" son, who was sixteen.

This was also the situation in the case of Louis Repouille, an elevator operator in New York, who worked at the Columbia-Presbyterian medical center and sold canaries and lovebirds part-time. Repouille had "spent his life's earnings trying to cure his incurably imbecile son, Raymond, 13 years old." Repouille chloroformed the boy in October 1939. He "soaked a rag with chloroform from a one-ounce bottle" and "applied it several times to the boy's face while he lay awake in a crib in the rear bedroom of a squalid four-room flat."[11] Repouille, who had four other children, was

[7] "Unaware He Slew Hazel, Says Blazer," *New York Times*, Nov. 10, 1925.
[8] "Dr. Blazer Is Freed, Jury Disagreeing."   [9] *New York Times*, July 13, 14, 17, 22, 1930.
[10] *New York Times*, Jan. 13, 14, 1939. On the Greenfield case, see Janice A. Brockley, "Martyred Mothers and Merciful Fathers: Exploring Disability and Motherhood in the Lives of Jerome Greenfield and Raymond Repouille," in Paul K. Longmore and Lauri Umansky, eds., *The New Disability History: American Perspectives* (New York: New York University Press, 2001), p. 293.
[11] "Despairing Father Kills Imbecile Boy," *New York Times*, Oct. 13, 1939. The case was national news; see, for example, "Blind, Crippled Boy Found Dead; Father Confesses 'Mercy Killing,'" *Atlanta Constitution*, Oct. 13, 1939. For a discussion of the case, see Brockley, "Martyred Mothers and Merciful Fathers."

found guilty of manslaughter in the second degree, but in fact went free; he received a suspended sentence of five to ten years. The judge said that "mercy killing" had no sanction in the law, and he warned that "leniency" might "encourage" others "to do what you did." But his actions belied these words. Prison, he said to Repouille, was inappropriate in this case; it would "greatly affect the lives of your children, who need your support and guidance."[12]

The Repouille case had a kind of grim echo when Lawrence Rougeau, a "26 year-old WPA worker," drowned his five-year-old stepson in the bathtub. Rougeau admitted he had been drinking and that he had "read and discussed accounts of recent 'mercy killings.'" Rougeau said he was afraid the boy was going crazy; he moaned at night and had a "foolish" smile. The neighbors, on the other hand, considered the boy, "a blond, blue-eyed youngster," a "lively, normal child."[13] Another echo of the case occurred in 1944. Repouille, who was not a citizen, filed a petition for naturalization. His petition was denied. The Nationality Act required evidence of "good moral character" for the five years preceding the petition. On appeal to the Second Circuit, Learned Hand, in a well-known opinion, upheld the denial of naturalization. Hand admitted that many people "of the most unimpeachable virtue" did not condemn what Repouille had done; they might consider it "morally justifiable to put an end to a life so inexorably destined to be a burden to others"; nonetheless, the decision denying Repouille's naturalization was in accordance with law.[14]

Repouille was not the only person accused of "old-style" mercy killing during this period. Margaret Cowen, a seventy-seven-year-old nurse in Allentown, Pennsylvania, killed her sister, who was in a mental institution, to "put her out of her misery." For whatever reason, she was shown no leniency. Indeed, she was convicted of first-degree murder in 1940 and sentenced to life imprisonment.[15] In 1941, Edith Reichert, a twenty-nine-year-old Brooklyn housewife, visited her brother, a patient in a mental hospital, with a gun concealed under her fur coat. She shot him to death. She was charged with first-degree murder. At the trial, her attorney stressed "legal insanity," rather than the "mercy-killing angle." This appeal was apparently successful. She was acquitted. But the jurors were surely aware of the "mercy-killing angle," whether or not the lawyer made this an overt part of his case.[16]

---

[12]   "Father Goes Free in Mercy Slaying," *New York Times*, Dec. 25, 1941.
[13]   "Stepfather Slays Boy, 5, By Drowning," *New York Times*, Oct. 16, 1939, p. 20.
[14]   *Repouille v. United States*, 165 F. 2d (C.A. 2, 1947). Judge Jerome Frank dissented. Frank pointed out that the decision was of "small practical import," even to Repouille. The law required "good moral character" only in the five years preceding the petition, and, as the majority itself admitted, if Repouille had waited until 1945, his petition would have been granted; the Hand opinion explicitly ordered Repouille's petition dismissed, "without prejudice to the filing of a second petition."
[15]   "Nurse, 77, Gets Life for Slaying Sister," *New York Times*, Apr. 5, 1940.
[16]   The newspaper accounts, on the other hand, referred to the case as one of mercy killing. "'Mercy Killing' Case Is Rested by State," *New York Times*, June 27, 1942; "Woman Acquitted in 'Mercy Slaying,'" *New York Times*, July 2, 1942.

The outcome troubled the judge. He refused to let Mrs. Reichert go free; instead, he committed her (temporarily) to the Matteawan State Hospital. Letting her go, he felt, might "influence the relatives of some of the 21,000 patients in state hospitals in Suffolk County to go out and do the same thing she did if they thought their dear ones incurable."[17] This is the familiar "slippery slope" argument (more on this in Chapter 6), but it reflects a real sense of unease. How "merciful" was it to kill mental patients like Margaret Cowen's sister?

THE EUGENICS MOVEMENT

Today, very likely, people who are in favor of assisted suicide, or at least the overwhelming majority of them, would agree with the judge. Putting severely disabled people to death is wrong, no matter how hard their lives or the lives of their families. These cases, however, have to be understood against the backdrop of the eugenics movement, which flourished between the late nineteenth and mid-twentieth centuries. Eugenicists thought we could (and should) try to use selective breeding to improve the human race. Farmers, after all, had bred better cows, sheep, and horses that way. Scientifically, the movement depended on Charles Darwin and Gregor Mendel, that is, on the theory of evolution, and the discovery of laws of inheritance. Whether these two honorary godfathers would have approved of the eugenics movement is, however, extremely doubtful.

Francis Galton was a key figure in the rise of the eugenics movement. His book on hereditary genius, which appeared in 1869, advanced the argument that real ability – genius, in fact – was an inherited trait and ran in families.[18] But if genius could be inherited, then the opposite might be true as well: perhaps idiocy, crime, and perversion also ran in families. If so, it would be sound policy to discourage the unfit from having babies. Dr. Warriner, as we saw, thought euthanasia was appropriate for "congenital idiots" as well as for "mangled car accident victims." Of the two prongs of eugenic policy, the negative one was more practical than the positive one. After all, it would be very hard to coerce elites, geniuses, and the like to spawn a bigger crop of babies.[19] But to keep inferiors from reproducing – by force, if necessary – seemed much more doable.

In 1874, the New York Prison Association dispatched R. L. Dugdale on a tour of county jails in New York State. Dugdale was astonished to find in the course of his

---

[17] "Release Is Denied in 'Mercy Killing,'" *New York Times*, July 3, 1942.
[18] Francis Galton, *Hereditary Genius: An Inquiry into Its Laws and Consequences* (London: Macmillan, 1869). Galton also argued that the "Anglo-Saxon race" was more talented than the "negro race." No doubt most "Anglo-Saxons" already thought so, but Galton's contribution was to wrap this idea in the mantle of science. Galton's work – and that of Dugdale, discussed in what follows–, of course preceded Gregor Mendel and the discovery of the laws of heredity.
[19] H. J. Muller, a distinguished scientist and winner of the Nobel Prize, believed in "germinal choice," popularly known as a "sperm bank for geniuses," an idea that quickly died. See Elof Axel Carlson, *The Unfit: A History of a Bad Idea* (Cold Spring Harbor, NY: Cold Spring Harbor Laboratory Press, 2001), p. 351.

tour that many criminals and other deviants were related to each other by blood and descent. In his book, he claimed that a family of such deviants (he called them the "Jukes" family, a made-up name) had a "long lineage, reaching back to the early colonies." Generation after generation of Jukeses were total good-for-nothings, "despised by the reputable community."[20] The message of Dugdale's book was plain: crime, pauperism, and indecency were inherited; they were passed on from parents to children and persisted over time.

In 1912, Henry H. Goddard followed up this study with his own findings; his book concerned a family he called the "Kallikaks" (another made-up name). The Kallikaks, he thought, formed a kind of "natural experiment in heredity."[21] During the Revolutionary period, according to Goddard, Martin Kallikak Sr., a man from a "good family," met a "feeble-minded girl" and she bore him a son. Of some 480 descendants of this union, 143 were feeble-minded and 43 were normal (the status of the rest was unknown). But there were 33 prostitutes, 24 alcoholics, 3 epileptics, and 8 who kept houses of ill fame.[22] Martin, after his fling with the "feeble-minded girl," married a decent girl, and their descendants were entirely different: "respectable citizens, men and women prominent in every phase of social life."[23] The lesson was obvious: heredity played a major role in the lives of Martin's descendants. The methodology was, to say the least, slip-shod; even at the time some scientists were skeptical. By now, the whole thing has been pretty much exposed as junk science.[24]

But the eugenicists, and, no doubt, millions of ordinary people, eagerly embraced the revelations about families like the Jukes and the Kallikaks. Arthur Estabrook and Charles B. Davenport published a study of another degenerate family, the "Nams," and other such studies appeared as well.[25] The whole country, it seemed, faced the danger of an absolute epidemic of degeneracy because of families of this sort – families that, moreover, tended to multiply like rabbits. What, if anything, was to be done? Some states were already experimenting with sterilization. Goddard himself was a bit hesitant; this was a mere "makeshift,"[26] but later on, he seemed to change his mind. In a 1915 book about murderous "imbeciles," he explained that, according to "[c]areful studies," at least "two thirds of these mental defectives have inherited this defect." What was to be done? One possibility was "segregation" in an institution; another might be "surgical interference."[27]

---

[20] R. L. Dugdale, *"The Jukes": A Study in Crime, Pauperism, Disease and Heredity* (New York: G. P. Putnam's Sons, 1877), p. 8.

[21] Henry H. Goddard, *The Kallikak Family: A Study in the Heredity of Feeble-Mindedness* (New York: Macmillan, 1912), p. 116.

[22] Ibid., pp. 18–19.   [23] Ibid., p. 30.

[24] J. David Smith, *Minds Made Feeble: The Myth and Legacy of the Kallikaks* (Rockville, MD: Aspen Systems Corporation, 1985).

[25] Arthur H. Estabrook and Charles B. Davenport, *The Nam Family: A Study of Cacogenics* (reprint edition, 2015, Philadelphia, PA: Andesite Press); the book was originally published in 1885.

[26] Smith, *Minds Made Feeble*, p. 117.

[27] Henry Goddard, *The Criminal Imbecile* (New York: Macmillan, 1915), pp. 106–107; Estabrook and Davenport favored segregating these people, which would be the "most radical measure, though

Some states had already launched themselves along the path of "surgical interference." A 1907 law in Indiana authorized the state to sterilize inmates of prisons and other institutions that housed "confirmed criminals, idiots, rapists and imbeciles," if a "committee of experts" agreed that "procreation" was "inadvisable."[28] Many other states adopted statutes along these lines. California's sterilization statute was passed in 1909,[29] and California eventually became the national champion of this dubious enterprise. Between 1921 and 1940, the state hospitals sterilized no fewer than 5,174 boys and girls under twenty-one, in an attempt to counteract the "menace" of the feeble-minded.[30]

The eugenics movement always had its critics, and the criticism increased in volume over time. Some state courts struck down sterilization statutes. The governor of Pennsylvania, Samuel Pennypacker, vetoed the Pennsylvania bill in 1905. The law called for a safe and effective operation "for the prevention of procreation." The governor, no doubt tongue in cheek, remarked that the "safest and most effective method ... would be to cut the heads off the inmates." The bill, he felt, would allow "experimentation upon living human beings."[31] The U.S. Supreme Court, on the other hand, gave the movement its blessing in the notorious case of *Buck* v. *Bell*,[32] decided in 1927. The state in question was Virginia. Carrie Buck, a poor white woman, was said to be feeble-minded, the daughter of a feeble-minded woman, and the unwed mother of a little girl, presumably also of weak intelligence. Should Carrie Buck be sterilized? Oliver Wendell Holmes Jr., who wrote the opinion, said yes, and famously declared that "three generations of imbeciles are enough."[33] In point of fact, none of the Bucks were "imbeciles"; the little girl (who died young) was considered "bright" by her teachers, and the case is now considered a monstrous miscarriage of justice.[34]

It is, of course, a long way from "surgical interference" to outright killing, but there is clearly an ideological connection. In the years leading up to World War II, there was some serious discussion of euthanasia – particularly in the case of severely

---

perhaps the most expensive." "Of course," they added, "asexualization would produce the same results," but they felt it would be politically difficult. *The Nam Family*, p. 84.

[28] Laws Ind. 1907, ch. 215. There is a huge literature on the eugenics movement in general; see Mark H. Haller, *Eugenics: Hereditarian Attitudes in American Thought* (New Brunswick, NJ: Rutgers University Press, 1963); see also, on the various state laws, Paul A. Lombardo, ed., *A Century of Eugenics in America: From the Indiana Experiment to the Human Genome Era* (Bloomington: Indiana University Press, 2011).

[29] Laws Cal. 1909, ch. 720, p. 1093.

[30] Mirosava Chávez-García, *States of Delinquency: Race and Science in the Making of California's Juvenile Justice System* (Berkeley: University of California Press, 2012), p. 134.

[31] Carlson, *The Unfit*, pp. 218–219.   [32] 274 U.S. 200 (1927).

[33] On the case, see Adam Cohen, *Imbeciles: The Supreme Court, American Eugenics, and the Sterilization of Carrie Buck* (New York: Penguin Press, 2016); Paul A. Lombardo, *Three Generations, No Imbeciles: Eugenics, the Supreme Court, and Buck v. Bell* (Baltimore, MD: Johns Hopkins Press, 2008). See also Ben A. Franklin, "Sterilization of Teen-Age Woman Haunting Virginia Decades Later," *New York Times*, Mar. 7, 1980, p. A16.

[34] On this point, see Lombardo, *Three Generations, No Imbeciles*.

abnormal babies. In 1915, at a Chicago hospital, a woman named Ann Bollinger gave birth to a "badly deformed" baby (her fourth child). The chief of staff of the hospital, Harry J. Haiselden, told the parents that the baby would die without surgery, and that it would be better to just let it go. They "tearfully agreed." The baby died. A coroner's jury, "composed of six leading physicians and surgeons," found the doctor "morally and ethically" within his rights in refusing to operate. But the jury also felt that the baby, with proper treatment, could have lived, and indeed, might have been able to live a normal life.[35]

This was not the only time Haiselden let "abnormal" babies die. In 1917, William and Eva Meier brought their baby to the hospital, microcephalic, and with an incomplete skull. Haiselden, among other things, "removed a ligature that had been used to stop an umbilical hemorrhage and let the baby bleed to death."[36] And Haiselden, along with others, felt that getting rid of "defective" infants was sound policy; many people agreed, including such well-known public figures as Clarence Darrow, not to mention church leaders and prominent reformers, such as Jane Addams. Curiously enough, Helen Keller sided quite strongly with Haiselden – one would think that a woman who had overcome an enormous physical handicap would be horrified at doing away with handicapped children, but this was not the case.[37] The incident with the Bollinger baby inspired a silent movie, *The Black Stork*, in which Haiselden himself made an appearance.[38] In the movie, Claude, one of the main characters, suffers from some sort of hereditary disease, due to the fact that his grandfather had an affair with a slave or servant girl. Claude marries Anne, and they have a "severely defective" baby. Anne has a vision of what will happen to the baby: a life of poverty and crime. She envisions the baby growing into a man and killing the doctor who had saved his life when he was an infant – the very doctor, in other words, who had "condemned" the baby to live. Anne, horrified, agrees to let the baby die, and "the infant's tiny soul leaps into the arms of a waiting Jesus."[39]

---

35 "Jury Clears, Yet Condemns Dr. Haiselden," *Chicago Tribune*, Nov. 20, 1915. One of the doctors on the coroner's jury was particularly critical. He felt that Dr. Haiselden's act, if "unchallenged," might be "the cause of many crimes. Many babies would be killed by unscrupulous physicians."

36 Martin S. Pernick, *The Black Stork: Eugenics and the Death of "Defective" Babies in American Medicine and Motion Pictures since 1915* (New York: Oxford University Press, 1996), p. 4.

37 John Gertz, "Disability and Euthanasia: The Case of Helen Keller and the Bollinger Baby," in Joseph W. Koterski, ed., *Life and Learning XVI: Proceedings of the Sixteenth University Faculty for Life Conference at Villanova University, 2006* (Washington, DC: University Faculty for Life, 2007), pp. 491–502.

38 Ian Dowbiggin, *A Merciful End: The Euthanasia Movement in Modern American* (New York: Oxford University Press, 2003), pp. 23–27; the full story is told in Pernick, *The Black Stork*. According to Pernick, no copies were known to exist until Pernick discovered and preserved a revision of the movie in 1927 and "subsequently located an unprojectable paper print of the 1916 original" (ibid., p. 143).

39 On the movie, and the Haiselden case in general, see Pernick, *The Black Stork*; Edwin Black, *War against the Weak: Eugenics and America's Campaign to Create a Master Race* (New York: Four Walls, Eight Windows, 2003), pp. 252–258. Black reprints, among the illustrations in his book, the image from the movie showing the euthanized baby ascending into the arms of Jesus. The Chicago critics apparently were not impressed by the movie; see "Black Stork Panned," *Variety* 46:28 (1917).

Some of the critics panned this movie, but it played in many cities, and was apparently still to be seen as late as 1942. No doubt many people agreed with its message.

Dr. Haiselden was surely not the only doctor who let newborn babies die if they were severely impaired. From the 1940s on, there were reports that some doctors followed a similar path. A blaze of publicity in the 1970s and 1980s involved "Baby Doe," in Indiana, and "Baby Jane Doe," in New York. The federal government chimed in; in 1983, the Department of Health and Human Services issued regulations to prevent hospitals from withholding treatment to such babies. The Supreme Court struck down these restrictions in *Bowen v. American Hospital Association*.[40] This was a highly technical opinion, somewhat muddled, and it commanded at most a bare majority of the court. It is not entirely clear (to me at least) exactly what, if anything, the case decided – except that the particular restrictions had no validity. No doubt the justices were aware of the underlying issue: a furious and passionate debate over treatment for these unfortunate babies (and the problems of their unfortunate parents). Should these babies be saved at all costs, regardless of what the doctors and the parents might want, and should government interfere with these very personal and very local decisions?

The discussions, along with proposed laws, executive actions, regulations, manifestoes, and debates, show that the issue has never been really put to rest. It is still controversial – especially when parents disagree with doctors or with each other. In 1969, a baby at Johns Hopkins, born with an intestinal blockage, could have been operated on. But the baby also had Down's syndrome. Briefed on the situation, the parents refused to allow the operation. The baby was "moved to a corner of the nursery" and allowed to "starve to death."[41] A study of deaths of infants in the Yale-New Haven hospital in the early 1970s found a small but definite number of cases where the doctor – with the agreement of the parents – simply withheld treatment, as a result of which the baby died. One baby had Down's syndrome "and intestinal atresia"; the parents "thought that surgery was wrong for their baby and themselves." The baby died seven days after birth. Many families wanted "maximal efforts to sustain life," but others, whose children had "severe defects," felt otherwise. They were afraid that they and their other children "would become socially enslaved, economically deprived, and permanently stigmatized, all perhaps for a lost cause."[42]

The issue of newborn babies became, rather naturally, entangled with the abortion issue. The "pro-life" camp has argued vigorously for the "rights" of severely handicapped babies. The Catholic Church, and some Protestant churches, have been powerful advocates for these babies. Perhaps a silent majority felt it was better

[40] 476 U. S. 610 (1986). See Pernick, *The Black Stork*, p. 168.
[41] David J. Rothman, *Strangers at the Bedside: A History of How Law and Bioethics Transformed Medical Decision Making* (New York: Basic Books, 1991), p. 191.
[42] Raymond S. Duff and A. G. M. Campbell, "Moral and Ethical Dilemmas in the Special-Care Nursery," *New England Journal of Medicine* 289:890 (1973).

to let these babies go than to use heroic methods to keep them alive.[43] For the "pro-life" camp, the death of these babies was, like abortion itself, a crime. Yet there were no trials, no arrests, nothing more than injunctions, lawsuits, and appeals to government. In a sense, then, if these were crimes, they were crimes without punishment.

In any event, newborn babies were something of a special case. On the larger or broader issue of euthanasia there was, to be sure, public discussion from time to time. On the whole, nothing came of the discussion. In a few states, bills of one sort or another were introduced. But no euthanasia law was ever actually enacted. Still, in the late nineteenth century and the first part of the twentieth, the subject of euthanasia was not wholly taboo. In the early twentieth century, a strong sense of cultural and demographic crisis erupted in America. A flood of immigrants seemed to threaten traditional values – a flood of what many people saw as inferior and unfit stock. And, of course, there were natives too of inferior and unfit stock. In the case of a child named Jerome Greenfield, somewhat similar to the Repouille case, the dead boy, it was hinted, could have grown up to be a menace: a "primitive, violent, sexual child's mind in an adult body," a danger to his own mother, among other things.[44] This was a theme of *The Black Stork* too: the baby that could grow up to become a kind of adult monster. Mercy killing would prevent a young Jukes or Kallikak from growing up to do harm or to reproduce his kind. This of course was also Dr. Haiselden's view.

The climate of opinion of course was not static. Events in Europe contributed to the changing winds of public opinion. Even before the actual outbreak of the Second World War (1939), the Nazi regime, in power in Germany from 1933 on, eagerly embraced the idea of sterilization. Eugenic circles in the United States found a lot to admire in the German attitude; Hitler was not yet quite so poisonous a brand name.[45] For the Nazis, sterilization was only a first step; next came a large-scale onslaught of murder. Undesirables, lives not worth living, had no place in the Nazi order. In 1939, the Nazis systematically murdered children born with Down's syndrome, microcephaly, and other disabilities; they also put to death more than 200,000 psychiatric patients.[46] This, of course, was hardly "mercy killing," and it was, in a way, itself only a prelude to an even more murderous cacophony: one of the most monstrous crimes in human history, the slaughter of millions of Jews – men, women, and children. The Nazis were also angels of death for Roma people, homosexuals, and untold numbers of Slavs. These had all been labeled as vermin, dangers to society, or totally subhuman. The Nazis also slaughtered anyone who

---

43   For a discussion, see Constance Paige and Elisa B. Karnofsky, "The Antiabortion Movement and Baby Jane Doe," *Journal of Health Politics, Policy, and Law* 11:255 (1986).

44   Brockley, "Martyred Mothers and Merciful Fathers."

45   Lombardo, *A Century of Eugenics in America*, p. 203; James Q. Whitman, *Hitler's American Model: The United States and the Making of Nazi Race Law* (Princeton, NJ: Princeton University Press, 2017).

46   Nicholas Stargardt, *The German War: A Nation under Arms, 1939–1945* (New York: Basic Books, 2015), pp. 82–87; Michael Burleigh, *The Third Reich: A New History* (London: Macmillan, 2000), pp. 382–404.

opposed the regime, and they ran, with monstrous efficiency, a whole series of death camps in which they murdered victims on an industrial scale. These incredible crimes were an almost fatal wound to the eugenics movement, and, ultimately, to the idea of sterilization. Most scientists had already come to reject the underlying premises. "Scientific racism" disappeared from the mind-set of scientists, surviving only in the fringe world of Neo-Nazis and white supremacists. It had never, in any event, really deserved the label of "science."

Even without the looming shadow of Hitler, eugenics suffered because of its moral boundary with euthanasia. Euthanasia, a "good death," has meant different things over the years, but most fundamentally, it refers to whatever affords a quick and pain-free death. It has always had bitter and committed opponents. To the Roman Catholic Church, human life is sacred, no matter how damaged. Hence Catholic doctrine is firmly set against euthanasia, just as it is dead set against killing the "Baby Does" of the world, or letting them die without treatment. Yet a poll taken in 1939 found that people in England approved of euthanasia (surely in this sense), by a substantial margin (70 percent to 30 percent); in the United States the public was divided 50-50 on the subject. Of course, nobody (we hope) meant the Hitler variety, or even the eugenic variety.

The sterilization laws were also abandoned over time. An important decision along the way was *Skinner* v. *Oklahoma* (1942).[47] Skinner had been convicted of such crimes as robbery and stealing chickens. He was slated to undergo a vasectomy under Oklahoma law. The Supreme Court found that the law in question violated the Equal Protection Clause of the Fourteenth Amendment. Skinner, the chicken thief, would lose the right to have children; embezzlers, on the other hand, were exempted from the law. The case was decided during the Second World War, a war against the murderous Nazi regime, which might have colored the decision, at least subconsciously. The Skinner case did not, in fact, hold that sterilization laws were per se unconstitutional. But the handwriting was on the wall. To be sure, mass sterilizations continued in California. In Virginia, state hospitals sterilized more than 100 people in 1958. The last state to abandon the practice – ironically – was Oregon, soon to be the first state to adopt assisted suicide. The last sterilization in Oregon took place in 1981. By then, all of the other sterilization laws had been consigned to the dustbin of history.[48]

LETHAL DOSING

In the twentieth century, euthanasia was formally illegal in every state. But "lethal dosing" was a common practice. Doctors gave pain medicine to suffering patients,

---

[47]   316 U. S. 535 (1942). The case and its background are discussed in Victoria F. Nourse, *In Reckless Hands: Skinner v. Oklahoma and the Near Triumph of American Eugenics* (New York: W. W. Norton, 2008).

[48]   Cohen, *Imbeciles*, p. 319.

patients who were terminally ill, at levels that were almost certain to bring on death, or at least make death come sooner. This was indeed arguably a kind of euthanasia, but it was considered far more acceptable. Even the Catholic Church was not unalterably opposed. Under the doctrine of double effect, with roots as far back as St. Thomas Aquinas, lethal dosing was not in itself an evil. The doctor did not intend to kill his patient; the drugs were given for a lawful purpose, though they could also have a fatal effect. A person was allowed to perform "an action from which a two-fold result follows, one good and the other evil."[49] Protecting life was an absolute duty, but keeping life going artificially was not. A patient who rejected certain end-of-life treatments, for example, was not committing a sin. Nor was the doctor committing a sin when she piled on painkillers. Probably few people were actually aware of this doctrine of double effect; but it fit in with what many, or most people, thought was ethical medical practice. Lethal dosing, then, was socially accepted, and even (to a degree) medically approved as well.

Some doctors, in fact, admitted openly that they were willing to help patients die – willing to commit a kind of quiet, subterranean act of mercy. In 1988, the American Medical Association approved of the practice, in a way. It took the position that it was acceptable to give drugs to "ease the pain of a patient," if the patient was terminally ill and in excruciating pain, even if "the effect of the drug may shorten life."[50] Legally speaking this was perhaps (technically) murder, and how often doctors actually did this is obviously unknowable, but nobody doubts that it took place.

The curtain was occasionally lifted. In 1988, a young doctor published a short and anonymous essay in the *Journal of the American Medical Association*. The essay was called "It's Over, Debbie." In it, the doctor described what he did for a young woman in her twenties dying of ovarian cancer; the patient was suffering from "unrelenting vomiting"; she had difficulty breathing, weighed only eighty pounds, had not "eaten or slept in two days," and had not responded to chemotherapy. It was a "gallows scene"; the woman said, "Let's get this over with." And he did. He gave her morphine sulfate, and she died quickly and quietly.[51] There were letters to the journal afterward – on both sides of the issue. The journal was subpoenaed for the name of the doctor but the journal refused to comply. The subpoena was later quashed.[52]

In 1991, a doctor in Rochester, New York, Timothy E. Quill, admitted, in a "rare disclosure," that he had helped a woman he called "Diane" to die; she was in pain, suffering from leukemia, with small chance of survival. He gave her barbiturates, knowing she wanted to die. Dr. Quill said he thought "many doctors had done what

49   Joseph Fletcher, *Morals and Medicine* (1954), p. 112.
50   Quoted in Lavi, *The Modern Art of Dying*, p. 127.
51   "It's Over, Debbie," *JAMA* 259:272 (Jan. 8, 1988).
52   Michael Specter, "AMA Won't Identify Mercy Killer: Medical Journal Rejects Subpoena," *Washington Post*, Feb. 17, 1988, p. A3; Linnet Myers and Jon Van, "Mercy-Killing Essay Subpoena Is Quashed," *Chicago Tribune*, Mar. 19, 1988.

he had done but not talked about it."[53] "Diane" had asked the doctor to help her. In other cases, no doubt, the patient is unconscious, and the doctor acts either on his own or at the request of the family. There are usually no consequences. A patient lies in a hospital bed, terminally ill, and dies (as expected). The hospital rarely investigates: why should it?

An article published in 1967 dealt with a son who shot his mother; she was suffering from terminal cancer (leukemia). The doctors had refused to carry out a mercy killing. One doctor, in an interview, admitted that doctors sympathized with mercy killers and that many doctors had, in fact, done something for patients who were hopelessly ill, action that was in effect a kind of mercy killing. He compared mercy killing to abortion (which at the time was illegal in many places); some doctors did perform abortions, despite the state of the law, and doctors similarly put dying patients out of their misery, even though this was, strictly speaking, also against the law. Both acts were (he thought) done with the best of motives; both were in the patient's best medical interest.

Mercy killing and lethal dosing were occasionally discussed in magazines and newspapers. In 1948, mercy killing was the subject of a movie, *Live Today for Tomorrow* (or, as it was renamed, *An Act of Murder*). The movie starred Frederick March and Florence Eldridge, who were major figures in Hollywood (March had won an Academy Award). In the movie, March plays a judge married to Eldridge (they were husband and wife in real life). They discover that Eldridge has a brain tumor and is doomed. March deliberately crashes a car they are driving in, not caring if he dies along with his wife. In fact, she is killed, but March survives. He confesses what he has done, and demands to be tried for murder. The movie ends with a kind of Hollywood cop-out. It turns out the wife (conveniently) was already dead at the time of the crash; she had taken an overdose of pills, a fact that March was not aware of. The murder charge is dismissed. March will not be punished. Despite the convenient Hollywood ending, the movie does suggest that mercy killing might possibly be deeply ethical at times, or that, at the very least, it poses a moral dilemma. Frederick March is presented in the movie as a wholly sympathetic character.

In 1963, on a television program, *Dr. Kildare*, a doctor is shown flipping the switch of a machine that kept a comatose patient alive. Like the movie, this was fiction, not reality, but the dilemma was real enough. As we have seen, doctors – usually with the tearful agreement of parents – continued to let some severely damaged babies die. Money was one issue: the fearful costs of treating these babies and of maintaining them later in life. Choice and autonomy were key issues – not for the babies, of course, but for the parents. Just as, in modern law (and society), people feel entitled to choose their sex lives, and just as women feel (in the main) the right to decide to

---

[53]   Lawrence K. Altman, "Doctor Says He Gave Patient Drug to Help Her Commit Suicide," *New York Times*, Mar. 9, 1991.

continue a pregnancy or not, some parents – many parents – feel entitled to decide whether they have to accept the burden of a child born with little or no chance of a meaningful life; but with profound and terrible consequences for parents.

In the last half of the twentieth century, mercy killing had little to do with eugenics or, for that matter, with babies. Probably most of the "victims" were very elderly people. Until the 1980s at least, cases of mercy killing, insofar as they came to public attention, fit a standard pattern: the patient was hopelessly ill and suffering; there was no real way to improve his or her condition. Ending that sort of life was (or could be considered) an act of mercy. A member of the family, or (probably more often) a doctor, actually did the deed.

It is impossible to tell how often this happened. Only cases that came out of the shadows, for one reason or another, were likely to be reported. As early as 1939, a jury declined to indict a sixty-five-year-old man who had killed his wife. She was suffering from terminal cancer. In 1953, an English judge confronted a case of an attempted mercy killing.[54] The husband of Mrs. Julia King was dying of cancer. She tried to suffocate him by putting a pillow over his face. The judge clearly sympathized: "only those who had kept the heartbreaking vigil by the bed of some beloved one who was slowly dying could realize the strain imposed." The situation no doubt made Mrs. King "distraught." He granted her a "conditional discharge"; he insisted he was not "lending countenance to what is sometimes loosely called 'mercy killing.'" What she did (he said) was "wrong and wicked" and she should realize this. Wrong, perhaps, but how can we interpret the judge's action except as a kind of tacit approval?

In 1950, Dr. Herman Sander went on trial in New Hampshire.[55] This was a case that gained nationwide attention. Dr. Sander was accused of killing a patient, Abbie Borroto, by injecting air into her veins. She was dying of cancer, bedridden, and in excruciating pain.[56] The newspapers called it a mercy killing.[57] At the trial, everybody seemed to be on Dr. Sander's side. This included the dead woman's family.[58] There was some dispute over the facts: what had Dr. Sander actually done, and when did he do it? But the real defense was a kind of unwritten law, and the strong feeling that Dr. Sander did not deserve any punishment, that he was a compassionate, devoted, and caring doctor and a "tireless and conscientious worker." The judge in this case did his official duty: if Dr. Sander caused the woman's death (he told the jury), then the act was murder, plain and simple.[59] The prosecutor told the jury that

54 See "Attempted Murder of Husband, *Times of London*, Oct. 16, 1953, p. 4.
55 Russell Porter, "4th Witness Heard against Dr. Sander," *New York Times*, Mar. 1, 1950, p. 6.
56 Russell Porter, "Defense Opens Case, Says Sander Will Testify Air Followed Death," *New York Times*, Mar. 3, 1950, p. 1.
57 See, e.g., Russell Porter, "Dr. Sander Denies He Killed Patient; Says Mind Snapped," *New York Times*, Mar. 7, 1950, p. 1.
58 Porter, "Defense Opens Case."
59 Russell Porter, "Sander Acquitted in an Hour; Crowd Outside Court Cheers," *New York Times*, Mar. 10, 1950, p. 1.

people "must abide by" the law; no one, "high or low, was entitled to take the law into his own hands and arbitrarily end the life of another person." But the jury – "twelve middle-aged and elderly men" – spent only a bit more than an hour before reaching a verdict: not guilty. When the news got out, "[w]omen spectators gasped and cried out in joy." Reginald Borroto, Abbie's husband, found the verdict "heart-warming."[60] Later, letters and telegrams "poured in" congratulating Dr. Sander.[61] He lost his license to practice, but the New Hampshire Board of Registration in Medicine later restored it.

To the community, and to Abbie's family, Dr. Sander was no murderer; he was a hero, a saint. No doubt many people agreed. An editorial in the *Chicago Daily Tribune*, commenting on the case, argued that a "doctor who puts an end to a life that promises nothing but anguish is no murderer in the sense that the word is applied to an assassin." The law, sooner or later, was bound to be "modified" to permit this result.[62] Jurors in other cases came to similar decisions. Carol Paight's father was diagnosed with terminal cancer. The cancer, according to his doctor, was sure to spread in coming months. She was horrified at the thought of his suffering. She took his service revolver, returned to the hospital, and shot him to death. She was put on trial in 1950. The defense was temporary insanity; "cancerphobia" had driven her out of her mind. The jury acquitted her.[63]

In 1973, the "chief resident surgeon at Nassau County Medical Center" in New York faced a murder charge. Dr. Vincent Montemarano was accused of "injecting deadly potassium chloride ... into the veins of Eugene Bauer." Bauer, suffering from cancer, was in a coma at the time. The superintendent of the hospital, suspicious about Bauer's death, reported the incident to the district attorney.[64] But Dr. Montemarano, after a sensational trial, was acquitted.

The newspaper account described this as "the first U.S. euthanasia case in 24 years involving a physician," in other words, that is, roughly since the Sanders case.[65] But surely there were instances in between, though perhaps they never came to light. In 1969, an (unpublished) poll of professors of medicine probed the extent of mercy killing. Less than 5 percent of the respondents were willing to admit that they had, in fact, indulged in mercy killing. This is a small percentage of doctors, but, none-theless, it implies quite a few mercy killings. The poll was reported in the *Washington Post*; the same article reported a Gallup poll showing that 53 percent of the American public favored physician-assisted euthanasia – this was roughly the same percentage as thirty years before.[66]

[60] Russell Porter, "Borroto Calls Verdict 'Most Heart-Warming,'" *New York Times*, Mar. 10, 1950, p. 23.
[61] Russell Porter, "Messages Flood in on Sander Verdict," *New York Times*, Mar. 11, 1950, p. 28.
[62] "Mercy Killing," *Chicago Daily Tribune*, Jan. 3, 1950, p. 12.
[63] "Carol Paight Acquitted as Insane at Time She Killed Ailing Father," *New York Times*, Feb. 8, 1950.
[64] "Hospital Surgeon Charged with Mercy Killing of N.Y. Patient," *Los Angeles Times*, June 29, 1973.
[65] This claim also appears in Giza Lopes, *Dying with Dignity: A Legal Approach to Assisted Death* (Denver, CO: Praeger, 2015), p. 77.
[66] Nancy L. Ross, "Mercy-Killing Issues Still Causing Debate," *Washington Post*, Jan. 13, 1974, p. B4.

A 1996 study of doctors, reported in the *New England Journal of Medicine*, found that 11 percent of them said they would be "willing to hasten a patient's death by prescribing medication"; 7 percent said they would provide a lethal injection. But, if the practice were legalized, 36 percent of the doctors would be willing to hasten death and 24 percent would be willing to give the lethal injection. Moreover, 18.3 percent of the doctors had "received a request from a patient for assistance with suicide"; 11 percent had been asked for a "lethal injection." Of the doctors, 4.7 percent said that "they had administered at least one lethal injection."[67] This is similar to the "unpublished" 1969 study reported earlier, where "something less" than 5 percent had reported conducting a mercy killing.

In the 1991 case of Dr. Timothy Quill, mentioned earlier in this chapter, Dr. Quill submitted a report to the *New England Journal of Medicine* in which he admitted helping a woman commit suicide. "Diane" (later identified as Patricia Diane Turnbull) had terminal leukemia; her chances of survival, even with treatment, were poor. She decided against treatment. Dr. Quill referred her to a mental health specialist, who told Dr. Quill that "Diane" was thinking clearly and was not depressed. "Diane" told Dr. Quill that she wanted to "take her life in the least painful way possible"; he recommended her to the Hemlock Society (about which more later). She returned and asked for "barbiturates for sleep." He recognized what this meant; it was a suicide process recommended by the Hemlock Society. Dr. Quill prescribed the drugs. He made sure she understood what the dosage was that produced sleep, and what dosage brought an end to life. Several months later, after a decline in her condition but after she had time to connect with her family, she notified the doctor and her friends and family that she would be "leaving soon," and two days later she committed suicide.[68]

Dr. Quill had made an admission, and openly. Yet a grand jury refused to indict him for aiding in Turnbull's suicide.[69] In addition, the state health department chose not to bring charges of professional misconduct, reasoning that "he could not know with certainty what use a patient might make of the drugs he has prescribed. Nor is it within any physician's power or authority to compel a patient to do one thing or another with any prescription. Ultimately, these are decisions left to the patients."[70] This was, perhaps, a bit disingenuous. Quill later became a figure in the euthanasia movement, testifying in front of Congress[71] and writing a book, *Death and Dignity: Making Choices and Taking Charge.*

[67] "A National Survey of Physician-Assisted Suicide and Euthanasia in the United States," *New England Journal of Medicine* 17:338 (1998), pp. 1193–1201.

[68] Timothy Quill, "Sounding Board: Death and Dignity – A Case of Individualized Decision Making," *New England Journal of Medicine* 324:10 (Mar. 7, 1991), p. 691. See Altman, "Doctor Says He Gave Patient Drug to Help Her Commit Suicide."

[69] Lawrence K. Altman, "Jury Declines to Indict a Doctor Who Said He Aided in a Suicide," *New York Times*, July 27, 1991.

[70] Lisa Foderaro, "New York Will Not Discipline Doctor for His Role in Suicide," *New York Times*, Aug. 17, 1991.

[71] The testimony was transcribed in Timothy E. Quill, A Physician's Position on Physician-Assisted Suicide, 74 Bull. N.Y. Acad. Med. 114 (1997).

In 1978, jurors in Texas found Dr. Robert Milton Raines guilty of *attempted* mercy killing. The victim was his own mother. He denied the charge. He was accused of trying to suffocate her, but he said he was merely applying a "glycerin soaked tissue" to her mouth to ease her dry lips. The jury recommended probation, a minimal sentence. Dr. Raines's mother lived another six months before she died of stomach cancer.[72]

In 1973, Lester Zygmaniak, in Freehold, New Jersey, was accused of murdering his brother, George. Lester (twenty-three years old), admitted shooting George in a room in a hospital. George, who was twenty-six, had been "paralyzed from the neck down after a motorcycle accident." Lester said he wanted to end George's suffering. He asked George if this was what he wanted. George "nodded yes." The defense was temporary insanity. Two psychiatrists testified that Lester had been deranged when he dispatched his brother; one of them, an instructor in psychiatry at Columbia University, Dr. Samuel Klagsbrun, had examined Lester and concluded that at the time of the shooting, "Lester suffered a psychotic reaction of a temporary nature." The second psychiatrist spoke about a "gross stress reaction," but added that Lester had "made a rapid recovery" and was "today apparently normal in every respect." A psychiatrist who testified on the prosecution side argued that Lester had "complete control of his facilities" when he shot his brother.[73] The jurors chose to ignore this testimony. They found Lester not guilty.[74] Here, as in classic cases of the unwritten law, variants of the insanity defense may appear, either in mitigation or as outright excuses. An English writer speaks about a kind of benign conspiracy between psychiatrists and courts to raise the defense of "diminished responsibility" in cases of mercy killing.[75]

In general, in cases that actually went to trial, acquittals were common. If juries convicted, then judges imposed very light sentences. In 1986, Wallace Cooper was accused of injecting a "deadly mixture of morphine and digoxin" into his bedridden uncle. Cooper, a "physician's assistant," had been caring for his uncle, a man "he regarded almost as a father," and whom he loved dearly. He was charged with first-degree murder. He "pleaded no contest . . . to voluntary manslaughter." For this, he might have gotten a sentence up to eleven years; instead, the judge, Coleman Swart of Pasadena Superior Court, put him on probation for five years. True, what Cooper did was a "crime," but there were no "ulterior motives"; it was an act of mercy.[76]

Other instances can be mentioned. In 1979, in Washington, DC, Patricia Stephens visited her critically ill father at Howard University Hospital. She "snipped

[72] "Jurors Felt Doctor Attempted Mercy Killing with Ill Mother," *Washington Post*, Nov. 23, 1978, p. A18.
[73] Richard J. H. Johnston, "Doctors Differ on Sanity in Jersey 'Mercy' Killing," *New York Times*, Nov. 2, 1973.
[74] "Mercy Killing: Jury Acquits Man in Slaying of His Paralyzed Brother," *Washington Post, Times Herald*, Nov. 6, 1973.
[75] Amanda Clough, "Mercy Killing: Three's a Crowd?" *Journal of Criminal Law* 79 (2015), pp. 358, 360.
[76] Mark Arax, "Man Given Probation in 'Unique' Mercy Killing of Uncle," *Los Angeles* Times, Jan. 8, 1986, p. A3.

the tubes that fed oxygen and liquid food to her father, who lay in a coma." Then she "unplugged the machine that kept her father breathing." She sat "quietly" by his side, and after his "final breath, she stood and made the sign of the cross over his body." She told detectives she "could not bear to see him suffer any longer." The medical examiner thought this was "euthanasia"; it was "to his knowledge ... the first such case in the District of Columbia." Evidence on the matter was put before the grand jury in the District, but the grand jury "declined to bring any charges."[77] In 1985, a woman in Lynchburg, Virginia, Ruth Davis, stabbed to death her seventy-two-year-old husband, Samuel Roscoe Davis, plunging an icepick into his chest. Samuel was dying of cancer. She acted, as her lawyer put it, "out of love." Davis reached a "plea agreement with prosecutors"; she was sentenced to two years' probation "in exchange for pleading guilty to one count of manslaughter." The judge "suspended the punishment on condition that [she] receive counseling and treatment from a mental health clinic."[78]

Once in a while, a case came out the other way. In 1950, a man who killed his blind brother, a cancer victim, was convicted of voluntary manslaughter and sentenced to twelve years in prison. The defendant had watched his brother get worse and worse; his brother, he claimed, begged to die. The jury, in its deliberation, had been heavily swayed by the "planned" nature of the crime; the defendant had visited several bars, in order to get drunk and build up enough courage to kill his brother. An article published in 1950 claimed to see a trend away from acquittals and toward criminal conviction of mercy killers. But conviction is not necessarily the end of the story. There is always the possibility of probation or clemency. In 2013, an eighty-six-year- old man faced trial for first-degree murder; he had killed his wife (they had been married more than forty years) in an apparent mercy killing. He was, however, eventually given probation.[79]

In 1985, newspapers reported the tragic case of an old man named Roswell Gilbert. Gilbert, of Fort Lauderdale, Florida, seventy-five years old, fired two bullets into his wife's brain; she had Alzheimer's disease and osteoporosis, which left her "disoriented and racked with pain." Gilbert was tried for first-degree murder. He was convicted, and the judge sentenced him to twenty-five years in prison.[80] Gilbert spent five years in prison; he was granted clemency in 1990.[81] The case was the subject of a TV movie in 1987, *Mercy or Murder*, which starred Robert Young as Gilbert.

In another 1985 case, Dr. John Kraai, a seventy-six-year-old doctor in Fairport, New York, injected a lethal drug into an eighty-one-year-old friend, Frederick

[77] Joseph D. Whitaker, "Daughter Freed after Mercy Killing of Father," *Washington Post*, May 24, 1979, p. A1.
[78] "Va. Woman, 69, Gets Probation in Mercy Killing," *Washington Post*, Aug. 23, 1985, p. D3.
[79] http://USnews.nbcnews.com/_newsd/2013/03/29/17515683
[80] "Man Convicted of Killing Wife Who Begged to Die," *New York Times*, May 10, 1985. The judge said he was "not without sympathies, but I am sworn to uphold the law."
[81] "Roswell Gilbert, 85, Who Killed His Ill Wife and Went to Prison," *New York Times*, Sept. 8, 1994.

Wagner, a retired farmer. Wagner had Alzheimer's disease and "severe gangrene on his legs," which would probably have meant amputation. Dr. Kraai, a "legend" in his community, had delivered more than 5,000 babies and was considered a kind, empathetic doctor. He was arrested and charged with murder. Three weeks later, he was found dead, leaving behind a suicide note. At a memorial service packed with people, he was declared a "living saint," the "Mother Teresa of Fairport." But the district attorney felt he had been almost compelled to bring charges: "no individual can decide what is an appropriate time to end another person's life."[82] Dr. Kraai was not the only "mercy killer" who chose suicide. In July 1977, Dr. Guy Shearman Peterkin, described as a "prominent urologist," thinking his son (after a "nervous breakdown") was "suffering from an incurable malady," shot the son to death; the newspapers described his act as a "mercy killing." Dr. Peterkin then took his own life.[83]

In 2012, John Wise, a former steelworker, shot his wife, Barbara, in her hospital room. She was sixty-six and had apparently suffered a triple aneurysm; the husband's lawyer claimed he acted to ease his wife's "agony, desperation and pain." He may have intended to shoot himself afterward, but the gun jammed. A grand jury in Akron, Ohio, charged him with aggravated murder. The press seemed to buy the theory that John was a quiet, devoted husband driven to despair by the suffering of his wife. The *New York Times* cited a comment from an expert on aging. According to the expert, the "numbers" of such acts, though "rare now," could rise in the future, as people lived longer and the generation of baby boomers would swell the population. John Wise went to trial, was convicted, and sentenced to six years in prison. He died while serving his sentence.[84]

In 1985, the police, nationally, reported twenty cases of supposed mercy killings. This may seem like a small number – and it was – but it amounted to something of an increase, since in the sixty-year period between 1925 and 1985, there were only twenty cases officially recorded. In a country the size of the United States, mercy killings were, in any event, only a minor problem in any statistical sense. But behind the figures, there were long-term trends that reflected important cultural and social processes. People were living longer lives. On the whole, these were better and healthier lives. But sometimes – and more and more often – people outlived a meaningful life. Medical science had made striking advances. This was wonderful news in most regards. But it also meant that doctors and hospitals could extend life artificially, sometimes to the point where it seemed to make no sense. They could keep patients alive who were, to be blunt, better off dead (at least in the opinion of

[82] Dirk Johnson, "Village Mourns Doctor Some Saw as a Saint," *New York Times*, Sept. 20, 1985.
[83] "Doctor Slays Son in 'Mercy Killing,'" *New York Times*, July 24, 1977.
[84] Ray Rivera, "Ohio Man's Shooting of Ailing Wife Raises Questions about 'Mercy Killings,'" *New York Times*, Aug. 24, 2012; for sentencing, see John Wise, "Ohio Man Gets 6 Years in Wife's 'Mercy Killing,'" CBS Crimesider, Dec. 13, 2013, available at www.cbsnews.com/news/john-wise-ohio-man-gets-6-years-in-wifes-mercy-killing/; for his death, see "Ohio Inmate Dies while Serving Time for Shooting Ailing Wife in Akron Hospital Bed," Associated Press/Cleveland.com, July 15, 2014.

family, friends, and perhaps the patient himself). This meant sharper and more frequent discussions of end-of-life issues. The hospice movement was one response. "Palliative care" was a new medical specialty, a mode of dealing with very ill, indeed, hopelessly ill, patients.

Many, if not most, people probably had no objection to lethal dosing, from either a legal or a moral point of view. The alternatives were dreadful: a slow, tortured death, at great expense to the taxpayers or the patient; or dreary scenes in nursing homes; or crushing burdens on caregivers. Medical expenses could add to these crushing burdens. Older people, if they had no family support, could live lives of terrifying isolation. Degenerative diseases slowly nibbled them to death. Horrific end-of-life dilemmas, in the twenty-first century, were a stark reality for millions of people. Probably no family of any size escaped the issue.

PULLING THE PLUG

In our times, mercy killing (including lethal dosing) still exists, and still exists in the shadows. One analogous situation has become a major legal and political issue. The patient is in a coma and, medically speaking, has lapsed into a kind of vegetative state; the doctors feel that there is no chance of recovery or even improvement. The patient is, in some sense, still alive. The heart beats. There is a feeding tube, and perhaps a ventilator. Can we and should we "pull the plug?" No doubt, most of the time, the plug *is* pulled; the grieving family, seeing a hopeless situation, agrees. Treatment ends, and the patient quietly dies. These patients, after all, are already dead, or brain dead, or at least not alive in any meaningful sense. The family buries its dead and moves on.

In a few spectacular cases, however, a major conflict erupts. The family refuses to give up or is split on the issue. Or doctors or hospitals refuse, sometimes because they are afraid of liability or of legal consequences. This was true in the case of Karen Quinlan (1975). Quinlan was a young woman, in a coma, with no real hope of any improvement. Her parents wanted to remove her respirator. The hospital was reluctant – a local prosecutor threatened legal action. The parents had to go to court to get permission to take steps to end Quinlan's life.[85] Later, in Missouri, a furious legal battle raged around the helpless body of Nancy Beth Cruzan, injured in a car accident in 1983.[86] At first, she appeared to be dead, but paramedics were able to kindle at least a minimal spark of life, and she was put on a life support system. For years, Nancy Cruzan lived in that twilight world of a "persistent

---

[85] *Matter of Quinlan*, 355 A.2d 647 (New Jersey, 1976). The case is discussed in Howard Ball, *At Liberty to Die* (New York: New York University Press, 2012), pp. 32–36. Ironically, when the respirator was removed, everybody expected that Karen would simply die, and quickly (although she was still getting nutrition). In fact, she lived for another ten years, until 1985. See also Rothman, *Strangers at the Bedside*, pp. 222–234.

[86] Ball, *At Liberty to Die*, pp. 37–47.

vegetative state." There was no improvement, or any hope that she would get better. By 1988, her distraught parents had had enough. They asked the hospital to end artificial feeding and hydration. The hospital refused to do any such thing without a court order. A lower court was willing, but there was bitter opposition; on appeal, the Missouri Supreme Court reversed. Missouri, according to its Supreme Court, required "clear and convincing evidence" that Nancy Cruzan would have wanted to have the tubes removed. No such evidence had been presented. From there, the case went to the very top, the U.S. Supreme Court, which affirmed the Missouri decision, five to four.[87] In some ways, it was a fairly narrow decision. The Court simply held that the criterion laid down by the high court of Missouri was not a violation of anybody's constitutional rights; for this reason, the Court refused to disturb the Missouri decision.

That was not the end, however. The family went back to court, this time to show what they claimed was in fact clear and convincing evidence of what Nancy would have wanted. This time a lower court judge decided that, yes, "clear and convincing evidence" showed that Nancy would have rejected life in a "vegetative state." The tubes were removed. The battle over Nancy's life, which had raged for years, continued until the very end. A minister from Florida appealed to the federal courts, asking for an order to reconnect the tubes.[88] This last-ditch effort failed. Nancy Cruzan died twelve days after the feeding tube was removed.[89]

Later courts faced similar issues and reached variable results. The most notorious and hotly contested instance was the case of Terri Schiavo.[90] Schiavo, who was twenty-seven and married, suffered cardiac arrest in 1990; for twelve minutes, her brain was cut off from oxygen, and she lapsed into a coma, which then turned into a vegetative state. Like Nancy Cruzan, she was kept more or less alive by virtue of a tube that fed her and provided hydration. Her husband, Michael, after eight years of this, petitioned the local Florida court for permission to remove the tubes. Terri's devoutly religious parents objected. Both the *legal* issues and the *policy* issues turned into matters of fiery controversy. In the background, of course, was the great debate over the "right to life," centered very often on abortion. Religious conservatives, both Catholic and Protestant, objected vigorously to any action that could even remotely be construed as killing someone. All these difficult policy issues had somehow come to a head in this instance and a furious personal and political struggle raged, over the

[87] *Cruzan v. Director, Missouri Department of Health*, 497 U. S. 261 (1990); for a discussion, see, in addition to Ball, *At Liberty to Die*, Anne Marie Gaudin, "Cruzan v. Director, Missouri Department of Health: To Die or Not to Die: That Is the Question – But Who Decides?" *Louisiana Legal Review* 51 (1991), p. 1307.

[88] Other religious leaders, however, "urged protesters to stop trying to force the state to resume intravenous feeding" ("End Fight on Dying Woman, Churches Urge," *New York Times*, Dec. 23, 1990).

[89] Tamar Lewin, "Nancy Cruzan Dies, Outlived by a Debate over the Right to Die," *New York Times*, Dec. 27, 1990.

[90] Ball, *At Liberty to Die*, pp. 51–66.

pitiful figure of Terri Schiavo, lying in bed in a vegetative state, attached to a feeding tube. The struggle lasted for years. The courts, of course, were major players in the drama. But the governor and legislature of Florida, the U.S. Congress, and even the president (George Bush) had their say as well – all of these on the side of the parents. Yet in the end, it was the husband – and the courts – who prevailed; the feeding tube was removed, and Terri Schiavo died quietly in March 2005.

There is no definitive, satisfying solution to the problem of those who lie in a vegetative state, helpless, unable to move or speak or feel, half dead and half alive. Or perhaps three-quarters dead. No legal solution, no political solution, no human solution. The problem refuses to go away. No doubt, the plug is quietly pulled every day, and many times, when all the players in the immediate circle of the drama – notably doctors, hospitals, and family members – agree. One doctor, Michael Halberstam, wrote in 1975 (about the Quinlan case) that every day "hundreds, perhaps thousands, of similar dilemmas present themselves"; they are "difficult, often agonizing," but they get resolved "in hospital corridors and in waiting rooms, not courts." The Quinlan case was a "failure of the usual."[91] This was almost surely the case. The *New York Times* reported an estimate, by the American Hospital Association, that 70 percent of all hospital deaths "are ... negotiated in some way," with an agreement to end life-support treatment, or not to begin it in the first place.[92] Most people want to live, of course, but in a "vegetative" state? Aside from ideology, why would anybody choose this kind of existence?

It is generally agreed, by the courts as well as by laypeople, that it would be a good thing if people decided for themselves. But of course you cannot decide anything if you are lying in a coma. One (partial) solution is to execute a document that at least *tries* to tell family and friends and doctors and hospital what we would like if we were in Nancy Cruzan's position. Whether these documents help is another question.

ASSISTED SUICIDE

In a handful of states (six, at the date of this writing), there is another twist to the story – the state has authorized assisted suicide. In orthodox mercy killings, the act is done, either by a doctor, or a member of the family, in response to the patient's wish. Assisted suicide cannot be called a form of mercy killing; rather, it might be called mercy suicide, and the moving actor is the "victim" herself.

But why legalize assisted suicide? Thousands of people commit suicide every year, for whatever reason – 42,773 in 2014, according to the National Center for Health Statistics; nothing prevents a sufferer from jumping off a bridge or otherwise ending a life that no longer seems worth living. Many old, sick people end their lives when their physical problems become more than they can bear or when they receive news

[91] Rothman, *Strangers at the Bedside*, p. 228.   [92] Lewin, "Nancy Cruzan Dies."

of a fatal, progressive illness. Still, suicide is on the whole socially illegitimate. It can leave behind a trail of guilt and regret, and there are few easy, pain-free ways to do it.

Assisted suicide differs from plain suicide in that it is social, open, legitimate, and has the explicit approval of the state. Mercy killing, as Shai Lavi pointed out, was often justified as a way out, not only for the patient, but also for the patient's suffering and heavily burdened family. Assisted suicide lifts some of this burden – and does it in an approved and legal manner. Suicide is often an impulsive act; assisted suicide is slow, deliberate, and even, to a degree, ceremonial. It fits in too with a strong norm of personal autonomy.

The movement to get legal approval for assisted suicide had its first success in the 1990s; the idea was quite a bit older. Euthanasia had been discussed, as we mentioned, for many years. It had always had proponents. The Euthanasia Society of America (ESA) was founded in 1938.[93] Until the 1960s, the organization had focused on promoting "active" euthanasia – what we think of now as assisted suicide. The organization was not particularly successful; by 1962, it had only 325 members.[94] At this point, the organization began to shift its policy focus; it emphasized "passive" euthanasia, such as the right to demand withdrawal of care. Joseph Fletcher, writing in 1954, saw "no real moral difference between self-administered euthanasia and the medically administered form when it is done at the patient's request."[95] Indeed, if lethal dosing and refusing treatment are accep-table, it is not clear why assisted suicide should be taboo. Even the pope in 1957 was willing to concede that it might be acceptable for a person to refuse "extraordinary medical treatment" (though the Church remains adamantly opposed to assisted suicide).[96]

At any rate the ESA, together with its tax-exempt charitable branch, the Euthanasia Educational Fund (later called Concern for the Dying), began to emphasize education and awareness – for example, helping people with "living wills." In the 1970s, the word "euthanasia" was not in good odor (it had overtones of Nazis and eugenics). The ESA changed its name to the Society for the Right to Die.[97] The new name had a better ring to it; the "right to die" sounded almost like a civil liberty – an extension of other human rights. Or so it could be argued.[98]

In 1980, Derek Humphry, a British journalist, founded the Hemlock Society. Humphry had written a book, *Jean's Way*, in which he told how he helped his first

[93] Dowbiggin, *A Merciful End* is a standard work on the history of the movement.   [94] Ibid., p. 107.
[95] Joseph Fletcher, *Morals and Medicine* (Boston, MA: Beacon Press, 1954), p. 184. Fletcher was an ordained minister and a sometime professor of theology.
[96] The pope's address can be found in James T. McHugh, ed., *Death, Dying and the Law* (1976), p. 72.
[97] Both Dowbiggin and Gorsuch note that revelations of Nazi euthanasian practices were a source of backlash; see Neil M. Gorsuch, *The Future of Assisted Suicide and Euthanasia* (Princeton, NJ: Princeton University Press, 2006), pp. 36–38.
[98] The Society for the Right to Die also merged with its offshoot, Concern for the Dying; the new organization was called Choice in Dying. And Choice in Dying became Partnership for Caring in 2000.

wife, Jean, to die. She had been in the last stages of breast cancer.[99] The Hemlock Society grew rapidly. It had dozens of local chapters by the 1990s, and thousands of active members.[100] The AIDS crisis helped Hemlock gain popularity. Between 1988 and 1990, during the height of this epidemic, Hemlock doubled its membership.[101] The Hemlock Society changed its name again in 2004 to End of Life Choices; it then merged with an organization formed in 1993 in Washington State, called Compassion in Dying. The new group was called Compassion and Choices.[102] This organization is very much a going concern. It played a role in the adoption of the Oregon law on assisted suicide, through a political action committee; it fought too in other states. Its letterhead states its goal as "Care and Choice at the End of Life."

No state had ever passed an assisted suicide law before 1994. In 1991, Washington voters narrowly turned down a measure that would have allowed doctors to help terminal patients to end their lives, if that was their wish. Then the breakthrough came in Oregon.[103] The legislature obviously felt the law was too hot to handle; the Death with Dignity Act actually became law through the referendum process. The vote, as it turned out, was quite close.

The Oregon law was cautious and carefully drafted. It specifically ruled out mercy killing: no "physician or any other person" had the authority "to end a patient's life by lethal injection, mercy killing, or active euthanasia."[104] That authority was vested exclusively in the patient. And the law applied only to a "capable" adult, who was a resident of Oregon, and who was "suffering from a terminal disease." To get medication that would end life "in a humane and dignified manner," the patient had to make "an oral request and a written request," and repeat the request to an "attending physician" no less than fifteen days after making the initial oral request. A doctor or organization or institution that takes part in an assisted suicide, and that follows the dictates of the law, is immune from civil or criminal liability. Since 1994, five more states – Washington, Montana, Vermont, California, and Colorado – have adopted a "death with dignity law." Six states is not nothing, but it is hardly a groundswell. Still, all of this is quite recent and may indicate a trend.

The battle for assisted suicide has been waged in the legislature, in the courts, and out in public (through referenda). As Alexis de Tocqueville long ago pointed out,

99   The book was originally published in 1978; it was reprinted and republished and became a bestseller some years later. The story is told in Derek Humphry and Mary Clement, *Freedom to Die: People, Politics, and the Right-to-Die Movement* (New York: St. Martin's Press, 1998), pp. 105–107.

100 Humphry became a controversial figure following his divorce from his second wife in 1989; she had helped him found the Hemlock Society, and he had helped her parents commit suicide. She successfully recovered from her own bout with cancer, but then committed suicide, leaving notes that suggested that Humphry was a "killer" and that he had wanted her to die. He then retired from the group and focused on writing. See Dowbiggin, *A Merciful End*, p. 151.

101 Dowbiggin, *A Merciful End*, p. 153.

102 Gorsuch, *The Future of Assisted Suicide and Euthanasia*, p. 221.

103 Mich. Laws § 730.329a; on the history of the movement, see Ball, *At Liberty to Die*.

104 O.R.S. § 127.800–897.

political and social issues in the United States almost inevitably find their way into the courts. Assisted suicide has been no exception. The opponents took their fight to the federal courts. They lost. The Ninth Circuit upheld the Oregon law in 1997.[105] The opponents had concocted a strange brew of claims, including freedom of religion and freedom of association. The court, however, pointed out that they had no real standing to complain; the law had not caused *them* any harm, nor was it likely to do so. Of course, their real argument was that the law was evil and harmful to society. They had already lost that battle at the ballot box. Later that same year, they tried again at the polls. They ran ads that warned about the law's awful consequences: it would "spur kids to kill themselves in droves." The attorney general of the United States then tried a different tactic. He used his powers, under the Controlled Substances Act, to forbid anyone from prescribing drugs for the purpose of assisted suicide. But in 2006, the Supreme Court overturned this decision, and rejected his action.[106]

The Supreme Court has never ruled directly on the subject of assisted suicide. In 1997, the Court did consider two cases that were more or less relevant, *Washington v. Glucksberg*[107] and *Vacco v. Quill*,[108] from Washington State and New York State, respectively.[109] Both states had old statutes on their books that outlawed any form of assisted suicide. The Washington statute made it a crime "knowingly" to cause or to help a person to commit suicide. A group of doctors in the state claimed they "occasionally treat terminally ill, suffering patients," and would like to "assist these patients in ending their lives," but the statute stood in the way. They argued that the ban deprived them of "liberty," in violation of the Fourteenth Amendment.

Essentially, this was an argument for a constitutional right to die, with your doctor's help. The Supreme Court saw no such right. According to Chief Justice Rehnquist, who wrote the majority opinion, a "fundamental" right, a right anchored in the constitution, had to be something "deeply rooted in . . . history and tradition." Many states had turned down assisted suicide laws, and public opinion seemed to be against these laws. Indeed, in 1997, the Federal Assisted Suicide Funding Act banned the use of federal funds for "physician-assisted suicide." The Court, however, did not in any way suggest that the Oregon statute (which was, of course, not before it) raised any constitutional issues.

In the *Vacco* case, decided on the same day as the Washington case, the Court upheld the New York ban on assisted suicide. Here too doctors wanted the right to "prescribe lethal medication" for their patients, if those patients were competent,

---

[105] *Lee* v. *Oregon*, 107 F.3d 1382 (9th Cir. 1997).
[106] *Gonzalez* v. *Oregon*, 546 U.S. 243 (2006). The decision was complex and technical; perhaps the heart of it was the argument that the attorney general, under existing statutes, had no power to intervene in this matter.
[107] 521 U.S. 702 (1997).   [108] 521 U.S. 793 (1997).
[109] For a general discussion of these cases, see Melvin I. Urofsky, *Lethal Judgments: Assisted Suicide and American Law* (Lawrence: University Press of Kansas, 2000), pp. 130–153.

terminally ill, "suffering great pain," and wanted "a doctor's help in taking their own lives."[110] In this case, the doctors referred to the Equal Protection clause of the Fourteenth Amendment. New York allowed patients to "refuse life sustaining medical treatment"; this, they claimed, was "essentially the same thing" as "physician assisted suicide." The inconsistency, it was argued, amounted to a violation of equal protection. But the Court disagreed. There is a distinction, the Court said, between helping somebody commit suicide and ending medical treatment. This distinction is "widely recognized and endorsed in the medical profession and in our legal tradition." Indeed, Washington State (for example) had in 1979 enacted a law, the Natural Death Act, which declared that "withholding or withdrawal of life-sustaining treatment," at the direction of a patient, is not to be considered suicide "for any purpose."

For several years, Oregon was the only state to recognize assisted suicide. In 1998, a "Physician Aid in Dying" law, proposed by an organization in Michigan, was roundly defeated at the polls – 71 percent voted no.[111] But in 2008, Washington State followed the lead of Oregon, also through a ballot measure.[112] Vermont[113] and California[114] followed suit in 2013 and 2015, respectively, through legislation. The laws in these states were modeled on the Oregon statute, and followed it closely, including the timing of oral and written requests, and the involvement of a second, consulting physician. Much of the language is very similar or even identical across these acts.

Montana followed a different path; assisted suicide reached Montana, not through legislative action, but through a court case in 2009. The named plaintiff, Robert Baxter, was a retired truck driver, "terminally ill" and suffering greatly from "lymphocytic leukemia with diffuse lymphadenopathy"; he had "no prospect of recovery." Baxter wanted "the option of ingesting a lethal dose of medication prescribed by his physician and self-administered at the time of Mr. Baxter's own choosing." He was backed in the case by four doctors, as well as by Compassion and Choices.

The Montana Supreme Court ruled in favor of Baxter. Under Montana law, the court said, "consent" can act as a valid defense against a criminal charge, unless the "conduct or the resulting harm" is "against public policy." Also, the law in Montana provided that a doctor who followed a patient's "directions to withhold or withdraw

---

[110]   *Vacco*, at 797.
[111]   The opposition was led and financed by the Catholic Conference, which outspent the proponents by a large margin. The Michigan voters "rejected by a 3-to-1 margin Proposal B," which would have legalized assisted suicide. *Detroit Free Press*, May 29, 2007, p. A-10. The organization in favor of the proposal was "Merian's Friends," an organization named after Merian Frederick of Ann Arbor, Michigan, who suffered from "Lou Gehrig's disease" (ALS) and who took her life with the help of Dr. Jack Kevorkian. CNN Interactive, "Michigan Group May Bring Physician-Assisted Suicide to Vote," Mar. 3, 1998, www.cnn.com/US/9803/03/assisted.suicide/index.html, visited Jan. 18, 2018).
[112]   See Wash. Rev. Code Ann. §§ 70.245.050-904 (West).
[113]   See Vt. Stat. Ann. tit. 18, §§ 5281–5293 (West).   [114]   Cal. Health & Safety Code § 443 (West).

life-sustaining treatment," would be immune from "criminal and civil liability." This law, said the court, made patients who were terminally ill "entitled to autonomous, end-of-life decisions, even if enforcement of those decisions involves direct acts by a physician."[115] The court dodged any constitutional issue and rested its decision on its interpretation of the statute. Legislation to undo the case and to make assisted suicide once more a crime passed the lower house in Montana, but stalled in the state senate.[116]

Brittany Maynard was a California woman who moved to Oregon to take advantage of that state's Death with Dignity Act. She had terminal brain cancer and committed suicide at the age of twenty-nine in 2014.[117] She had been active in the assisted suicide movement; she had worked with Compassion and Choices, and she tried to reach a mass audience, spreading the word through the media, YouTube, and Facebook.[118] She had recorded video testimony for the California assembly, and the video was shown at hearings on the California bill to legalize assisted suicide.[119] One of the authors of the bill talked about a "sea change in public opinion"; Brittany's willingness to be "public and courageous" had, in his opinion, a real impact.[120]

Brittany Maynard's efforts were also a factor in New York, New Jersey, and Connecticut.[121] In New Jersey, a Death with Dignity Act was proposed in 2014; a poll found that 63 percent of the voters supported the idea. The governor was against the law, however, and the act never became law.[122] New York has not passed as yet any legislation on the subject.[123] In 2012, Massachusetts voters rejected assisted suicide 51 percent to 49 percent; polls had suggested it would pass, but in the end it failed narrowly. After Brittany Maynard died, a state representative introduced new legislation, specifically citing Brittany Maynard's experience.[124] On November 8, 2016, the voters of Colorado approved Proposition 106, closely modeled on the Oregon law. This brought the number of states to six.

---

[115] *Baxter* v. *State*, 224 P.3d 1211, 1222 (Mt. 2009).

[116] Associated Press, "Senate Panel Rejects Making Physician Suicide a Crime," *The Missoulian*, Apr. 1, 2015.

[117] Melody Gutierrez, "Reports: Right-to-Die Advocate Brittany Maynard Dies," *San Francisco Chronicle*, Nov. 2, 2014, www.sfgate.com/news/article/Reports-Right-to-die-advocate-Brittany-Maynard-5865382.php.

[118] Anthony Zurcher, "A Cancer Patient's Decision to Die," BBC News, Oct. 10, 2014; Josh Sanburn, "Brittany Maynard Could Revive the Stalled 'Death with Dignity' Movement," *Time*, Nov. 1, 2014.

[119] Melody Gutierrez, "Assisted-Death Bill Passes State Senate Committee," *San Francisco Chronicle*, Mar. 25, 2015.

[120] Ibid.

[121] See, e.g., Lindsey Bever, "How Brittany Maynard May Change the Right-to-Die Debate," *Washington Post*, Nov. 3, 2014.

[122] "Editorial: Coming Soon to Gov. Christie's Desk: The Right-to-Die Debate," *Star-Ledger*, Oct. 6, 2015; Patrick T. Brown, "Push for Legalizing Assisted Suicide Stalls Out in New Jersey Senate," *National Catholic Reporter*, Jan. 19, 2016.

[123] Brittany's husband, Daniel Diaz, lobbied for the bill.

[124] Colleen Quinn, "Renewed Interest in 'Death with Dignity' Law for Massachusetts," *22 News*, Feb. 17, 2015; Sanburn, "Brittany Maynard Could Revive the Stalled 'Death with Dignity' Movement."

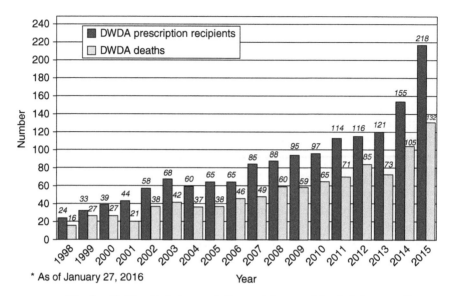

FIGURE 4.1 Death with Dignity Act prescription recipients and deaths*, by year, Oregon, 1998–2015

ASSISTED SUICIDE IN PRACTICE

Oregon's law was passed in 1994, but an injunction prevented it from going into effect until late 1997; data on the impact of the statute begin only in 1998. As Figure 4.1 shows, use of the law has grown steadily over the years.[125] The state reports that 78 percent of patients who actually took the drugs were over sixty-five, well educated, and white. (The median age over the 1998–2014 period is seventy-one years old.) More than 90 percent died at home and had hospice care. Most had been suffering from cancer.[126] The Washington experience is very similar to Oregon's. In 2014, 176 Washington citizens were prescribed lethal drugs, of whom 126 actually took the medication. Just as in Oregon, most were white, educated (76 percent had at least some college education), and died at home. And most were victims of cancer.[127] Figure 4.2 summarizes the facts about the Washington's Act.

Why did people choose assisted suicide? In both Oregon and Washington, people gave as their reasons, first, loss of ability to do things that make life enjoyable, second, loss of autonomy, and, third, loss of dignity.[128] Surprisingly, in the light of the history

[125] Oregon Public Health Division, *Oregon Death with Dignity Act: 2015 Data Summary*, http://public .health.oregon.gov/ProviderPartnerResources/EvaluationResearch/DeathwithDignityAct/ Documents/year18.pdf.

[126] Ibid. at 4.

[127] Washington State Department of Health, 2014 Death with Dignity Act Report at 1, www.doh.wa.gov /portals/1/Documents/Pubs/422-109-DeathWithDignityAct2014.pdf.

[128] See Oregon Report at 4; Washington Report at 7.

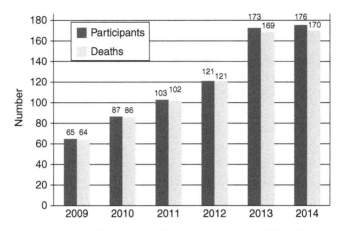

FIGURE 4.2 Washington State Participants and Deaths

of mercy killing, only 22 percent of those who asked to die, according to a recent study, mentioned fear of the pain of their illness.

What does the American public think of assisted suicide? In a 2013 study by the Pew research group, 47 percent of the respondents were in favor of legalization, 49 percent were opposed; the numbers were basically the same as in a survey taken in 2005.[129] A Gallup poll suggests that a lot depends on the way the question is worded; 70 percent supported permitting a physician to "end the patient's life by some painless means," but only 51 percent supported physicians helping a patient "commit suicide."[130] (The Pew survey used the word "suicide," which may explain why its results are close to the results of the Gallup poll that used the word). The Pew survey suggests that support for legalization is *not* a matter of age or stage of life. Among young people eighteen to twenty-nine years old, 45 percent approved of assisted suicide; 54 percent were against.[131] Perhaps Americans are more conflicted on this issue than people in other countries. This seems to be true, for example, of Canada, though in Canada too a lot depends on how survey questions are worded.[132]

[129] "Opinion about Laws on Doctor Assisted Suicide," Pew Research Center (Nov. 21, 2013), www .pewforum.org/2013/11/21/chapter-1-opinion-about-laws-on-doctor-assisted-suicide/.
[130] Lydia Saad, "U.S. Support for Euthanasia Hinges on How It's Described," Gallup (May 29, 2013), www.gallup.com/poll/162815/support-euthanasia-hinges-described.aspx.
[131] Michael Lipka, "Americans of All Ages Divided over Doctor-Assisted Suicide Laws," Pew Research Center (Oct. 22, 2014), www.pewresearch.org/fact-tank/2014/10/22/americans-of-all-ages-divided-over-doctor-assisted-suicide-laws/.
[132] Isabelle Marcoux, Brian L. Mishara, and Claire Durand, "Confusion between Euthanasia and Other End-of-Life Decisions: Influences on Public Opinion Poll Results," *Canadian Journal of Public Health* 98:3 (2007).

THE OPPOSITION

Opposition remains strong – to assisted suicide, to "lethal dosing," and to mercy killing. The Catholic Church remains unalterably opposed to all of these. Eli Stutsman, who drafted the Oregon law, told a magazine that "[y]ou could put this issue on the ballot anywhere in the country, and if there were no political campaigns organized around the issue, it would pass in every state. But if you look at where the money comes from and the political expertise and organization, it's always the Catholic Church."[133] The Church, or "individuals associated with it," provided $4,000,000 in the campaign to defeat the ballot measure in Massachusetts (2012). The Vatican also specifically criticized Brittany Maynard, and denounced assisted suicide as "an absurdity."[134] The U.S. Conference of Catholic Bishops called assisted suicide a "threat to human dignity" and proposed, instead, an emphasis on palliative care.[135]

Many laypeople agree with the Church's position. Neil Gorsuch, who is now a member of the U.S. Supreme Court, earlier wrote a learned book in opposition to assisted suicide and euthanasia. He based his view on the principle that life is "inviolable," that life is a good, an end in itself, and that life should not, under any circumstances, be intentionally destroyed. "[P]rivate intentional acts of homicide are always wrong." If you treat human life "as intrinsically, not instrumentally valuable," this would "rule out assisted suicide and euthanasia."[136] Many doctors too express disapproval. The American Medical Association (AMA) has officially stated that "Physician assisted suicide is fundamentally inconsistent with the physician's professional role."[137] The AMA submitted amicus briefs in *Glucksberg* and *Quill*, arguing that "physician-assisted suicide" was "incompatible with the physician's role as healer."[138] When, later, the Massachusetts Medical Society opposed legalizing assisted suicide, its president used identical language.[139] The *New England Journal of Medicine* surveyed its U.S. readers (who presumably all worked in health care); 67 percent were against the idea of physician-assisted suicide for a seventy-two-year-old man suffering from terminal pancreatic cancer.[140] But a 1995 study in Oregon found that 60 percent of physicians in that state who were "qualified

[133] Sanburn, "Brittany Maynard Could Revive the Stalled 'Death With Dignity' Movement."
[134] "Vatican Official Condemns Maynard Assisted Suicide Case in U.S.," Reuters, Nov. 4, 2014.
[135] "To Live Each Day with Dignity: A Statement on Physician-Assisted Suicide," U.S. Conference of Bishops, June 16, 2011.
[136] Gorsuch, *The Future of Assisted Suicide and Euthanasia*, p. 218.
[137] American Medical Association, H-140.952 Physician Assisted Suicide, www.ama-assn.org/ssl3/ecomm/PolicyFinderForm.pl?site=www.ama-assn.org&uri=/resources/html/PolicyFinder/policyfiles/HnE/H-140.952.HTM.
[138] Yale Kamisar, "The Rise and Fall of the 'Right' to Assisted Suicide," in Kathleen Foley and Hubert Hendin, eds. *The Case against Assisted Suicide* (Baltimore, MD: John Hopkins University Press, 2002), p. 88.
[139] Quinn, "Renewed Interest in 'Death with Dignity' Law for Massachusetts."
[140] James A. Colbert, Joann Schulte, and Jonathan N. Adler, "Physician-Assisted Suicide – Polling Results," *New England Journal of Medicine* (2013).

to serve as attending physicians" within the meaning of the Oregon law thought assisted suicide "should be legal in some cases," and nearly half were willing to prescribe a fatal dose of medication, provided it was legal to do so.[141] The California Medical Association shifted from opposing legalization to being officially neutral during the debates over the bill.[142]

Some terminally ill patients and their advocates worry about possible pressure, or guilt-tripping, over end-of-life choices. In New Jersey, a terminally ill patient expressed the fear that "[t]he legal option to commit suicide with a physician's help would be perceived as an obligation by many terminally ill patients," if they felt they were "a burden to loved ones," and that it might encourage patients, even some with years to live, "to give up hope."[143] Critics also worried that legalization might have a bad effect on poor people and on members of marginalized communities; would they feel pressure to put an end to their lives, because that would be cheaper than the alternatives?[144] They cited the case of Barbara Wagner (2008). She lived in Oregon and had state-provided insurance; she had late-stage cancer and wanted to take an expensive experimental drug. The insurance company (it was said) refused to pay for the drug, but it did offer to cover the cost of assisted-suicide drugs – about $50.[145] Compassion and Choices claimed that the insurance company probably would have covered hospice and palliative care, hence the situation was not so bad as it was made out to be.[146] There is also often fear that, in states like Oregon, the mentally ill would feel encouraged to commit suicide, rather than ask for treatment.[147]

Then there is the case of Efren Saldivar. Saldivar, a respiratory therapist, confessed to killing up to fifty patients at the hospital where he worked. The hospital fired him. The police at first had no choice but to release him; they had no evidence to back up his confession. The press called him the "angel of death." At various points, he admitted killing more than 100 patients. He also claimed he did this to reduce his workload and that he had talked others into killing patients. One of the hospitals he worked for suspended its entire respiratory therapist staff; after an investigation, it cleared them.[148] But at least a few of these workers apparently

---

[141] Katrina Hedberg and Susan W. Tolle, "Physician-Assisted Suicide and Changes in Care of the Dying," in Louis Snyder and Arthur L. Caplan, eds., *Assisted Suicide: Finding Common Ground* (Bloomington: Indiana University Press, 2002), p. 8.

[142] Ian Lovett, "California Legislature Approves Assisted Suicide," *New York Times*, Sep. 12, 2015.

[143] Patrick T. Brown, "Push for Legalizing Assisted Suicide Stalls Out in New Jersey Senate," *National Catholic Reporter*, Jan. 19, 2016.

[144] Lovett, "California Legislature Approves Assisted Suicide."

[145] Susan Donaldson James, "Death Drugs Cause Uproar in Oregon," ABC News, Aug. 6, 2008.

[146] Barbara Coombs Lee, "Sensationalizing a Sad Case Cheats the Public of Sound Debate," *The Oregonian*, Nov. 29, 2008.

[147] See, e.g., Stephen Mendelsohn, "Op-Ed: Assisted Suicide Would Be Fraught with Problems and Abuses," *CT Mirror*, Mar. 6, 2015; John B. Kelly, "Opinion: Assisted Suicide Laws Are More Dangerous Than People Acknowledge," *Star-Ledger*, Oct. 31, 2014.

[148] "22 Cleared in Hospital Mercy Killing Investigation," *New York Times*, Mar. 31, 1998.

suspected that Saldivar was up to no good, with a "magic syringe" and lethal drugs.[149] The police exhumed bodies to find proof that Saldivar's patients did not die natural deaths, but had been murdered by Saldivar. Saldivar was eventually sentenced to life without parole.[150]

Of course, Saldivar's crimes had nothing to do with mercy killing or assisted suicide laws. But a fog of suspicion does hang over the idea of making it easier to help people die. If those in favor of assisted suicide could point to Brittany Maynard, opponents could point to Dr. Jack Kevorkian. This man, "Dr. Death," helped polarize the debate. In a blaze of publicity, Kevorkian helped patients commit suicide. There was nothing quiet and refined about his behavior; he was not a cautious doctor pulling the plug. Kevorkian was irreverent, noisy, and eager for publicity. He was both loved and reviled, scorned and admired. He was even the subject of a movie, *You Don't Know Jack*, in which he was portrayed by Al Pacino.[151] Dr. Kevorkian used chemicals in his work, and also machines he had devised himself. He was happy to tell the press, in detail, what he had done.[152] His first suicide patient, who had Alzheimer's disease, died in 1990; Kevorkian claimed he helped 130 others in the following years.

The AMA was no fan of Dr. Kevorkian; it called him a "reckless instrument of death" in 1995.[153] It labeled him a "criminal" and a "killer" who "perverts the idea of the caring and committed physician." Kevorkian sued for defamation; there was a motion for summary judgment, but the trial court refused to grant it.[154] The appeals court reversed. Kevorkian, according to the court, was "possibly the best known and most controversial proponent of assisted suicide." This made him a public figure, and a "public figure" cannot sue for defamation, unless the defendant had lied deliberately or acted with "reckless disregard for the truth."[155] Besides, the subject of assisted suicide was a matter of great public interest; this made Kevorkian essentially "libel proof."[156] No doubt the court got it right, at least in the label it pinned on Jack Kevorkian. He lusted after publicity and inserted himself blatantly into the debates over assisted suicide.

[149]   Paul Lieberman, "'Angel of Death' Co-workers Targeted," *Los Angeles Times*, Mar. 14, 2002.
[150]   Paul Lieberman, "Hospital 'Angel of Death' Gets Life without Parole," *Los Angeles Times*, Apr. 18, 2002.
[151]   *You Don't Know Jack* (HBO Films, 2010).
[152]   Lisa Belkin, "Doctor Tells of First Death Using His Suicide Device," *New York Times*, June 6, 1990.
[153]   Keith Schneider, "Dr. Jack Kevorkian Dies at 83: A Doctor Who Helped End Lives," *New York Times*, June 3, 2011.
[154]   *Kevorkian v. Am. Med. Ass'n*, 602 N.W.2d 233, 235 (Mich. Ct. App. 1999).
[155]   This refers to the crucial decision *New York Times v. Sullivan*, 376 U. S. 254 (1964) and the cases that followed. See Kermit L. Hall and Melvin L. Urofsky, *New York Times v. Sullivan: Civil Rights, Libel Law, and the Free Press* (Lawrence: University Press of Kansas, 2011).
[156]   Basically, too, there was no chance the AMA statements could have an actual impact on his reputation (ibid). This seems correct: Kevorkian was too famous, too much in the center of the stage to be affected by the comments made by the AMA.

Kevorkian, whatever motivated him, was in constant hot water. He was put on trial, in fact, five times. The first three times, he was acquitted. The fourth trial resulted in a mistrial.[157] The fifth trial, however, was Kevorkian's undoing. At issue was the death of Thomas Youk, a fifty-two-year-old man who suffered from ALS (commonly known as Lou Gehrig's disease). Kevorkian himself injected Youk with lethal chemicals and taped the event; the tape was shown on the television show *60 Minutes*. (It is now available on YouTube.) With this video as key evidence, Kevorkian was brought to trial for premeditated murder in Michigan (in the previous trials, he was accused of assisting suicide, which was a separate and less serious offense). Kevorkian acted as his own lawyer at the trial (this is usually a mistake). He tried to introduce evidence to show that Youk had wanted to die. The judge refused to allow this evidence. Consent is not a defense to murder. Perhaps people approved of the general idea of assisted suicide, but Kevorkian's behavior and his methods were a naked challenge to the methods and aims of assisted suicide laws. Moreover, doctors were supposed to be like Dr. Sander, not like "Dr. Death." In this fifth trial, Kevorkian was convicted of second-degree murder, and also of use of a controlled substance. He was sentenced to a long prison term. After eight years in prison, Kevorkian was released. He promised to give up his role as "Dr. Death." He died four years later.[158]

Dr. Kevorkian scandalized large segments of the community. He shattered the quiet reality of mercy killing. Assisted suicide laws brought mercy killing (in a sense) into the open. But they did this carefully, discreetly, and hedged about with procedural safeguards. Dr. Kevorkian was a bomb thrower. That was not to be tolerated.

In previous chapters, we saw many examples of "crimes without punishment." Some were blatant and open: indeed, that was almost the point. Lynching is the prime example. Yet even with regard to lynch mobs, sheriffs and other authorities behaved in a crucial way; they quietly refused to prosecute and even insisted (against all evidence) that they had no idea who had led the lynch mob. The women who killed newborn babies were also secretive, quiet, restrained. Blatant, open behavior, defiance of conventional norms; these were never the case. And defendants who invoked the "unwritten law" hid behind such notions as temporary insanity. Dr. Kevorkian, however, thumbed his nose at proprieties, at an elaborate system of masks and screens. That led to his downfall.

---

[157] "Dr. Kevorkian's Client," *New York Times*, Mar. 25, 1999.
[158] The original charge was assisted suicide, as in the prior cases. But when the judge ruled that evidence of Youk's pain and suffering was permitted in a case of assisted suicide, but not in a murder case, the prosecutors dropped the idea of proceeding on an assisted suicide theory. On Kevorkian's trial, see Pam Belluck, "For Kevorkian, a Fifth but Very Different Trial," *New York Times*, Mar. 20, 1999; "Dr. Kevorkian's Luck Runs Out," *New York Times*, Mar. 27, 1999; "Jail Time for Dr. Kevorkian," *New York Times*, Apr. 15, 1999; "Kevorkian Stumbles in His Self-Defense," *New York Times*, Mar. 24, 1999. See also Fred Charatan, "Dr. Kevorkian Found Guilty of Second Degree Murder," *British Medical Journal*, Apr. 10, 1999; "Kevorkian Released after 8 Years," *Washington Post*, June 2, 2007, and Schneider, "Dr. Jack Kevorkian Dies at 83."

WHERE DO WE STAND?

At the present time, as we pointed out earlier, six states allow assisted suicide; the topic remains controversial; mercy killing is still illegal everywhere, but it continues, at least in the form of "lethal "dosing"; medical practices come close to the edge of euthanasia, and sometimes go beyond. But euthanasia is still in some ways taboo. The actual word surely is. But, of course, "passive" euthanasia is very common – intentionally withdrawing care, with the patient's consent, rather than prolonging suffering. Usually nobody knows this has happened. If nobody makes a fuss, the law takes no notice. Passive euthanasia, and even lethal dosing, remain, on the whole, crimes without punishment.[159]

The issue today cannot be separated from a bigger and broader one: how to deal with the sad and complex situations that arise at the end of life. Longevity has increased remarkably in the past century or so. A long life can be a blessing, can be rich, full, and healthy, and, somewhat surprisingly, a time of happiness and contentment. Yet life can also, at times, go on too long; it can become a burden, a long and drawn-out curse. What results is a human tragedy of incalculable proportions. The cost to society, in dollars, is calculable, but immense. Some help comes from the hospice movement and the development of "palliative care" as a medical specialty. The quality of life *can* be improved for people in the last act of the drama of life. But not always. And sometimes at great expense.[160]

Most people do not want to outlive meaningful mental and physical life. Also, they do not want to die in slow-motion agony. Lying in a hospital bed, attached to tubes, alive only in some technical sense: nobody wants this. People need to talk frankly, to family, friends, doctors, about the kind of end stage they would like: how, to be blunt, they want to die. This kind of conversation is tough. People put it off. It is painful for everybody. It is easier to put your wishes in writing. There are formal documents designed to do this. The most important, or at least the best known, is the Advanced Health Care Directive (AHCD). The states provide statutory forms, which anybody can print out and use. In theory, you can design your own. Most people simply take the official form and fill in the blanks.

An AHCD basically does two things: first, it gives agents the power and the right to make medical decisions if and when patients cannot do it on their own. Second, the document gives instructions to "health care providers and others involved in [one's] care" on how to deal with end-of-life situations. The California form gives two basic options: one is, essentially: do not prolong my life if it seems pointless, or if I am unconscious and will not wake up; or if I have an "incurable and irreversible condition" that will kill me "in a relatively short time." The other option is to

---

[159] See Gina Kolata, "'Passive Euthanasia' in Hospitals Is the Norm, Doctors Say," *New York Times*, June 28, 1997.

[160] Among the many books and articles on the subject, perhaps the best and most informative is Atul Gawande, *Being Mortal: Medicine and What Matters in the End* (New York: Henry Holt & Company, 2014).

prolong life "as long as possible within the limits of generally accepted medical treatment standards." The signer can change or revoke the form at any time.

The second form, less well known, is the Physician Orders for Life-Sustaining Treatment (POLST). This is also available in a statutory form, which can be printed out and used. The form states plainly that it is "a legally valid physician order." It is between a patient and a doctor. It "complements" the AHCD and "is not intended to replace that document." The POLST is more specific than the AHCD. The signer has choices for different situations and conditions – for example, if the patient "has no pulse and is not breathing," the signer can check a box that says, do not try to resuscitate; or a box that says, try it. The heart of the form is Section B, which provides three options (for patients who do have a pulse and are breathing). The options are "full treatment," "selective treatment," and "comfort-focused treatment."

No doubt these are helpful for some people, helpful in the sense that they provide a certain amount of peace of mind. But they raise almost as many problems as they solve. Unfortunately, situations at the end of life are so various, so complex, so full of dilemmas and uncertainties, that no document can really cope with all the problems that might arise. And do people understand what they are signing? "Full treatment" under POLST includes "intubation, advanced airway interventions, mechanical ventilation, and cardioversion." How many laypeople know what these things mean? Then there is the problem of family dynamics. POLST is "binding," but how binding is it in fact? If anxious, distraught family members disagree with the form, what is the doctor to do?

AHCD and POLST seem, on the surface, to have little or nothing to do with the history and practice of mercy killing, or assisted suicide for that matter. But if you dig a little deeper, you can find a connection. There is a long-term evolution, or rather coevolution, of science and culture, of medical skill and practice, on the one hand, and of a strong cultural shift toward personal autonomy, on the other. The organization Compassion and Choices, in letters to contributors (or potential contributors), talks about the "right to self-determination."[161]

In the early history of mercy killing, both in its eugenic phase and in the phase of "pure" mercy killing, and even when the patient presumably wanted to die, the focus was on another actor: a family member or a doctor. This actor made the ultimate decision. To be sure, there was an important difference between, say, Louis Repouille, putting to death his helpless son, who certainly never wanted to die, and the "orthodox" mercy killers, who responded to a request from a patient who actually did want to die. The latest theme is to empower the patient more directly. Assisted suicide, and the development of such forms as AHCD and POLST (however clumsy and imperfect) have, at their core, the idea of transferring that power, as much as possible, to the patient.

---

[161] Fund-raising letter, summer 2016, received by the author (and no doubt by tens of thousands of other people).

At one time, the concept of a "good death" (which is what "euthanasia" means in Greek) had religious overtones. A good death was a calm acceptance of fate. Suicide was a sin, if not a crime. It took death away from providence and put it in the hands of mere men and women. The Catholic Church continues to oppose suicide, including assisted suicide, for much the same reason. Life is sacred, no matter how minimal, no matter how truncated, no matter how debased. But the question is, sacred to whom? To the Church, it is and must be God, and God only, who chooses life or death.

To be sure, there are reasons besides religion to reject both mercy killing and assisted suicide. But these reasons themselves reflect the primacy, in our times, of the ideal of personal autonomy. Will a regime of assisted suicide put pressure on people? Will it add to the psychological burdens of handicapped people? Choice should be free and unfettered. In some cases, the "autonomy" has to be transferred from the patient. For a Nancy Cruzan or a Karen Quinlan, the question is: what would they have chosen? It is impossible to ask them, so the autonomy shifts to the surrogates. It does not shift, people feel, to the government. The government should not play a role.

In any event, "good death" now means a chosen death. Medical science is a double-edged sword; it can keep life going artificially; it can also cut it short. That is what assisted suicide – and for that matter, lethal dosing – is all about. Many people, millions of people (there is no way to count them), have the awful experience, for themselves or some family member, of facing an end-stage dilemma. They must decide, personally or for somebody else, whether to hang on to a truncated life or to welcome the final embrace of death. For these people, on the whole, mercy killing, lethal dosing, and assisted suicide are not crimes at all. Or, if they are still defined as crimes, they are or should be crimes without punishment.

5

Black Swans

In the earlier chapters, we discussed *patterns* of homicides that escaped punishment. Single cases can be idiosyncratic; patterns tell a story. Juries were quite consistent, for example, in using the unwritten law to excuse a man who killed his wife's lover. Vigilante action took place all over the West – there were hundreds of examples. Though a little less clear-cut, there were also patterns in cases of unmarried women who killed newborn babies, and in mercy killings. In this chapter, I want to consider what we could call "black swans," situations that are rare and extreme, and therefore fail to form a pattern. But the "black swans" of this chapter were also crimes without (significant) punishment.

A famous English case, *The Queen* v. *Dudley & Stephens*, decided in 1884, is one of our black swans.[1] Dudley and Stephens, the two defendants, had been adrift in a dinghy, "cast away in a storm on the high seas 1600 miles from the Cape of Good Hope."[2] They had been members of the crew of the *Mignonette*, a yacht bound for Australia, which sank in the south Atlantic, and left them stranded in a small boat in the trackless ocean. Four men were in the boat: Dudley and Stephens, a man named Ned Brooks, and a seventeen-year-old boy, Richard Parker. The four men were slowly starving to death.[3] Dudley and Stephens, desperate to save their own lives, decided to kill Parker, who was "lying at the bottom of the boat quite helpless, and extremely weakened by famine."[4] Brooks refused to go along with this plan. But Dudley and Stephens did the deed. Dudley, who was in charge, dispatched Parker, then the three survivors "fed upon the body and blood of the boy." This kept them alive for four days, at which point they were rescued by a passing ship and carried back to England. Here, somewhat to their surprise, they were put on trial for murdering Parker. Many people considered them heroes, and they were released on bail – something quite extraordinary for

---

[1] (1884) 14 Q.B.D. 273 (Eng.). A full account of this case, its background, and what followed, is in
    A. W. Brian Simpson, *Cannibalism and the Common Law* (Chicago: University of Chicago Press,
    1984).
[2] *Dudley & Stephens*, 14 Q.B.D. at 273.   [3] Ibid. at 273–274.   [4] Ibid.

men facing a murder charge.[5] At the trial, a jury found them guilty, which was, in a way, expected. After all, the basic facts were not in dispute. The sole question on appeal was a question of law. Had Dudley and Stephens committed a crime? They were in a desperate situation, dying of hunger: they killed out of "necessity," to save their lives; otherwise they would all have died. Could this be a valid defense in a murder trial?[6]

Emphatically not, according to the court. Lord Coleridge, who wrote the judgment, admitted that the men faced "terrible" temptations; they found themselves in a situation in which hardly anybody could be trusted to keep their conduct "pure," in other words, to follow the rules.[7] Still, he said, extreme and desperate conditions are not an excuse: "[w]e are often compelled to set up standards we cannot reach ourselves, and to lay down rules which we could not ourselves satisfy." There was no question in his mind but that the men were guilty of murder. Under English law, this meant the death sentence, and the judge duly imposed it with the usual formula: "hanged by the neck until . . . dead."[8]

Yet, as a matter of fact, the death sentence was never carried out. Indeed, people had expected all along that the men would be pardoned or that the sentence would be commuted. As it happened, in government circles, there was something of a dispute over exactly what to do. Technically, mercy was the prerogative of Queen Victoria; normally she followed the advice of the Home Secretary. After some delay, the Queen did commute the sentences; she reduced them to six months (though without hard labor). Even so, this was a "painful surprise" to the defendants and their families; they expected no punishment at all.[9] In any event, six months in prison is hardly a severe punishment for a case in which, originally, the death penalty was imposed. Here the formal rule remained intact; murder is murder, and the punishment for murder is death. The judge made this clear. To everyone – the government, the general public – it seemed somehow important to cling to the formal rule and to close their eyes to the fact that the rule was not really going to be applied.

Dudley and Stephens benefited from a kind of unwritten law. In extreme and desperate situations, the law bends and adjusts; it does this even when the charge is murder. The bending and adjusting, though, is not done openly. A jury might do it, or the executive (in England, the Queen and her advisers). But the bending and adjusting will definitely take place.

The trial of William Holmes in Philadelphia could be considered a kind of precedent for Dudley and Stephens. In 1841, an American ship, the *William*

[5] Simpson, *Cannibalism and the Common Law*, pp. 79–80. The case is usually considered unprecedented, almost one of a kind. Simpson has shown, however, that cases of cannibalism, in situations of this sort – not all of them at sea (think of the Donner Party) – were by no means as rare as is usually supposed.

[6] *Dudley & Stephens* at 287–288.   [7] Ibid. at 288.

[8] Simpson, *Cannibalism and the Common Law*, p. 239.   [9] Ibid., pp. 242–248.

Brown, sailed from Liverpool for Philadelphia, with a crew of seventeen and sixty-five passengers, mostly Irish emigrants.[10] The ship hit an iceberg and sank. The *William Brown* carried a "long boat," and a so-called jolly boat. But only half the passengers could fit in these boats. The rest simply went down with the ship. The captain and some of the crew set off in the jolly boat. The long boat was jammed with forty-one people; eight of these were seamen, the rest were passengers. It was cold and rainy, and the sea was full of ice. The crew felt the long boat was seriously overloaded. The boat would somehow have to be lightened. Otherwise, the boat would sink, and they would all drown. Whether this was true is not at all clear. In any event, the crew felt that a crisis loomed. There was only one way out, and they took it. They started throwing passengers overboard, where of course they drowned. Sixteen passengers died in this way. Almost all of the victims were men. None of them were members of the crew. The next morning, a passing ship rescued the remaining people in the long boat.

One of the sailors, William Holmes, was put on trial in federal court in Philadelphia, charged with "manslaughter on the high seas." Holmes had in fact played a key role in the affair. He was also something of a hero: he had rescued a young woman from the sinking ship, at great danger to himself. The dramatic trial was big news in Philadelphia. The prosecution argued for conviction. Sailors had no right, and no power, to save their own lives by making "jettison of human beings, as of so much cargo." Holmes's lawyer, in defense, invoked the "law of necessity," and asked the jury to think of the situation as it was: "a long-boat, sunk down to its very gunwale with 41 half naked, starved, and shivery wretches – the boat leaking from below ... a hundred leagues from land ... [an] utterable condition."[11] The judge's instructions to the jury practically dictated a guilty verdict. Nonetheless, the members of the jury were troubled by the case. They deliberated for some sixteen hours. They told the judge at one point they were unable to agree; he sent them back to their room; in the end, they returned a verdict of guilty, but with a strong recommendation of mercy. The judge sentenced Holmes to pay a fine and to serve six months in jail. Many people thought even that was too severe a punishment.[12]

One other case might be mentioned: *Queen v. Cocks* (1887).[13] The defendants (there were four of them) were part of the crew of the *Lady Douglas*, a British ship, which sailed out of western Australia. A Malay crew member, Hassin, seemed to

[10] The story is told in detail in Tom Koch, *The Wreck of the* William Brown: *A True Tale of Overcrowded Lifeboats and Murder at Sea* (Camden, ME: International Marine, 2004); the case report is *United States v. Holmes*, 1 Wall. Jr. C. C. 1, 26 F. Cas. 360, No. 58,383 (1842).

[11] 26 F. Cas. at 363, 364.

[12] According to Koch, *The Wreck of the* William Brown, p. 181, Holmes appealed to President John Tyler for clemency, but this appeal was not successful. Presumably, Holmes did go to prison. What happened to him later is apparently unknown; there is no record of what became of him in the rest of his life.

[13] Reported in Proceedings of the Old Bailey (the central criminal courts of London), June 27, 1887; these proceedings are available online; reference number t18870627-718.

have lost his mind. He hid in various parts of the ship; the crew locked him up, but he escaped; his behavior seemed extremely threatening. He was wounded badly, but the crew decided "the best way was to kill him right out," so they finished him off and chucked the body into the sea. The men were found guilty by a London jury, but the jury strongly recommended "mercy." The men were sentenced to death, but then were reprieved. The captain (Cocks) got a five-year sentence, two others had to serve eighteen months, and the fourth received a twelve-month sentence.

Brian Simpson, whose book was mainly about the case of Dudley and Stephens, noted other instances in the nineteenth century in which desperate men, facing death from hunger on the high seas, resorted to human flesh to keep themselves alive. A storm turned the schooner *Sallie M. Steelman* into a "drifting derelict." The crew was starving; after more than a month of drifting, a black seaman "lost his reason and threatened to shoot the captain." The seaman was shot and then his corpse was "butchered"; his flesh was "boiled and fried," and tasted "as good as any beefsteak."[14] Nobody was ever called to judgment for these acts.

Holmes was convicted, but he had never been accused of murder. Murder carried the death penalty. His crime was "manslaughter on the high seas"; for this, the maximum sentence was three years. And even this seemed too severe to many people. Defendants in the Cocks case did worse, but at least they were spared the death penalty. Dudley and Stephens were sentenced to death. The English judge had had no choice: once a defendant was convicted of murder, the judge was bound to impose the death sentence. But the sentence against these two men was, as we saw, never carried out. Clemency and reprieves were, actually, quite common in English criminal justice. As Brian Simpson put it, there would have been an "alarming" number of executions "if all murderers had been hanged."[15]

As it happened, there was no "alarming" epidemic of hangings. In England, a semi-formalized system of clemency saved the necks of many of those who were convicted of homicide. In American law, homicide had been sliced into degrees and types: first- and second-degree murder, voluntary and involuntary manslaughter. Choosing a charge was itself a way to squeeze some leniency into the system, in both England and the United States. Judges and juries tended to react to extreme and desperate situations by bending and adjusting the law, though not always openly. In the "black swan" cases, the legal system – juries, judges, executive officials – declined to treat men as murderers when these men faced situations of extreme stress, of utter desperation, or at the brink of life and death. There are not quite enough cases for us to talk about patterns. But the results in the "black swan" cases hint at yet another type of crime without punishment.

---

[14]   Simpson, *Cannibalism and the Common Law*, p. 139.   [15]   Ibid., p. 242.

6

The Meaning of Unwritten Law

The phrase "unwritten law," in the nineteenth century, came to mean, above all, one particular situation: killing a rival in a love triangle, and getting away with it. But it was clearly not the only example of "unwritten law." All of the situations described in this book could be called examples of unwritten law. Impunity for lynch mobs was unwritten law. Failure to prosecute vigilantes was an unwritten law. Patterns in cases of neonaticide, and in mercy killing, and in the black swan cases, suggest still other unwritten laws.

Officially, in these instances, a crime had been committed – a crime conventionally and formally defined as murder. Yet, in practice, for the most part, no punishment or mild punishment followed. A good deal of the material comes from accounts of trials, especially jury trials. But often men and women who killed never faced a courtroom. Certainly not the executive committee of the second San Francisco Vigilance Committee, not to mention its 6,000 members; and certainly not the lynch mobs in the South or their leaders, even when photographs and dozens of witnesses could identify those who were guilty of the crime. Nor was there punishment for doctors who quietly "pulled the plug"; nobody, in most cases, was ever the wiser.

The examples discussed in this book all fit this pattern. Otherwise, they do not seem to have much in common. Vigilantes claimed they were plugging holes in the dykes of law and order. Noble Dr. Sander is about as ethically distant from a lynch mob as one could get. And it is hard to compare a friendless, trembling servant girl giving birth in secret with the macho characters who fill their sexual rivals full of lead. Moreover, each of our examples is itself a complicated fabric of individual instances. One study lists more than 300 separate vigilante movements; there were thousands of lynchings; there are countless instances of "lethal dosing." It would be odd if all of the instances could be squeezed into a single box. Still, there are (as we said) patterns. And, we believe, commonalities.

Take the vigilantes, for example. What tied many of the movements of these "roughnecks" together was the *message* they thought they were sending: a message about the justice system, about law and order, about social hierarchy in the far West. Lynch mobs, too, were sending a message: a message of white supremacy. The ordinary courts were too weak, too namby-pamby, to send a comparable message. This despite the fact that the ordinary courts were in the hands of white supremacists; the courts, to be sure, dealt quick, harsh justice to African-Americans, but, for the lynch mobs, the message was not quick and harsh enough. The message of a lynching was far more vivid, to say the least. And, in many cases, it had a kind of "ritual" element: "the use of fire . . . the symbolic taking of trophies of the victim's remains, the sense of celebratory anticipation" – all these suggest that lynching was a "kind of tribal sacrifice."[1] Lynching was, in short, didactic theater, the drama of white supremacy.

Among the examples treated in this book, the lynch mobs most resemble their contemporaries, the vigilantes. Vigilante actions, on the whole, lacked the sheer sadism and brutality of Southern lynch mobs; vigilantes did not torture, did not tear bodies limb from limb, did not burn desperadoes alive. That was reserved for the lynch mobs. A pessimist might argue that there are potential lynch mobs in all societies, that all societies have a dark underside, a stagnant pool of sadism, of mindless brutality, which only traditions and institutions and perhaps moral leadership can keep in check. Strip these away, and the veneer of decency, of civilization, vanishes. The South was a wounded, destroyed, disturbed society in the years after the Civil War. Soon after the war, the Ku Klux Klan and other hate groups wallowed in blood; the Klan committed acts of incredible savagery against blacks – and even against whites who stood in the way of total white supremacy.

Each of the situations described in this book sent some sort of message. Many of the messages were, if not benign, at least somewhat defensible. Official law refused to recognize a right to kill. Its message was simple: human life is sacred. Hell is paved with good intentions. To kill out of love, or desperation, or for the good of society, will set a dangerous precedent. No one has the right to set aside the formal law. A jury that disregards the formal law is a lawless jury. But the message of the living law was different. There was a gap – sometimes a yawning, unbridgeable gap – between official law and particular social norms. Each was sending its own conflicting message about what was right and what was wrong.

But this raises a basic question, which I have already discussed, at least in part. Why did the unwritten law *remain* unwritten? If jurors thought a man was justified in killing his wife's lover, and jurors reflected what many or most people actually thought, why did the law refuse to recognize the practice? Why did the law refuse to crown the act with legitimacy? Law, after all, is a reflection of social norms. True, official law and actual behavior never coincide exactly. But when the discrepancy is really huge, when we seem to face separate systems of thought and behavior, when we see a flat-out contradiction, some sort of explanation is called for.

---

[1] Philip Dray, *At the Hands of Persons Unknown: The Lynching of Black America* (New York: Random House, 2002), p. 79.

People might *think* they know the reason; they might express an explanation, if you pressed them, but, on the other hand, there might also be a different reason, an underlying reason, a social reason, that people might even be unaware of. One obvious, popular explanation for "unwritten laws" is that old chestnut, the floodgates argument. Open the sluices, even a little bit, and waters might pour in and drown the whole city. Give an inch, and you lose a mile. If you recognize, if you legitimate, certain behaviors, you invite catastrophic consequences. Exceptions turn into rules. It is important, then, not to take the first step; it is important to avoid the first step, at all costs.

We have met this argument already. It is wrong to encourage killing, even killing that seems justified. If a woman can kill her wretched and abusive husband, and get away with it, won't unfaithful and unhappy women start doing away with their men? If you let doctors pull the plug, are you encouraging nurses and doctors to become angels of death? And indeed, there are alarming cases, where we find just such angels of death – men like Saldivar, who murdered scores of patients. In short, you have to draw a line. People must not take the law into their own hands. If you allow this, things will end badly. Of course, acquitting Dr. Sanders or Congressman Sickles or some mercy killer *is* letting people take the law into their own hands. Vigilante leaders thought there were times when people *should* take the law into their own hands. But they did not give out a license to kill.

Granted: but how does it help to have an unwritten law? Perhaps, if you keep quiet about the license to kill, if you refuse to legitimate crimes without punishment, you can discourage overuse of the privilege. You are (supposedly) putting some kind of cap or limit on the process. Formal law, then, acts like a kind of speed limit. We set the speed limit at 65; in practice, we let people drive at about 70. If we set the limit at 70, they would drive at 75. And if we took the speed limit off altogether, some people would drive at crazy, reckless speeds. The speed limit (we think) puts a lid on speeding. Another sort of limit is what we might call crowdsourcing of murder. Vigilantes and lynchers did not act alone. The need for mass action, for gathering a mob, acted as some kind of limit or cap.

This argument, the floodgates argument, or the argument about a "slippery slope," has a certain amount of power. People do believe in it. But the argument, basically, is an empirical argument. Would assisted suicide laws cheapen human life, if we legalized it? Would we see pressure to get rid of handicapped people? Are we inviting women to kill husbands, if we are open and aboveboard about letting women kill abusive husbands? Would more unmarried women strangle babies if the law openly promised light sentences, or perhaps no sentences at all? Of course, we have no answers to these questions. The fears seem exaggerated. But we have no proofs.

In the world of today, cultural changes have removed many of the fears just mentioned. There are, to be sure, still qualms about assisted suicide or about the overuse of the battered woman defense. But the same questions could have been asked, and were asked, about the historical examples, about unwritten laws that are now obsolete. The floodgates argument is pretty much unconvincing too in the case of what we have called "black swans." These were and are, after all, rare situations. Even for more common situations, the floodgates argument is fairly implausible – if it implies that the *official* norm still has a great deal of power, even when everybody knows that this norm exists only on paper.

If we dismiss the floodgates argument, can we think of a better explanation? A social explanation? The most obvious explanation is, that in each case, we confront a genuine clash of norms. Unwritten law flourishes in situations where one powerful social norm collides with another, which is perhaps equally powerful. Think, for example, of the norm that human life is sacred and that killing can almost never be justified. Almost nobody holds this norm absolutely (otherwise, armies would be impossible). But a fairly strong version is official policy among members of some religious denominations. It affects attitudes toward the unborn, toward people in irreversible comas, and it leads to opposition to assisted suicide. The formal law reflects this view: all lives are equal, as far as criminal law is concerned. Everybody is entitled to life. Every human being. Every living soul has a sacred right to life.

But unwritten laws often imply something quite different: all lives are not equal. Certain lives or types of lives are worth less than other lives. To put an end to these lesser lives is not murder, and may not even be a crime. On the contrary, society might be better off. The life of an African-American was cheap to a lynch mob, if the African-American had violated the Southern code, or was thought to. Vigilantes felt thugs and highwaymen deserved to die. In one way or another, the lives of victims described in this book were discounted: seducers, newborn babies, people dying of terrible diseases, and even the poor, helpless lad adrift on the trackless ocean. In every case, at least some people (never everyone) defined the lives as low in the scale of values. The perpetrator killed someone who (in some sort of social judgment) deserved to die or whose life was valued at zero or close to zero. Indeed, in the case of some dying men and women, the "victims" themselves denied that their lives had value. Many victims of "mercy killing" clearly thought their lives were not worth living – indeed, assisted suicide laws presuppose this kind of valuation. Many people – most people? – think that withdrawing life support is not murder under these conditions. English poet Arthur Hugh Clough (1819–1861), in his satirical poem, "The Latest Decalogue," included these two often-quoted lines: "Thou shalt not kill, but needst not strive, Officiously to keep alive." Whatever these lines meant to Clough, they seem relevant to modern policy issues.

The valuation can be in some instances comparative: the "victim's" life is not valueless; but it falls short measured against the needs and wants and the very life of the perpetrator. This applies, of course, to desperate women who kill their newborn, illegitimate babies. Perhaps, in the case of neonaticide, it would be more accurate to say that it was the mother's situation that was crucial: it reduced the value of the baby's life. Or consider Richard Parker, helpless and dying in a dinghy. Captain Slade, the hell-raiser. Or consider an abusive husband. Someone, or some group, felt that lives of this sort did not matter, that they had no intrinsic worth, no claim to the right to stay alive, or relatively little. In this category, we can put newborn lives, and, at the other end of the road, the life of someone very old, a suffering life, a dying life, in the grips of some painful disease, or a person in an irreversible coma.

The motives of the killer also has relevance. The vigilantes certainly thought they were making their towns better off by getting rid of bad guys. Lynch mobs were preserving white supremacy. "Mercy" killing is thought to be, well, merciful. Congressman Sickles and others who killed sexual rivals felt they were defending their honor, not to mention their macho self-concept, and perhaps also the integrity of family life in general. Not to mention the fact that the scoundrels they killed deserved to die. Sheer necessity, and the instinct for self-preservation, can act as a kind of excuse for Dudley and Stephens in their ghastly situation on the high seas.

Each of these unwritten laws also represents some sort of struggle between groups, factions, strata of society. Analysis in terms of social norms, in terms of a struggle between groups and factions, is essentially different from analysis in terms of the slippery slope. Both sides had concrete interests and aims. The vigilantes, in some cases, were merchants and elites at war with common folks, foreigners, and other "undesirables." Lynch law was clearly white against black; it was also, to a degree, rural as opposed to urban, masses as opposed to elites. Mercy killing pitted Catholics, for example, against non-Catholics. In San Francisco, in the 1850s, the Vigilance Committee represented a Protestant elite facing a Catholic (mostly Irish) working-class. In the case of neonaticide, the pulpits could threaten hellfire for sinners, the elites could condemn women who had sex outside of marriage, but jurors (all men) had different interests, different ideologies. At least we can infer this from their behavior.

Is there some sort of larger pattern? The law harbors a number of what we might call dual systems: situations where the living law departs radically from the formal law. I have elsewhere used the terms "high law" and "low law."[2] The idea is that *formal* law, official law, "high law," reflects the moral code of the elites; it hews to traditional moral or religious standards. "Low law," the living law, is the law of a larger public; it often reflects consumer demand for an illegal status or substance. One can even analyze lynch law in these terms. Lynch mobs were low law (one could hardly get lower); it reflected a crude, savage racist streak, mostly in small Southern towns; the high law was itself racist to the core, but it had at least a minimal commitment to law and order, some surface respect for due process, or the appearance of due process, and also, perhaps, a genuine fear of mob rule.

Consider the law related to houses of prostitution. Religious leaders and others condemned prostitution as an unmitigated evil. Running a brothel was illegal under

[2] Lawrence M. Friedman, "High Law and Low Law," *FIU Law Review* 10:53 (2014).

American law. But brothels flourished in every American city in the nineteenth century. At times they were even regulated by police codes, although this had absolutely no basis in formal law. Brothels were pretty much tolerated, so long as they stayed in designated vice areas – the so-called red light districts. City officials winked at the practice. Corruption explains part of the situation, but by no means all of it. Houses of prostitution, after all, had plenty of customers. The city of St. Louis, in 1870, embarked on an experiment unique for this country: licensing and regulating prostitution. A firestorm of criticism quickly put an end to the experiment.[3] But an "unwritten law" protected the houses inside the red light districts.[4] As a Minneapolis Vice Commission Report put it in 1911, people felt that "houses of prostitution" were "necessary evils"; they were "permitted to exist in the localities given over to them," and were even (informally) licensed by the city.[5] The "red-light abatement movement" of the early twentieth century tried to stamp out vice districts, once and for all.[6] The movement had some initial success. Some districts were closed down. But of course vice never really disappeared. In the end, not much changed. The moralists got their law. The customers got their sex. "Mercy killing" too was a kind of battle between high law and low law. High law was the sanctity of human life, at all costs and under all circumstances. Lethal dosing was in practice low law; so too was the occasional open act of mercy killing.

There was, paradoxically, sometimes unwritten law on both sides of moral wars. Vigilantes in some areas rode out at night to enforce rules of traditional morality, to stamp out houses of prostitution, and to horsewhip men (and women) whose sins offended the night riders. Lynch mobs strictly enforced rules that outlawed sexual contact between blacks and whites. Those who backed lynch law in the South ranted and raved about black rapists, "beasts" who (they claimed) hungered for the bodies of white women and girls. The classical "unwritten law" – killing a sexual rival – visited punishment on illicit sex, on the vile and cunning seducer. On the other hand, in the big cities (and elsewhere), "unwritten laws" gave the green light to red light districts, and made nonsense of (formal) laws on sexual behavior, gambling, and general hell-raising. The sexual behavior of poor, desperate women who gave birth to unwanted babies, met also with sympathy and solicitude. In both England and the United States, middle-class morality in the Victorian era strongly condemned a woman who had sex outside of marriage. The data on neonaticide,

---

[3] Lawrence M. Friedman, *Guarding Life's Dark Secrets: Legal and Social Controls over Reputation, Propriety, and Privacy* (Stanford, CA: Stanford University Press, 2007), p. 136.

[4] See Lawrence M. Friedman, *Crime and Punishment in American History* (New York: Basic Books, 1993), p. 227.

[5] Report of the Vice Commission of Minneapolis 23 (1911). The "indirect license system" consisted of "regular monthly fines" paid into the municipal court. The brothel owners would come to court "without the formality of arrest," and plead "guilty to a charge ... of keeping a house of ill-fame." A fixed fine would then be paid.

[6] Friedman, *Crime and Punishment in American History*, pp. 186–188; Peter C. Hennigan, "Property War: Prostitution, Red Light Districts, and the Transformation of Public Nuisance Law in the Progressive Era," *Yale Journal of Law and the Humanities*, 16:159 (2004).

however, complicate our understanding of Victorian morality. High law condemned the killing of newborn babies. Low law was otherwise.

I have spoken of clashing norms. Of course, in our complex societies, clashing norms are nothing special. The whole legal system is shaped by clashing norms, in one way or another. But in the instances discussed here, we have high law and low law: one side stakes out what it considers the moral high ground; the other side occupies a more popular (or populist) view. Prostitution, as we mentioned, is the classic case. Legalizing this business was politically impossible. But it survived and even flourished. Something similar was at work for the classic unwritten law.

Not all of our cases can be neatly analyzed as high versus low, morality versus consumer demand for behaviors or commodities condemned by high morality. Vigilante action was at times the reverse; the "high" element led the movement and appealed to the demand for law and order; the low element served on juries and ran local government. Mercy killing is perhaps better analyzed as secular norms against religious norms. Both sides claim a kind of moral high ground. I leave it to the reader whether either side is right.

High law was open, overt, and, often, elite. But it would probably be wrong to think of it as narrowly conservative and nothing more. Many people, high or low, think that law should express noble values, should espouse an ideal morality, a mountain we can never climb, but is still meaningful to us in the valley. Lord Campbell, in *Dudley and Stephens*, said that the law expresses and enforces standards that we cannot, perhaps, live up to. But if so, what use are these standards? Hard to say, but people are convinced that the standards have value – a symbolic value, if nothing else, although symbolic values are hard to define or specify, and whether they have an impact on behavior is an open question.

TRIAL BY JURY

This is a book about *law*, after all, and the conflicts described have played out within the legal system. Legal norms, procedures, and institutions are important aspects of the stories told here. What all of the examples have in common is that the acts involved are or were "against the law" in a formal sense, but did not get punished, or were punished very lightly. In most instances, the non-punishment also happened through law, that is, through a decision or some other behavior of a legal institution.

There are many points in the system where unwritten laws can make their mark. Sheriffs, coroners' juries, and local officials can turn a blind eye to lynching or vigilante action. Or prosecutors can simply fail to prosecute doctors who do "lethal dosing" (we have, of course, no data on this). Judges can dismiss cases or impose laughable sentences. Governors can pardon or commute. An unwritten law might work to prevent the wheels of the system from turning at all. How many cases of "lethal dosing" or mercy killing ever came to light in the first place? How many doctors simply kept quiet? In the "black swan" cases, there were actual trials.

The defendants were convicted and there were pious speeches about duty, human life, and the law. In the end, though, the defendants were hardly punished at all.

In many of the examples, the work of non-punishment falls to that old and sacred institution, the common law jury. Federal and state constitutions guarantee the right to trial by jury. But the jury is, in some ways, a bizarre institution. A key virtue of the jury – or a key vice (take your pick) – is the power of the jury to twist or modify the law, or even to ignore the law, and do it moreover on the sly. It is perfectly positioned for a kind of benign lawlessness. We have seen many examples: refusal to convict men like Dan Sickles, sympathy for poor, desperate women who give birth out of wedlock, to mention two prominent instances.

Jury behavior of this kind goes back rather far in history. In eighteenth-century England, it was a capital offense to steal property worth more than a certain amount. A jury could come in with a verdict of guilty but spare the defendant's life by simply assigning some absurdly small value to stolen goods. There are American examples as well. In Maryland, in the 1660s, a man named Pope Alvey was charged with stealing a "Certaine Cow of black culler" worth two pounds and ten shillings.[7] The jury found him guilty of the crime, but assessed the value of the cow at "eleven pence and no more" – a figure that seems almost ridiculous.[8]

Cases on the unwritten law, on neonaticide, and on mercy killing richly illustrate the jury's power to modify the living law. Juries, after all, deliberate in secret. They work in a closed-off room. And they simply decide. They never explain. The jury comes out of its room and makes a pronouncement – a terse phrase or two, nothing more. If the jury acquits, the state cannot appeal. The defendant gets up and walks out of the courtroom.[9] Once in a while, a juror talks about what happened in the jury room, but this is rare, and frowned upon. For Max Weber, the great German sociologist, the common-law jury was a prime example of "irrational" decision-making.[10] He put the jury in the same category as oracles, trial by ordeal or battle, or reading the entrails of birds. Jury decisions, like these other examples of "irrational" decision-making, did not lend themselves to logical analysis.[11] But precisely *because* the jury never gives reasons, it can bend the law without owning up to what it

---

[7] See J. Hall Pleasants, ed., *Archives of Maryland: Proceedings of the Provincial Court of Maryland 1663–1666* (Baltimore, MD: Maryland Historical Society, 1932), pp. xix–xx.

[8] The judge reprimanded the jury members and sent them back into their room to reconsider their valuation. This of course could not happen in later times: judges today have much less power to treat juries like naughty children.

[9] Even when a jury convicts, the state can appeal only on technical, formal grounds; it can only complain about "errors" at the trial – bad evidence let in or good evidence kept out – or flaws in the judge's instructions to the jury.

[10] *Max Weber on Law in Economy and Society*, Max Rheinstein ed., Edward Shils and Max Rheinstein, trans. (Cambridge, MA: Harvard University Press, 1954), p. 63. Lawmaking and law finding are "'formally irrational'" when they use "means which cannot be controlled by the intellect, for instance when recourse is had to oracles." The jury, according to Weber, resembles the oracle, "inasmuch as it does not indicate rational grounds for its decision" (ibid., p. 79).

[11] See ibid.

is doing. In a way, then, juries who acquitted under the unwritten law were performing a classic function. They were acting as a kind of brake or check, modifying the rigidity of formal law. You can call this "lawless"; you can argue that the system should not work this way. And surely this can often lead to abuse: white juries in the South that refused to convict men who assaulted or murdered African-Americans. On the other hand, you might admire juries that showed sympathy to young mothers or men like Dr. Sanders. In any case, jury "lawlessness" is hardly an aberration; it is baked into the system, integral to the structure and function of the jury.

The jury can bend and check, but its work is, on the whole, not random. Weber was, in a way, wrong to label juries as irrational. A jury decision is not at all like trial by battle, or reading the entrails of birds. A jury, after all, is a panel of human beings. Members of a jury can be, and very often are, quite rational. They rarely tell us why they do what they do, but that does not mean they decide the case by tossing a coin. Juries deliberate, they argue, they consider. And what they do always reflects their time, place, culture, and context.

DECLINE AND FALL

This has been a study in legal and social history. The topics have been forms of unwritten law in homicide cases, roughly from the mid-nineteenth century to a generation or so ago. It has also been, by implication, a study of social change. The unwritten laws we discussed reflected, as they must, the norms and values of their times. Our values and norms are quite different.

The unwritten laws described in the pages of this book have not, on the whole, survived. Or survived only in altered form. Social and cultural changes have doomed them: notions about sex and gender, race, law and order. When white supremacy lost legitimacy, lynching came to an end. Lynchers lost impunity, and lynching died along with the impunity. Racial segregation has been outlawed. Whites and blacks are free to marry. Race prejudice is still very much alive, but it cannot express itself in quite the blatant forms it once did. As law and order became normalized in the West, vigilante movements virtually disappeared. They are not extinct, but they have been marginalized.

The modern sexual code is miles away from the Victorian code. Sex outside of marriage is no longer scandalous. Bastardy has lost most of its sting and become exceedingly common. Adoption, Baby Moses laws, and the general culture have combined to make neonaticide a rare event. When it happens, we are, paradoxically, less indulgent than during the nineteenth century; we think of it now as actual murder – or, more often, as the product of a diseased mind. The debate over mercy killing has merged with the debate over assisted suicide. The eugenics movement is dead; that element of the debate is history. The end-of-life issue is, of course, very real, very current, but the terms of the debate have changed.

Assisted suicide has gained legality in only six states, but people everywhere probably approve of euthanasia in its original sense: a good – and peaceful – death.

We live in an age of expressive individualism. People think of themselves as unique individuals. The culture encourages people to do their own thing, to develop their own personalities, to follow their own paths through life. This cultural message begins almost from the day of birth – childrearing practices, "show and tell" in kindergarten, the push for people to achieve their "personal best," to find the right fit, to marry for life, and to divorce when love curdles; to have children or not as one pleases. (New technologies of birth control, of course, have helped enormously.) Moral codes are always with us, but their contents change. The current American moral code is more flexible, more permissive, more nuanced, less hierarchical, less deferential, than the code of our great-grandparents. The civil rights movement helped strengthen the women's rights movement, and there are also movements on behalf of old people, aliens, ethnic and sexual minorities, deaf people, illegitimate children – the list goes on and on. All of these movements have in common the demand for individual autonomy: the right to be judged as an individual, not as a woman, a black, a Mormon, a Jew, or a person in a wheelchair. The law of the twenty-first century is necessarily the law of twenty-first-century culture, and the "unwritten laws" of the nineteenth century have consequently failed to survive.

UNWRITTEN LAW TODAY

The unwritten laws described in this book are thus obsolete or much modified today. None of them survive in their classic form. Does that mean that unwritten laws do not exist anymore? Is this species extinct?

In fact, unwritten laws are still with us. They are a common feature of many legal systems, maybe all legal systems; this is certainly true of all advanced, formalized systems. Whatever the theory, in practice, real-life systems never follow the rules exactly. They tend to be flexible and case-specific. They are shot through with discretion. At least in certain contexts, they are what we might call dual systems: systems where the formal law and the law in action are almost totally at odds with each other.

Of course, unwritten laws go beyond the usual gap between theory and practice, or the usual leeways and flexibilities. They represent patterns that flatly *contradict* formal law but are nonetheless at times overt and well respected, if not by the majority of the public, then at least by substantial parts of it. Indeed, as the *Atlanta Constitution* argued in an article from the early twentieth century, the trouble with the (classic) unwritten law was that it was not unwritten *enough*. The writer thought it was best just to leave matters to juries; they would do the right thing quietly, in their locked rooms and secret discussions.[12] No need to talk about unwritten laws. Just let them happen.[13]

This book has focused on the history of homicide. But unwritten laws are not just a feature of criminal justice. Other examples are or were just as important, possibly more so. A good example is the law of divorce in the United States (and elsewhere). During the long years before no-fault divorce, the law absolutely forbade consensual divorce.[14] People could decide to get married, when both parties wanted to; but they definitely could not get a divorce simply because both parties were sick of the marriage and wanted out. There was no such thing as consensual divorce. To get a divorce, you had to go to court; and one party – the supposedly innocent party – had to accuse the other party of committing a sin against the marriage: adultery, desertion, or cruelty, depending on the particular state statute. Yet judges from roughly 1870, continuing for about a century, did in fact allow consensual divorce. A wife would file for divorce, alleging (say) cruelty; the husband would simply not respond. Or the court would shut its eyes to a kind of pious perjury. It was impossible to change the law for almost a century: moral elites were dead set against "easy" divorce. They got their law. Couples got their divorce. It was messy, it satisfied nobody, but it worked.

And today? No-fault put an end to the "unwritten law" of consensual divorce. But careful empirical study of the legal system would surely reveal other unwritten laws. A police officer shoots an unarmed African-American. Is there an unwritten law that protects the officer from suffering any adverse consequences? Many African-Americans (and others) think there is. A whole series of raw, disturbing incidents (some of them captured on videotape) lends credence to the belief that the police can get away with almost anything. The core of the movement called "Black Lives Matter" is a revolt against what can be seen as a modern "crime without punishment." In fact, the only thing "modern" about it is the pushback, not the killings themselves. True, in many recent cases, the officer claims self-defense; his own life, he says, was in danger. Sometimes, this is no more credible than the old defense of "temporary insanity" in cases of the unwritten law. Police brutality (not only against

---

12 See "The Menace of 'Unwritten Law,'" *Atlanta Constitution*, Nov. 14, 1907, p. 6.
13 The editorial huffed and puffed and called the unwritten law a device to "shackle justice and to chloroform the judgments and consciences of jurymen." The author continued: "Like many of the quasi-truths of civilization and legal jurisprudence, its chief deadliness lies in the fact that it wears no bridle and admits no check." He was commenting on the case of Anne Bradley, who shot a man who (she claimed) had used his "wiles" to "lay her life in ruins." No, the writer insisted, the written law must prevail. But his point was not a demand to send this woman to prison. Rather, it was a criticism of the blather that surrounded the unwritten law, the "hysterics and melodrama," the "intoxicated and unrestrained emotions." Simply lay the facts before the jury – "men with mothers and sisters and wives of their own" – and they would be able to "discern the provocation" that led to the shooting and reach a verdict "based on mercy and equity; and yet founded in the law of the land."
14 See Lawrence M. Friedman, *Private Lives: Families, Individuals and the Law* (Cambridge, MA: Harvard University Press, 2004), p. 29; Joanna L. Grossman and Lawrence M. Friedman, *Inside the Castle: Law and the Family in 20th Century America* (Princeton, NJ: Princeton University Press, 2011).

minorities) has a long and disgraceful history, and with very little in the way of punishment. Until fairly recently, too, only rapists who raped middle-class women, women with good characters (and who were not their wives), were likely to be convicted of rape.

No doubt there are many other unwritten laws, at all levels of government. There are today (2018) federal laws criminalizing the sale and use of marijuana. These federal laws have not been enforced in states like Colorado, which have legalized marijuana. (At this writing, there are hints that the policy might change.) President Obama announced a policy protecting "dreamers," people brought to the United States as children by undocumented parents; the "dreamers" were technically illegal aliens, but under the policy, they were not to be deported. (The Trump administration here too announced in 2017 that it was reversing this policy). Unwritten laws, we argued, arise out normative clashes, especially the clash between high law and low law. This has a long history and is certainly not extinct.

Some unwritten laws – today as well as yesterday – may be unspoken as well as unwritten. They live underground, in the dark. If we studied *patterns*, if we studied how prosecutors and judges and juries behaved, we might unearth these subterranean practices. Of course, the more unwritten and unspoken the law, the deeper its obscurity. Sometimes patterns that change, like soft-bodied animals, leave little behind in the way of fossilized remains. Unwritten laws may change in unwritten ways.

Index

Abarta, Lastencia, 46
abortion, 71, 101
abortion rights, 2
abusive husbands, 59
adultery, 20, 22–24, 31. *See also*
    unwritten law
Advanced Health Care Directive (AHCD), 122, 123
agency, 29
Aiken, Sam, 51–52,
Alvey, Pope, 136
American Bar Association, 37
American Hospital Association, 110
American Medical Association, 118, 120
Andrews, Edwin, 10
Annis, William E., 56
anti-lynching bills, 16
anti-Semitism, 16
Aquinas, Thomas, 100
assisted suicide
    current thoughts about, 122–124
    introduction to, 89, 110–115, 116f
    opposition to, 118–121, 131–132
    in practice, 116, 117f,
    support for, 138
Atlanta Constitution newspaper
    neonaticide, 67, 69, 74
    unwritten laws, 24, 25, 26, 42, 56, 138

baby-farming, 70–72
Baby Jane Doe, 97
Baby Moses laws, 82–83, 86
Baca, Onofrio, 12
Backhouse, Constance, 77
Bancroft, Hubert, 6
Barbour, Charles, 51
Barnett, Frank, 49
Bartley, Francis A., 30

Bastard Nation, 84
battered woman syndrome, 59
Battice, Earl, 52
Bauer, Eugene, 103
Baumberg, Anton, 54–55
Baxter, Robert, 114
Beers, Andrew, 91
beloved roughnecks, 4–11, 129–130
Bennett, George, 42
Bergin, Jack, 50–51
Biddle, John, 75
Big Nose George, 4
Birdsong, Angie, 42
Bishop, Warren L., 78
Black Lives Matter, 139
black swan cases, 3, 125–128
Blazer, Harold E., 90–91,
Bollinger, Ann, 96
Borroto, Abbie, 102–103
Borroto, Reginald, 103
Boston Globe newspaper, 78
Bowen v. American Hospital Association, 97
Bowker, Frank, 75
Boyce, Al, Jr., 21, 26, 54
Boyce, Al, Sr., 21
Boyer, Nicole, 82
Brady, James, 6
Bransfield, Thomas, 75
breach of promise, 72
Brooks, Walter B., 51
Browder, Mary, 75
Brown, Hannah, 65
Brown, Richard Maxwell, 5, 6, 8
Brown, William, 16
Buck, Carrie, 95
Buck v. Bell, 95
burning alive, 13

Burroughs, Adoniram J., 45
Bywaters, Viola, 38
Bywaters, William, 38

California Gold Rush, 5
California Medical Association, 119
Campbell, Hellen, 68–69
Carter, John T., 51
Catholic Church, 97, 99, 100, 118, 124
chastity, 86
Chatterton, Fennimore, 8–9
Chicago Daily Tribune newspaper, 103
civil rights movement, 138
Clark, James E., 56
Clark, Ruby, 44
clashing norms, 11, 135
Clement, Susan, 65
Cline, George, 50–51
Clough, Arthur Hugh, 132
cohabitation and neonaticide, 79
Cole, George, 26, 32–33, 34, 54
Coleman, William T., 5
Colfax massacre in Louisiana, 13
Collins, Kate, 65
Comer, B. B., 39
Compassion and Choices, 112, 114, 119, 123
concealing birth of child, 64
Constable, Marianne, 43–44
contraception, 79
Controlled Substances Act, 113
Cook, Katie, 41, 46–47
Cook, Tom, 41
Cooper, Wallace, 105
Cordena, Jose Maria, 12
Corwell, Estelle, 42
Cowen, Margaret, 92
Crittendon, Alexander, 44–45
Cruzan, Nancy Beth, 108–109, 124
Culley, R. E., 49
Cusick, James, 5, 6
Cyrus, Mary, 65, 78

Dakan, E. W., 49
Daniels, James, 8
Darley, Gabrielle, 42–43
Darling, Clyde N., 26, 54
Darrow, Clarence, 28, 96
Darwin, Charles, 93
Davenport, Charles B., 94
Davis, Carrie, 58
Davis, Ruth, 106
Death and Dignity: Making Choices and Taking Charge (Quill), 104
death squads, 19

Death with Dignity Act, 112, 115
democracy in United States, 85–86
Department of Health and Human Services, 97
diminished responsibility in mercy killings, 105
Dimsdale, Thomas, 7–8, 9, 10
divorce, 56, 138, 139
Doke, Judson, 50–51
Dorsey, George, 14
double infanticide, 74–75
Down's syndrome, 97
dreamers, protection of, 140
Drexler, Melissa, 82
Dubois, James, 75
Dugdale, R. L., 93–94
dumpster babies, 83

Earp, Wyatt, 42
economic desperation and neonaticide, 61–62
Edwards, Alexander, 27
Elfring, H. B., 76
emotional insanity defense, 38, 40
end-of-life treatments, 100
Equal Protection Clause (Fourteenth Amendment), 99, 114
Errett, Alice, 74
Ertell, Mary, 25–26, 53–54
Estabrook, Arthur, 94
Estes, Theodore, 48–49
ethical democracy in England, 86
eugenics movement, 89, 93–99, 137
Euthanasia Educational Fund, 111
Euthanasia Society of America, 111
Ewing, George B., 69

Fair, Laura, 44–45, 47
Falmer, Clara, 40–41, 47, 48
Farnham, Mina, 76
Federal Assisted Suicide Funding Act, 113
feminist movement, 56–57
Fenton, Rebecca Latimer, 12, 13
Finn, Margaret, 20–21, 46–47
first-degree murder, 1, 25
floodgates argument, 131, 132
Forster, Francisco, 46
Fortescue, Grace, 28
founding homes, 73
Fourteenth Amendment (U.S. Constitution), 99, 113
Frank, Leo, 16, 17
Freeman, Sarah, 64

Galton, Francis, 93
Garcia, Inez, 58
Garrett, J. W., Mrs., 60

Index 143

Gaskell, Charles, 38
gender issues. *See also* women
  male jealousy, 30
  manhood and unwritten law, 21,
    24, 30
  stereotypes, 30–31
  unwritten law and, 56–57
  victimhood and neonaticide, 86
Georgia law (1833), 64
get-out-of-town warnings, 5–7,
Gibson, J. L., 50
Gilbert, Roswell, 106
Glascock, John Henry, 58
Goddard, Henry H., 94
Golden Age of unwritten law, 34–40
Gordon, Nellie, 53
Gordon, W. Lee, 38–39
Gorsuch, Neil, 118
Gossett, F. C., 39
Great Lakes Naval Training station, 17
Greenfield, Jerome, 98
Grossberg, Amy S., 82
"guiltless" woman, 40

Hains, Peter C., Jr., 56
Haiseldon, Harry J., 96, 98
Harlan, Charles, 43
Harris, Jean, 58
Harris, Mary, 45
Harris, Walter, 52
Hartog, Henrik, 29
hate crimes, 18
Hattman, Byron, 57
Hemlock Society, 104, 111–112
Herrin, Shelton W., 39
Hess, Charles, 38
high law, 133, 134
Hiscock, L. Harris, 32–33
Hollingshead, Lamar, 50–51
Holmes, Oliver Wendell, Jr., 95
Holmes, William, 126–127, 128
homicide law, 1
honor and unwritten law, 21
Hopkins, Willie, 15
How the Other Half Lives (Riis), 70
Humphrey, Derek, 111–112
Hunter, Bobby Gene, 58
Huntsman, Megan, 84

illegitimacy, 86
Infanticide Act (1922), 80
Infanticide Act (1938), 81
insanity defense, 36, 45–47
Ireland, Robert, 32, 45

Irish-Catholic Democrats, 10
Irwin, Rush, 39

Jansen, C. J., 5
Jenkins, John, 5
Jim Crow South, 16, 27
Johnson, Eddie, 15
Johnson, James, 54
Jones, Elizabeth, 80–81
Jones, John C., 15
Journal of the American Medical Association, 100
justifiable homicide, 22–23, 50

Kahahawai, Joe, 28
Hurricane Katrina, 19
Keller, Helen, 96
Kentucky law, 26
Kevorkian, Jack, 120–121
Key, Philip Barton, 20, 23, 31
Kidder, Harry L., 27
Kilgore, Ray, 30
Kimmel, John B., 53
King, Julia, 102
Kinkead, Ellis, 58
Kraai, John, 106–107
Ku Klux Klan, 10

Lack, Jules H., 57–58
LaDue, Charles, 40–41
Langford, Nathaniel Pitt, 6, 8
Larkyns, Harry, 33–34
Lavi, Shai, 88, 89, 90, 111
law of necessity, 127
Leek, Susan, 76
lethal dosing, 89, 99–108, 122–124, 135–136
Lindsay, Matthew, 52
Lohman, Ann (Madam Restell), 71
Los Angeles Times newspaper, 24, 71
Loving, William, 48–49
low law, 133, 134
lynchings
  anti-lynching bills, 16
  impunity for, 129
  introduction to, 4
  overview of, 11–19
  vigilantism and, 130
  white supremacy and, 130, 133, 137

Mahaffey, J. E., 20–21
maiming *vs.* killing, 22
Malcolm, John, 54–55
Malcolm, Roger, 14
male jealousy, 30
manhood and unwritten law, 21, 24, 30

manslaughter, 1, 80
Manuel, James J., 27
Martinez, Andres, 12
Massachusetts Medical Society, 118
Massey, Bert, 58
Massie, Thalia, 27–28
Maxon, Will, 27
May, Nancy, 26, 44, 54
Maynard, Brittany, 115, 118
McDaniel, Annie, 65
McFarland, Daniel, 33, 34
McGregor, Dud, 27
McGuirt, M. I., Mrs., 39
McKibbin, Elsie Maye, 47
Mendel, Gregor, 93
menstruation defense, 45
mental illness and neonaticide, 62, 80
mercy killing. *See also* assisted suicide
  current thoughts about, 122–124
  dawn of, 89–93
  eugenics movement, 89, 93–99
  introduction to, 2, 88–89
  lethal dosing, 99–108
  pulling the plug, 108–110
Meyer, Cheryl, 81
misdemeanor crime, 1, 14
Montemarano, Vincent, 103
Moody, John George, 39
Moore, James C., 38–39
Morman, Charles, 12
Moynahan, Johanna, 62
murder
  first-degree murder, 1
  introduction to, 1
  lynching as, 14
  second-degree murder, 1
Murphy, Thomas, 6
Murrill, Nancy, 44
Muybridge, Eadweard, 33–34

National Center for Health Statistics, 110
Natural Death Act, 114
Nazis in Germany, 98–99
Neely, Andrew Frederick, 55
Neely, Robert, 10–11
neonaticide
  baby-farming, 70–72
  in Britain, 79
  founding homes *vs.*, 73
  incidence of, 66–73
  introduction to, 60–66
  in modern times, 79–84
  summary of, 84–87
  in United States, 74–79

neovigilante groups, 11
New England Journal of Medicine, 104, 118
New York Times newspaper
  Baby Moses laws, 84
  mercy killing, 90, 107, 110
  neonaticide, 70, 74–75
  unwritten law and, 24, 33
newspaper databases on neonaticide, 66–67
nightriders, 13
no-fault divorce, 139
North Ward Citizens' Committee, 10
Nutt, James, 50

Obama, Barack, 140
Oberman, Michelle, 81
Old Bailey papers, 64, 75, 80
Olson, Oscar, 26, 54
Osborne, John, 4

Paight, Carol, 103
palliative care, 108, 122
pardons in unwritten law, 39–40
paroxysmal insanity, 45
patriarchy and unwritten law, 28–31
penal codes
  introduction to, 1–2,
  neonaticide, 61
  unwritten law and, 22
Pennypacker, Samuel, 95
periodic homicidal mania, 45
Perry, Margaret, 76
Perry, Sidney S., 40
persistent vegetative state, 108–109, 110
Peterkin, Guy Shearman, 107
Peterson, Brian C., Jr., 82
"Physician Aid in Dying" law, 114
Physician Orders for Life-Sustaining Treatment
  (POLST), 123
Planned Parenthood, 87
Plummer, Henry, 9, 10
police shootings of African-Americans,
  139–140
political movements, 9
Populist Party, 13
Prager, Robert, 17
premarital sex laws, 84
Prescott, Harry F., 49
Pritchett, Dolly, 77–78
pro-lifers, 87, 97
Proctor, Carrie, 75
Proctor, W. E., 49
prostitution, 133–134
pulling the plug, 108–110
Purdue, Letha, 39

Queen v. *Cocks*, 127–128
The Queen v. *Dudley & Stephens*, 125–126
Quickel, John A., 39
Quill, Timothy E., 100–101, 104
Quinlan, Karen, 108, 124

racial issues
  demographics among killers, 3
  lynchings, 11–19, 132
  Nazis in Germany, 98–99
  neonaticide, 67, 69, 74
  police shootings of African-Americans, 139–140
  scientific racism, 99
  white supremacy and, 130, 133, 137
Raines, Robert Milton, 105
Ramsey, Carolyn, 40, 52
rape crimes, 16, 29, 35, 58
Reconstruction period, 13
Regan, Mary, 77
Reichert, Edith, 92
Repouille, Louis, 91–92, 123
reputation and neonaticide, 62
Rhodes, William J., 49
Richardson, Albert, 33
Riegel, Joseph, 17
right to die, 111. *See also* assisted suicide
Riis, Jacob, 70
Ringold, Cecilia, 60, 63, 65, 74
Roberts, Ellen, 70
Roe v. *Wade*, 2, 87
Rogers, Earl, 42–43
Rosas, Maggie, 67, 76
Rougeau, Lawrence, 92
Royle, Edwin Milton, 36
Rutledge, Robert C., 57

"safe haven" law, 82, 83
Sage, Abby, 33
Saldivar, Efren, 119–120
Salley, Alexander, 18
San Francisco Foundling Asylum, 73
San Francisco Vigilance Committees, 9
Sanders, Herman, 102–103, 129, 131
Schiavo, Terry, 109–110
Schultz, Charles, 75–76
scientific racism, 99
second-degree murder, 1
seduction, as crime, 72
self-defense plea, 37–39, 41–42, 59
self-induced abortions, 71
sexual betrayal, 42
sexual insecurity, 30
Sherman, Lawrence Yates, 17
Shill, W. E., 39

Sickles, Daniel Edgar, 20, 23, 31, 34, 54, 131
Sickles, Teresa, 29
Sikora, Rudolph, 26, 54
Simon, John, 54
Simpson, Brian, 128
Simpson, Emma, 43–44
Skinner v. *Oklahoma*, 99
Slade, J. A., 7, 12
slippery slope argument, 93
Small, Kenneth B., 57–58
Smith, Alice, 26, 44, 54
Smith, Henry, 14
Sneed, John Beal, 21, 26, 54
Society for the Right to Die, 111
Solomon, Edward, 54
South Carolina Regulators, 5
Steinmetz, Joseph L., 52–53
Stenhouse, Robert, 27
Stephens, Patricia, 105–106
sterilization, 95, 99
Stewart, Elgin, 50
Stone, Olivia, 58
Strother, James and Philip, 38
Stuart, Granville, 8–9
suicide, 111. *See also* assisted suicide
Sullivan, Lizzie, 78

Talbot, Al, 43
Talbot, Mae, 43
Tarnower, Herman, 58
Taylor, Bert, 39
Temple, Emma, 80
temporary insanity pleas
  mercy killing, 91
  unwritten law and, 21, 31, 32, 34, 37
  by women, 40, 44
Terry, Mary, 44
Thaw, Evelyn Nesbit, 34–37
Thaw, Harry K., 26, 34–37, 54
Thompson, Ralph, 49
Till, Emmett, 18
Tocqueville, Alexis de, 112
trial by jury, 135–137
Tropp, Leonard, 42–43
Trump, Donald, 87
Turnbull, Patricia Diane, 104
Twain, Mark, 7

unwritten law
  black swan cases, 3, 125–128
  fall of, 55–59, 137–138
  Golden Age of, 34–40
  insanity defense and, 36
  introduction to, 20–28

unwritten law (cont.)
  meaning of, 129–135
  modern existence of, 138–140
  patriarchy and, 28–31
  rise of, 31–34
  self-defense and, 37–39
  success and failure of, 47–55
  trial by jury, 135–137
  women and, 40–47

Vacco v. Quill, 113
Vance, Myrtle, 14
variegated vagabondizing, 7
Victorian sexual code, 84, 137
vigilante committees, 5–6, 9, 129, 133
vigilante movement/tradition
  beloved roughnecks and, 4–11, 129–130
  death squads as, 19
  introduction to, 2, 4
  lynch mobs and, 130
  neovigilante groups, 11
  unwritten law as, 31
Vigilante Parade, 5
Vinson, Willie, 16

Wagner, Barbara, 119
Wagner, Frederick, 106–107
Wallis, Gwendolyn, 44
Warriner, M. A., 89–90, 93
wartime killing, 1
Washington, Jesse, 14
Washington Post newspaper, 68, 103
Washington v. Glucksberg, 113

Waters, Margaret, 69–70
Weber, Max, 136
Welshorn, C. W., 74
Wendell, R. P., 51
Werner, Ada, 46
West, Fred, Mrs., 71
White, Sanford, 34–37
white supremacy, 130, 133, 137
Wibie, W. F., 39
Williams, J. D., 40
Winston, John Anthony, 40
Wise, John, 107
women
  battered woman syndrome, 59
  feminist movement, 56–57
  "guiltless" woman, 40
  menstruation defense, 45
  rape crimes, 16, 29, 35, 58
  as subordinate, 28–31
  unwritten law and, 40–47
  as victims, 86
women's rights movement, 138
Woolsteen, Hattie, 43
Wright, Charlie, 13–14
Wright, Paul A., 53

Yates, Andrea, 60
Yatko, 27
yellow journalism, 34
Yonan, Victoria, 47
Youk, Thomas, 121

Zygmaniak, Lester, 105